The Commons

Critical, Digital and Social Media Studies

Series Editor: Christian Fuchs

The peer-reviewed book series edited by Christian Fuchs publishes books that critically study the role of the internet and digital and social media in society. Titles analyse how power structures, digital capitalism, ideology and social struggles shape and are shaped by digital and social media. They use and develop critical theory discussing the political relevance and implications of studied topics. The series is a theoretical forum for internet and social media research for books using methods and theories that challenge digital positivism; it also seeks to explore digital media ethics grounded in critical social theories and philosophy.

Editorial Board

Thomas Allmer, Mark Andrejevic, Miriyam Aouragh, Charles Brown, Melanie Dulong de Rosnay, Eran Fisher, Peter Goodwin, Jonathan Hardy, Kylie Jarrett, Anastasia Kavada, Arwid Lund, Maria Michalis, Stefania Milan, Vincent Mosco, Safiya Noble, Jack Qiu, Jernej Amon Prodnik, Sarah Roberts, Marisol Sandoval, Sebastian Sevignani, Pieter Verdegem, Bingqing Xia, Mariano Zukerfeld

Published

Critical Theory of Communication: New Readings of Lukács, Adorno, Marcuse, Honneth and Habermas in the Age of the Internet
Christian Fuchs
https://doi.org/10.16997/book1

Knowledge in the Age of Digital Capitalism: An Introduction to Cognitive Materialism
Mariano Zukerfeld
https://doi.org/10.16997/book3

Politicizing Digital Space: Theory, the Internet, and Renewing Democracy
Trevor Garrison Smith
https://doi.org/10.16997/book5

Capital, State, Empire: The New American Way of Digital Warfare
Scott Timcke
https://doi.org/10.16997/book6

The Spectacle 2.0: Reading Debord in the Context of Digital Capitalism
Edited by *Marco Briziarelli and Emiliana Armano*
https://doi.org/10.16997/book11

The Big Data Agenda: Data Ethics and Critical Data Studies
Annika Richterich
https://doi.org/10.16997/book14

The Commons:
Economic Alternatives in
the Digital Age

Vangelis Papadimitropoulos

University of Westminster Press
www.uwestminsterpress.co.uk

Published by
University of Westminster Press
115 New Cavendish Street
London W1W 6UW
www.uwestminsterpress.co.uk

First published 2020

Cover design: www.ketchup-productions.co.uk
Series cover concept: Mina Bach (minabach.co.uk)

Print and digital versions typeset by Siliconchips Services Ltd.

ISBN (Paperback): 978-1-912656-83-7
ISBN (PDF): 978-1-912656-84-4
ISBN (EPUB): 978-1-912656-85-1
ISBN (Kindle): 978-1-912656-86-8

DOI: https://doi.org/10.16997/book46

The full text of this book has been peer-reviewed to ensure high academic
standards. For full review policies, see: http://www.uwestminsterpress.co.uk
/site/publish.
Competing interests: The author has no competing interests to declare.

Suggested citation: Papadimitropoulos, V. 2020. *The Commons:
Economic Alternatives in the Digital Age.* London: University of Westminster
Press. https://doi.org/10.16997/book46 License: CC-BY -NC-ND 4.0

To read the free, open access version of this book
online, visit https://doi.org/10.16997/book46
or scan this QR code with your mobile device: 

Printed and bound by CPI Group (UK) Ltd, Croydon, CR0 4YY

Contents

CHAPTER 1

Introducing the Commons

The last decades have witnessed the rise of peer production driven by three main interdependent and mutually reinforcing factors: 1) the sustainability crisis; 2) neoliberalism, and 3) low-cost information and communication technologies (ICTs). Peer production is a type of social relations, a technological infrastructure and a new mode of production and property, whereby participants have maximum freedom to cooperate and connect (Bauwens et al. 2019, 1). Peer production disrupts centralised capitalist production through the decentralised use of the Internet and open source technologies. It is a relational dynamic playing out in terms of sharing, openness, co-creation, self-governance and bottom-up eco-techno-social innovation (Bauwens et al. 2019, 2). 'Peer production (often also "P2P Production") has been broadly portrayed as a generic form of self-organisation among loosely-affiliated individuals that volunteer on equal footing to reach a common goal' (Bauwens et al. 2019, 4).

Peer production is often referred to in the literature as the collaborative economy, comprising various sorts of economic models (Morell et al. 2017). This book, however, will stick to the term 'peer production', since, as will become evident later on, the term 'collaborative economy' is often attached to models that are rather extractive than collaborative, that is, they centrally coordinate online decentralised peer production downstream to disproportionally reap the benefits upstream.

The literature (Bauwens et al. 2019; Benkler 2006; Morell et al. 2017; Kostakis and Bauwens 2014; Scholz 2016a; 2016b; Troxler and Wolf 2016) has documented thus far three main streams of peer production: 1) firm-hosted peer production or platform capitalism (user-centric open innovation business models, the so-called sharing and gig economy); 2) the commons (local and digital commons, the solidarity economy); and 3) and a hybrid commons-based peer production operating on the models of platform and open cooperativism.

The commons consist of distributed or common property resources/ infrastructures (natural resources, technology, knowledge, capital, culture),

How to cite this book chapter:

Papadimitropoulos, V. 2020. *The Commons: Economic Alternatives in the Digital Age.* Pp. 1–30. London: University of Westminster Press. DOI: https://doi.org/10.16997 /book46.a. License: CC-BY-NC-ND 4.0

self-managed by their user communities in accordance with collectively established rules or norms (Bollier and Helfrich 2012; Ostrom 1990). While platform capitalism solely focuses on creating company value and maximising profits from leveraged user knowledge, commons-based peer production introduces new and radical forms of ownership, governance, entrepreneurship and financialisation in a mission to promote sustainability and empower individuals and communities against the pervasive economic inequalities and power asymmetries generated by neoliberalism.

This book focuses on commons-based peer production, or briefly the commons, which is facilitated today by the architectural design of the Internet and free/open source software/hardware, supporting various grassroots initiatives operating in terms of sustainability, decentralisation, openness, self-governance and equitable distribution of value (Benkler 2006; Scholz 2016a). Whereas plenty of diverse theoretical approaches to the commons have been developed over the last decades, only two comprehensive critical accounts of the commons are currently available in the literature. Alexandros Kioupkiolis (2019) and Pierre Dardot and Christian Laval (2014) have recently offered two illuminating critical studies on contemporary theories of the commons. This book deviates from these two influential works in at least one major respect: it takes into account a number of techno-economic factors, the cross-examination of which is deemed appropriate to introducing a multidisciplinary approach to the commons.

This work attempts to contribute to the contemporary discussion over the commons, which revolves around three main axes: a liberal (Benkler 2006; Lessig 2001; Ostrom 1990), a reformist (Arvidsson and Peitersen 2013; Bollier 2003; Kostakis and Bauwens 2014; Rifkin 2014; Rushkoff 2016; Scholz 2016a; 2016b; Wright 2009) and an anti-capitalist (Caffentzis 2013; Dardot and Laval 2014; Dean 2009; 2012; De Angelis 2017; Dyer-Witheford 1999; 2015; Federici 2012; Fuchs 2008; 2011; Gibson-Graham 1996; 2006; Hardt and Negri 2000; 2004; 2009; Harvey 2003; 2010; Kioupkiolis 2019; Laclau and Mouffe 1985; Mason 2015; Söderberg 2008; Žižek 2008; 2010).

This book is not all-inclusive. It covers only authors who do not rest on a piecemeal approach to the commons that singles out one dimension over others – collaborative consumption (Botsman and Rogers 2010), free/libre and open source software (Raymond 1999; Weber 2004), open culture (Leadbeater 2010; Stalder 2005), firm-hosted peer production and open innovation business models (Tapscott and Williams 2006; Benyayer 2016), networking (Castells 2000; 2009; 2010), intellectual communal property (Wark 2004), produsage (Bruns 2008), access (Belk 2014; Bardhi and Eckhardt 2012), decentralisation (Crowston and Howison 2004) or stigmergy (Siefkes 2010). This book, instead, grapples with the work of authors who intend to make or extend a more or less systematic theory out of the commons in terms of an alternative socio-economic paradigm that opposes neoliberalism.

The classification of liberal, reformist and anti-capitalist authors is but a schematic one since arguments often intersect. It does not, therefore, seek to produce any sort of dualities. The classification criterion corresponds to the position where each argument situates the commons in relation to market and state operation. Advocates of the liberal argument take a stand in favour of the coexistence of the commons with market and state operation. The reformists argue for the gradual adjustment of the state and capitalism to the commons, while the anti-capitalists differ from both liberals and reformists by placing the commons against capitalism and the state.

The core thread that penetrates both the reformist and the radical argument dates back to Karl Marx's claim that the technological evolution of the means of production will force capitalism to transform into communism in the long run. Marx was of course a humanist and not a techno-determinist theorist. This conviction, however, does not detract from the fact that technology assumes a central role in his political economy. Today, the presumed advent of communism is projected through the prism of a post-capitalist transition powered by the Internet of Things (IoT), free software/hardware (FOSS), the digital commons and Blockchain. The commons literature portrays multiple variants of this potential transition.

A similar reading of the politics of the commons has been recently undertaken by Antonios Broumas (2017; 2018), though to a limited extent. Broumas classifies theories of the commons into two basic strands: social democratic and critical, with the social democratic diversifying into liberal and reformist versions, and the critical into poststructuralist and anti-capitalist ones. However, Broumas's work focuses on the intellectual commons, that is commons referring to the production, distribution and consumption of information, communication, knowledge and culture, whereas this book examines all types of commons, whether material or immaterial, local or global. This book purports to cover the overall political landscape of the commons, while elaborating a unique critical perspective on the commons.

Drawing on the work of Kioupkiolis and Dardot and Laval, the main thesis of this book is that there is a significant lack of the political in the post-capitalist argument. The political is understood in the theoretical framework of Cornelius Castoriadis's (1988; 1993) concept of the commons as the self-instituting power of the people, exercised against capitalism and the state. The political embraces democracy as the core moral value of society, promoting individual and collective autonomy. Real democracy is based on the equality of all people participating in the creation of the law governing society (Papadimitropoulos 2016).

Whereas all approaches to the commons substantiate the self-instituting power of the people as the key concept of the common, they do not fully address the political in terms of radical democracy, agonistic freedom, conflict and power structures (Kioupkiolis 2019; Mouffe 2005, 15–16, 22, 33–34; Tully 2008, 306–314). Theorists often rest on a limited or ideological standpoint that runs counter to a holistic account of the political, which would translate into a set of cross-disciplinary policies conducive to the sustainability of the commons against the current neoliberal hegemony.

This book intends to produce a critical dialogue between the different approaches to the commons. By no means can it cover all the issues, nor is the coverage of any particular issue complete. The book serves as an introduction to the commons. It aims to provide an in-depth analysis of the core arguments on the commons. Yet the book does not limit itself to a broad-brush approach. It rather seeks to put forward a multidisciplinary account of the commons with the aim of bringing together technology, finance, politics, economics, sustainability science, education and law under commons governance. It does not elaborate another systematic theory of the commons, nor does it reproduce another postmodern, 'anything goes' narrative. It rather maps key proposals that stand out in the literature in a mission to integrate them into a holistic, multi-format political strategy that could variously advance the self-instituting power of the people beyond capitalism and the state. By 'multi-format' strategy this book does not introduce a politics à la carte, but an arsenal of policies that could variously pursue a unique goal: the advancement of the commons into the dominant socio-economic paradigm. The objective here is to critically reconstruct the current theoretical framing of the commons in the networked information economy and unravel the potential of ICTs for the creation of an economic democracy based on sustainability, openness, solidarity and cooperation.

The core argument running through this book is as follows: for the commons to become a fully operational mode of peer production they need to reach a critical mass. Economic democracy cannot exist without a critical mass participating in it. To do so, the commons need to create compelling benefits and use cases for people. They need to provide a steady income to their members along with the incentive to join an alternative socio-economic paradigm anchored in openness, sharing, cooperation, sustainability and democracy. Much of this depends on the degree to which technology can democratise finance and politics, while offering user-friendly solutions to citizens' concrete needs, supported by commons-friendly state policies. In short, to rephrase Bauwens and Kostakis's dictum, it all depends on whether commons-based peer production can become competitive with capitalist production.

The commons could be viewed as vehicles for the creation of a more inclusive social economy, aiming to eliminate the gaping inequalities and power asymmetries of neoliberalism by establishing a sustainable mode of production anchored in openness, sharing, democratic self-governance and the equitable distribution of value. The intent here is not to carve out a unique path but rather to encompass alternative visions of a commons-orientated transition under a holistic, post-hegemonic perspective that contrasts the liberal conception of the commons as 'club' goods, as niche markets coexistent with capitalism and the state. It also disengages from the anarcho-capitalist or libertarian strand of the commons that champions individualism as the core moral value of our times.

My perspective is post-hegemonic in that it seeks to embed the market into the political by socialising the state and economy. The goal is to transform capitalism into the post-capitalism of the commons, that is, a social economy self-organised around the commons. Post-hegemonic holism expresses the need to radically transform the core structure of society by cross-fertilising commons policies and practices across the entire psyche and body of the social. It is often underestimated in the literature that the key to this social change is first and foremost the moral transformation of society; the replacement of 'everyday libertarianism' with 'everyday cooperativism'. This requires the reinvention of humanism and community, the expansion of the politics of care and the overall improvement of the quality of life, including tackling climate change, securing health, food quality and well-being, promoting culture, affection, gender equality, sexuality and self-realisation, which are all primarily tasks of politics, everyday education and collective action.

My argument develops against the backdrop of the struggle between the commons and neoliberalism, which mutates today into the struggle of the digital commons (Aigrain 2012; Griffiths 2008; Morell 2010; Stalder 2010) against platform capitalism. This book situates this struggle within the broader normative framework of Marxism and liberalism, where major political concepts such as power, democracy, freedom, justice and equality are debated (Freeden 1996; Swift 2019). This book cannot but draw some basic lines of argument that serve as an introduction to the struggle between the commons and neoliberalism. Central theoretical categories (i.e. the commons, the political, Marxism, neoliberalism) are outlined upfront to help the reader connect the dots, when necessary, and gain a solid understanding of the core argument. Several other major concepts such as 'platform capitalism', 'the digital commons', 'digital labour', 'immaterial labour', 'post-Fordism', the 'general intellect', 'cognitive capitalism' and 'the multitude' are recurrent themes variously worked out in the course of the book. My argument, thus, disassembles into several modules to be reassembled at the conclusion in a set of concrete policies intended to put forward a post-capitalist, commons-orientated transition beyond neoliberalism.

1.1 The Contours of the Commons

Historically, the term 'commons' has served diverse theoretical contexts, charged with heterogeneous philosophical, religious, legal and economic connotations. To begin with, the etymology of the word 'commons' (*cum* = with and *munus* = obligation), analysed through the prism of ethnology and sociology (Clastres 1989; Godelier 1999; Lévi-Strauss 1969; Mauss 1967), implies a political principle of shared responsibility in the collective practice of public tasks, which is of theological-mythical origin, dating back to primitive societies (Dardot and Laval 2014, 25). The commons represents the 'common good' inherited from Gods/ancestors and further 'incarnated' in the communal institutionalisation of society and nature (Dardot and Laval 2014, 24–27). It is not society and nature in terms of objects or properties that constitute the commons, but the very collective activity of *the instituting*.

The sense of community through unity and equality took a juridico-political and philosophical turn in Greek and Roman thought, without ever losing its theological component, especially after the birth of Christianity (Dardot and Laval 2014, 24–27). Aristotle's *Politics* defines the 'common good' in terms of the collective activity of the *demos* to autonomously decide on the law governing the city. The 'common good' is less a common land and more a public deliberation over the city's common interests. Thus, in Aristotle, the 'common good' refers to the political self-institutionalisation of the city by citizens themselves (Dardot and Laval 2014, 24–27). Cicero revived the Aristotelian republican content of the commons by reconfiguring the 'common good' under the invention of the Roman law (Dardot and Laval 2014, 24–27). The officials of the Roman Empire were obliged by law to serve the 'common good', which was replaced by the public good as represented by the state. Roman republicanism nationalised the 'common good'. The state now held the monopoly of the commons. The common good translated into the public good run by the state and its officials.

The commons republicanism had at least two counter-effects. It highlighted, on the one hand, the juridico-political dimension of the commons over the theological dimension, while limiting, on the other hand, the knowledge of the commons to the experts, namely the legislators or the sovereign. Rousseau would, in one sense, redemocratise the commons by rendering the 'common good' the object of the general will. The 'common good' identifies with what is common between the particular interests of the citizens, turning the sovereignty of the general will against the monopoly of the state (Dardot and Laval 2014, 30, 241–242, 385). Thus, Rousseau prioritised anew the concept of the common as the self-instituting power of the people, which would take an economic turn in the Ricardo school of socialists and the work of Saint-Simon, Fourier, Proudhon and Marx.

Marx, in particular, radicalised the content of the common by integrating the economy into the 'common good'. *Contra* the separation of the economy from the 'common good' and the representation of the latter by the state, adopted by both republicanism and liberalism, Marx locates in the primitive communism of tribal societies the socio-economic model of the free association of producers that would replace capitalism and state despotism with future communism (Dardot and Laval 2014, 67).

The last two centuries have witnessed the emergence of a post-Marxist and post-foundational political ontology of the commons (Marchart 2007). Following the rupture with the philosophical foundations of modernity brought about by Nietzsche, Freud and Heidegger, a number of authors have embraced a post-Heideggerian notion of community and the common with the aim of 'commoning the political', that is, refiguring politics in light of an ontological sense of coexistence, aiming to clear the ground for social openness, solidarity, plurality and autonomy.

Drawing on the conceptual difference between the 'political' and 'politics', first introduced by Carl Schmitt, a number of authors such as Jean-Luc Nancy, Giorgio Agamben and Roberto Esposito elaborate on a concept of the common that welds together a plurality of singularities in a way that overcomes the fragmentation and exclusion of gated communities marked by fixed ethnic, cultural and ideological boundaries (Kioupkiolis 2017). Contrary to economics, the political is the ontological substratum that sustains the different areas of politics, including the economy, culture and state policies. Politics is the concrete instantiation of the political, which is the very ontological possibility of the social (Marchart 2007).

Nancy (1991; 2000), Agamben (1993) and Esposito (2011; 2012; 2013) attempt to address the 'retreat of the political' caused by the current hegemony of neoliberalism by bringing to the fore the political as an open, plural and 'inessential commonality', thereby aiming to reinvigorate the politics of the common. Contrary to variants of liberal communitarianism (Freeden 1996) that conceive of the community in terms of tradition, family, state and nation, the common represents the being-with a plurality of singularities, thus opposing closed identities of blood, soil, community or self. The political brings to the fore an ontological community that determines politics in terms of a collective deliberation that constitutes the common accordingly.

Alexandros Kioupkiolis, among others, has pointed out the political limits of this existential thought. He argues that Nancy, Agamben and Esposito reproduce an abstract level of philosophising, detached from any actual politics (2017, 284). Conversely, he attempts to politicise the common by comparing the ontologies of the common with the political theory of hegemony set out by Ernesto Laclau and Chantal Mouffe.

Laclau and Mouffe (1985) draw on the work of Schmitt and Gramsci, among others, to put forward a politics of the common predicated on the premises of hegemony and antagonism. Hegemony is the articulation of a precarious chain of equivalence among political alternatives, subject to constant change due to the antagonism inherent in the political. Conflict, power and representation are necessary components of democratic politics due to the unavoidable division between oppositional blocks.

In Laclau and Mouffe's hegemonic politics, the commons refers to a multiplicity of spaces, social relations, movements, forms of identification and democratic practices, which retains its partial autonomy with regard to the ever-changing hegemonic articulation of the social (Laclau and Mouffe 1985, 176–193). Kioupkiolis (2017, 300) detects a tension, however, between the hegemony of a particular chain of equivalence and the autonomy of the commons. The hegemony of hierarchy is the cause and effect of uneven power, which contrasts the plurality and horizontality of the commons. To mitigate the tension, he situates hegemony and autonomy at different sites of the political, calling for the post-hegemonic alignment of the former with the latter.

Post-hegemony is the democracy of the common that seeks to balance out hegemony and autonomy.

Michael Hardt and Antonio Negri (2004) were the first to dissolve the misconception of the commons as certain properties or natural resources by introducing the notion of the common in the singular, thereby describing the peer production of the multitude, that is, a network of individuals spontaneously self-organising around common resources. The common stands beyond the private and public sphere of capitalism and the state respectively. It is not so much about destroying or protecting the commons, but about producing the common as the trans-historical political principle of governing nature and society according to collective rules and norms.

David Bollier and Silke Helfrich (2015, 1–12) describe the commons as shared resources, co-governed by their user community, according to the rules and norms of that community. They (2015, 1–12) emphasise the activity of commoning as a social process. The commons is neither the resource nor the community that determines protocols for its stewardship, but the dynamic interaction between all these elements. The term commoning, popularised by historian Peter Linebaugh, signifies the relationship between physical resources and the communities that utilise them and depend upon them for essential human needs. Massimo De Angelis (2017, 119) defines the commons as social systems in which resources are pooled by a community of subjects engaging in commoning, that is, the self-governing and reproducing of the community and the resources. Therefore, the commons consists of three elements: 1) the common-pool resources or common wealth, 2) the community and 3) commoning.

Dyer-Witheford (2006) and Gibson and Graham (1996; 2006) champion the circulation of the commons alongside the capitalist economy with the aim of transforming the latter into a post-capitalist economy. In the same vein, Bauwens and Kostakis (Scholz 2016b, 163) treat the commons as 'a new logic of collaboration between networks of people who freely organise around a common goal using shared resources, and market orientated entities that add value on top of or alongside them'. Arvidsson and Peitersen (2013) refer to the commons as productive publics that help rationalise the public sphere along ecological and democratic lines. Kioupkiolis (2019) approaches the common as a post-hegemonic regime of agonistic freedom, radical democracy, conflict and antagonism. Similarly, Dardot and Laval (2014) conceive of the common as a new type of collective right best exercised under regimes of direct democracy.

Yochai Benkler (2006) discovers this new type of right in the digital commons of the Internet and free/open source software. For Benkler, the commons constitute a third institutional axis of civil society that coexists alongside capitalism and the state. He introduces the term 'commons-based peer production' to demarcate a non-market sector of information, knowledge and cultural production, not treated as private property but as an ethic of open sharing, self-management and cooperation between peers having access to fixed capital, namely computers and software (2006, 59–90).

The commons are also often used with a neoliberal connotation. Corporate terms such as 'flat hierarchies', 'community spirit', 'the sharing economy', 'consumer tribes' and 'the collaborative economy' are euphemisms and marketing buzzwords that aim to exploit commons-based peer production. Neoliberalism occasionally manages to infuse a competitive mentality into the commons themselves, alienating them into extractive enterprises adopting capitalist criteria.

On the flipside, several values of the commons such as common ownership, egalitarianism and collective self-government throb at the heart of communism. Yet the commons are at odds with several features of orthodox communism such as the centrality of the state and the party, top-down direction, totalitarian control, authoritarianism, violence, terror and the idolatry of leaders. Therefore, the signifier is not up for resignification, since it contrasts with the self-instituting power of the people, advanced here as the quintessential concept of the common.

Paradoxically, the digital commons meet with neoliberalism at the crossroads of cyber-libertarianism and cyber-collectivism. Whereas cyber-libertarianism advocates for a minimal state that protects the social and economic freedom of the individual to voluntarily reach mutual, consent-based, online agreements, cyber-collectivism embraces a state that promotes the cybernetic 'general will' or 'common good' (Thierer 2009). Maximum freedom and autonomy for the individual are common moral values within cyber-libertarianism and cyber-collectivism. But the digital commons part ways from both cyber-libertarianism and cyber-collectivism by opposing capitalism and the state. By reformatting the mechanisms of managerial hierarchies, property rights, contracts and prices, the digital commons play out in a variety of formats ranging from networked socialism to spontaneous networked anarchism or anarcho-communism (Benkler 2006; Wright 2009).

Ultimately, the concept of the common as the self-instituting power of the people today has three major and often entangled interpretations: a liberal, a reformist and an anti-capitalist. Yet all three interpretations falter to a lesser or greater degree upon the problem of collective action, formalised today by neoliberalism.

1.2 Neoliberalism and the Problem of Collective Action

The task of this chapter is to explore the problem of collective action posed by neoclassical economics which sustains the bedrock of neoliberalism, which, according to Michel Foucault (2004), is a new form of governmental reason, expanding the corporate model into state management. After exposing the problem of collective action in the normative framework of neoliberalism (1.3), the chapter goes on to introduce a number of challenges to neoclassical economics posed by non-mainstream currents of economic thought (1.4). The task of the latter section is to highlight some crucial heterodox economic points of view that could support a commons-orientated transition.

1.3 The Tragedy of the Commons

Aristotle (1932, Book II, ch. 3) observed long ago that individual interest often prevails over what is considered common to the greater number. Thomas Hobbes's parable of man in a state of nature indicates that the innate selfishness of humans culminates in a war of all against all, whence the need for a Leviathan state to settle conflict and prevent civil war. Most recently, Garret Hardin (1968) introduced the famous 'Tragedy of the Commons' to pose the free-rider problem in economics. He called on us to picture a pasture open to all, in which each herder acts as a self-interested actor, aiming to maximise his/her gain by adding more and more animals for grazing. Self-interest alone eventually results in overgrazing and pasture depletion. Hardin's metaphor has been often formalised as a prisoner's dilemma game expanding from economics to international relations and politics. To address the alleged tragedy, Hardin advocates for private–public control of common-pool resources, which resonates today with neoliberalism, that is, a contemporary version of economic liberalism.

The crux of the classical economic liberal argument is that the basic motive of behaviour is self-interest, the unintended consequences of which generate common welfare (Smith 1977/1776). By trying to maximise her own benefit via commerce and entrepreneurship, each individual unwittingly serves the common good. Unfettered markets are the most efficient means of allocating scarce resources, ensuring that everybody does what they are best suited for and gets what they deserve. Value derives from scarcity and, hence, is confronted by an opportunity cost, that is, the benefit one misses out by choosing one alternative over another. Unrestricted individual exchange guarantees the flow of scarce resources to the highest valued uses. Collective action, on the other hand, cannot produce the 'spontaneous order of the market' due to a lack of the information necessary to coordinate economic activity (Hayek 1944). Collective action either planned by the state or by groups misallocates resources, resulting in societal malfunction.

Classical economic liberal responses to the problem of collective action combine Hobbes's Leviathan approach – central command and control – with Smith's theory of the 'invisible hand' of the market that matches supply and demand through property rights and contracts enforced by the state. Cycles of the Leviathan state and the invisible hand of the market intersect historically at the overlapping peripheries of liberal democracy and the market economy, which demarcate multiple variants of state capitalism.

Neoclassical economics built on classical liberalism's ethics of individualism to construe a utilitarian theory of economics that laid the moral foundation for neoliberalism. David Hume and Jeremy Bentham introduced the notion of utility to argue that each individual aims to satisfy her economic preferences. This ethical idea spilled over into economics to replace the labour theory of value with the theory of utility maximisation. Whereas in classical economics value is synonymous with the labour necessary for the production of a commodity, in neoclassical economics the value of a commodity resides in its utility to a buyer (Mazzucato 2018, 57–74).

Alfred Marshall (2013/1890) shifted thinking about value from the study of capital, labour and technology inputs to that of marginal utility measured by the usefulness of a commodity to a consumer. The value of chocolate is not solely determined by the means of production (land, labour, capital, technology), but is also proportional to the degree of customer satisfaction. Utility translates into the price a customer is willing to pay for the chocolate. Money is not concealed labour, as Marx would have it, but the measure of utility, which varies between individuals, reflecting the evolution of human preferences over time. Marginalism, thus, inverted the objective theory of value measured by labour into the subjective theory of value measured by consumer utility.

Neoclassical economic explanations of behaviour are anchored in the assumption of a fundamentally self-interested rational actor motivated by financial and other incentives (Lowenberg 1990). Humans mutate into economic 'rational' agents using a cost–benefit analysis to choose the market alternative that best satisfies their preferences (Mazzucato 2018, 65). Scarcity and marginal utility – that is, the added satisfaction a consumer garners from consuming additional units of goods or services – determine prices and the relative supply and demand equilibria. Scarcity renders resources rivalrous and subtractable. Hence, private property, contracts and compensation incentives are necessary for individuals to invest in the resource, exchange their valuable products and maximise their subjective utility. Prices, and not labour, are now the sole markers of value. Thus, market allocation produces more efficiency by directing resources to the highest valued use.

The 'tragedy of the commons' is, then, due to the absence of clear property rights, resulting in either underinvestment in resources or overuse and depletion. Motivation is considered lacking in collective action, since no one will invest time, money and energy in a project if they cannot appropriate its benefits. Power to organise collaboration is absent. Therefore, organisation lacks and collaboration necessarily fails. The 'tragedy of the commons' represents, thus, a version of the prisoner's dilemma game, implying that rational strategies of self-interested maximisers can lead to collectively irrational outcomes.

In neoliberal versions of rational choice theory, there can be no common good save for the coincidence of individual ends (Downs 1957). The common good is served best if no one is there to serve it except for the invisible hand of the market. Neoliberalism is predicated on the assumption that collective action fails to manage the economy owing to the uncertainty and complexity inherent in information-processing, which renders coordination and planning impossible (Hayek 1944; Reisman 1990). Complexity and uncertainty impede collective action – the prisoner's dilemma game renamed. Given that centralised planning lacks substantial information on markets and goods, privatisation is the most efficient method for managing resources. Only pricing in markets produces good information and coordination.

Marginalism, the economic bedrock of neoliberalism, suggests that government should limit itself to regulating the economy and intervening only under conditions of market failure. Democracy is merely 'a utilitarian device' for assessing the interests of competing elites (Schumpeter 1994). Voter apathy is then explained on the grounds of massive 'rational ignorance' adopted on the grounds of opportunity costs (Downs 1957). The citizen considers obtaining information on complex policy issues as a highly costly and time-consuming activity. Based on Kenneth Arrow's (1950) theorem pointing out the mathematical impossibility of aggregating individual preferences, some theorists have even been arguing for the complete dismissal of democracy, since, when citizens are faced with three or more alternative options, there is no rational way to reach a consensus and therefore account for democratic governance (Riker 1982).

Capitalism, on the other hand, is considered a peaceful economic system that encapsulates the liberal ideal of self-regulating markets, operating as sites of voluntary exchange based on free trade and property rights, designed to foster technological progress and rising labour productivity to satisfy the wants and needs of all (Mazzucato 2018, 63). An ideal capitalism is supposed to produce multiple equilibria, allocating scarce resources under conditions of 'perfect competition' and perfect information fully accessible to all (Mazzucato 2018, 63–64). The democracy of the market, thus, comes to represent an ethical pluralism that breeds on freedom of choice, tolerance and the rule of law.

1.4 Mainstream vs Non-mainstream Economics

Michel Foucault (2004) describes neoliberalism as a normative order of governmental reason that differs from classical economic liberalism in a number of respects. Government intervention replaces the 'invisible hand' of the market, which is supposed to naturally serve the common good out of individual self-interested actions. The naturalism of liberalism gives way to the constructivism of neoliberalism (Brown 2015, 84). Government intervention should not identify with central planning. Rather, it aims to regulate market operation and facilitate entrepreneurship (Foucault 2004, 121, 131, 145, 164). The liberal image of humans as creatures of needs who contribute to the common good by pursuing individual interest through market exchange is now replaced by the image of humans as entrepreneurs, epitomised in the model of *homo oeconomicus* (Foucault 2004, 276–278).

In neoliberalism, capital replaces labour and entrepreneurship production (Foucault 2004, 116–118). Humans are now managers and self-investors of human capital, rather than solely sellers, workers, clients or consumers. Each person is a mini-capitalist susceptible to the uncertainties, risks and contingencies of the market. Responsibility becomes the indispensable component of self-sustenance inasmuch as the cost–benefit analysis of economic behaviour meshes with state constituencies and the overall health of the economy, the latter standing now as the main site of veridiction (Brown 2015, 68, 84, 131–134). Economic metrics and market prices hold as the only truth valid for legitimising state policies. State governance, finally, breaks down to a neoclassical cost–benefit analysis subject to the dictates of the market.

Neoliberalism, thus, signals a two-way transformation of the economy and the state. On the one hand, the economy becomes the model of the state, marketising all sectors of governance, while, on the other hand, it becomes denaturalised and loses its liberal status as autarchic and self-regulated, requiring the intervention of the state to correct market failures and stimulate competition and growth.

Competition replaces exchange as the fundamental dynamic of the market economy, creating winners and losers and, by extension, inequality (Brown 2015, 64). In the neoclassical model, inequality is a non-issue, since utility is subjective and, therefore, non-comparable. There can be no inequality of utility, but only varying degrees of utility among economic actors (Varoufakis 1998, 43–113). Whereas political equality in the rule and application of law is both the norm of market exchange and the founding principle of the social contract in liberal democracy, economic inequality is considered a structural indicator of meritocracy and an additional incentive for the overall improvement of the economy. Economic inequality is both a cause and an effect of competition, resulting in multiple equilibria that render liberal democracy a contested terrain of corporate interests competing for favourable state policies through negotiation, lobbying, consensus and win–win public–private partnerships (Varoufakis 1998, 43–113). Both persons and states are now construed on the model of the contemporary firm, aiming to maximise their capital value and utility through entrepreneurialism, self-investment and/or attracting investors (Brown 2015, 22). The model of the market expands to all domains and activities, thus reconfiguring human beings first and foremost as market actors.

Simon Springer (2012) describes neoliberalism as a complex discourse articulated in various forms: a hegemonic ideology, a policy and a programme, a form of governmentality. Wendy Brown (2015) makes the case that neoliberalism inaugurates a new era of de-democratisation, thus marking the substitution of politics by technocracy and economics. William Davies (2017) argues that neoliberalism is the disenchantment of politics by economics. From a Marxist standpoint, David Harvey (2005) perceives neoliberalism as a class project aiming at consolidating class power through accumulation by dispossession, that is, the privatisation of public goods and services by financial institutions and state mechanisms.

From a neoclassical standpoint, neoliberalism is supply-side economics born out of the failure of Keynesian demand-side economics to maintain the mixed economy of the post-war period (Stiglitz 2016). Put simply, the state is too costly to sustain and prone to the periodic crises of capitalism. The goal should be, instead, to shrink the state, remove regulation and lower taxes at the top to incentivise the economy and lead to faster economic growth that would trickle down to all and 'lift all boats' to prosperity. Neoliberalism, thus, has been hailed as a solution to the problem of collective action manifested in markets and institutions.

Yet neoclassical economics acknowledges that markets fail under various circumstances. Monopolies, information asymmetries between consumers and producers, externalities not reflected in market prices and the provision of public goods are all instances of market failure (Jacobs and Mazzucato 2016, 16). Governments should intervene and seek to 'correct' market failures, where appropriate, by promoting competition, requiring more available information for consumers, forcing firms to pay for externalities and providing or subsidising public goods. Neoclassical economics insists that competitive markets produce on average positive outcomes that maximise welfare (Jacobs and Mazzucato 2016, 17). Therefore, they should be allowed to operate with the least state interference possible. Governments should limit themselves to a minimum regulatory framework of employment, low taxation, consumer and environmental protection. Excessive regulation is considered to slow economic activity to a crawl and precipitously reduce government revenues, eventually 'killing the goose that lays the golden eggs'.

Yet a number of mainstream economists (Blanchard and Summers 2017) admit today that the market is not a self-stabilising system; the financial system, in particular, becomes over time more complex and is still poorly understood. Therefore, the market needs the state to stabilise the economy with proper policies. The basic difference between mainstream and non-mainstream economics – and between non-mainstream economics themselves – lies in the degree of state intervention and the mixture of policies necessary to regulate the economy.

1.4.1 Post-Keynesian Economics

Post-Keynesian economics considers neoclassical economics an inadequate model for understanding how capitalism operates. A number of authors claim that there are different kinds of market behaviour and several varieties of capitalism (Jacobs and Mazzucato 2016, 17–23). Post-Keynesian economics builds on Keynes's key insight that private investment is volatile and procyclical. It therefore requires public investment to balance it out. Governments should do more than 'levelling the playing field'. They should help tilt the playing field towards publicly chosen goals by investing in education, training, health, childcare, social care and infrastructure:

> Public policies are not 'interventions' in the economy, as if markets existed independently of the public institutions and social and environmental conditions in which they are embedded. The role of policy is not

> simply of 'correcting' the failures of otherwise free markets. It is rather to help create and shape markets to achieve the co-production, and the fair distribution, of economic value. Economic performance cannot be measured simply by the short-term growth of GDP, but requires better indicators of long-term value creation, social well-being, inequality and environmental sustainability. (Jacobs and Mazzucato 2016, 23)

Joseph Stiglitz (2013; 2016) argues that neoliberalism has failed, since it has produced immense income and wealth inequalities from the 1980s onward, exacerbated by the credit-fuelled boom and bust cycles of the market, as in the case of the 2008 financial crisis. Thomas Piketty (2014) describes a patrimonial capitalism of inherited wealth where the rate of return of capital surpasses the rate of growth in the long run. Monopoly rent creates an oligarchy of the 1% that undermines democracy. The winners of the capitalist competition are not compensating the losers, but speculate and hoard profits through rent-seeking mechanisms instead. Rather than expanding the economic pie by means of reinvestment, innovation and job creation, they occupy an even larger space in the economy, with idle capital circulating in the finance sector in the form of share buybacks, derivatives, options, and the like. Asset prices inflate while wages rest more or less stagnant.

For conventional economics, finance performs a number of essential functions for the economy: it allocates capital by recycling surpluses across the globe from surplus countries to deficit countries in the form of investment and credit, it mediates between savers and investors providing credit to individuals and companies, it promotes innovation and job creation, it manages risk, it provides liquidity, and it runs the payment mechanism (Stiglitz 2016, 40). Finance adds value to the real economy by completing markets, thereby propelling the Arrow-Debreu general equilibrium momentum: if only all different agents create as many contracts as possible, complete all markets and trade continually among them, the economy will reach the Pareto-efficient maximum possibility of human welfare.

However, Stiglitz (2013; 2016) has shown that trading in financial instruments is not trading between different people with different consumer preferences or production possibilities. It is rather trading between different people with different points of view over the state of an uncertain future wherein more trading can be actually harmful. One of the justifications of high-frequency trading is that it increases price discovery, thus contributing to perfect information. Yet the Grossman–Stiglitz theorem (Grossman and Stiglitz 1980) has revealed that high-frequency trading reduces the informativeness of the price system. Opaqueness and leverage produce a zero-sum game, a casino activity that impacts all sectors of the economy, from retail to wholesale. By creating leverage, that is, speculation, finance shifts risk from one sector to another, with risk eventually ending up in the public sector due to the interconnectedness of the financial sector and its spreading into the real sector.

The 2008 crisis proved that finance failed in every dimension: it misallocated capital, it did not provide credit for new job creation, it mismanaged risk, it misguided innovation, it prioritised exploitation and market manipulation and created an exorbitantly expensive payments mechanism (Stiglitz 2016, 108). Finance became, finally, a negative sum game, creating enormous profits for corporations and benefiting the affluent few at the expense of the rest. Many of the profits were achieved as a result of predatory lending, abusive credit card practices, market manipulation and excessive market power. The economic consequences of the failures of finance have been gaping inequality, low growth, high instability, and high levels of private and public indebtedness.

The sociopolitical result has been the revival of the nightmares of the 1930s in the form of the rise of racist, xenophobic and neo-fascist far right-wing populism. Wealth and income inequality, economic nationalism, deglobalisation, trade wars, geopolitical tensions and the migrant crisis accompany the sustainability crisis, in which global warming increases, pandemics spread, ecosystems degrade, fossil fuels are diminishing and food remains insecure (Dedeurwaerdere 2013).

To reverse the neoliberal tide, Stiglitz (2016, 97–168) suggests changes to executive compensation schemes, combat against short-termism, the reduction of rent seeking, the elimination of racial and gender discrimination, macroeconomic policies to restore full employment, the regulation of the shadow banking system, greater investment in education and infrastructure and the reform of capital taxation, among other things. Mariana Mazzucato calls for the 'socialisation of investment' by an 'entrepreneurial state' investing in innovation to address major societal problems such as climate change and elderly healthcare (Jacobs and Mazzucato 2016, 14). Yanis Varoufakis (2011) calls for a Green New Deal funded by the issuing of Eurobonds as a first step before reimagining the corporation. Piketty (2014) advocates for a global wealth tax and higher top marginal tax rates.

1.4.2 Radical Economics

Theorists coming from the radical left call for a socialist transition to an economic democracy via either more or less direct state intervention. Erik Olin Wright (2009) is one of the most prominent scholars to have advocated for radical reforms wherein the state should assume a central role towards a socialist transition. He argues for the creation of a more democratic financial system where we should reimagine the role of governments in private capital markets.

Under neoliberalism, the state is considered a drain on taxpayers' private money, with its capacity to print money causing inflation. Conventional economics considers money a scarce resource that is more efficiently managed by the law of supply and demand. Money is a market innovation that replaced the barter economy with a more efficient economic system (Mellor 2019, 638). It dates back to the invention of coinage, that is, the adoption of precious metal as a valued commodity. Given the scarcity and the physical properties of gold and silver (durability, divisibility, transferability, storability, usability), money in the form of coins is considered the embodiment of economic value, circulating in the market as the general equivalent of goods and services. Money functions simultaneously as a unit of account, a medium of exchange and a store of value.

Yet money is also a means of social and economic power. What fuelled the market and the growth of capitalism was not the invention of coinage but the proliferation of bank-issued debt (Mellor 2019, 639). Money accumulates into profit, which then transforms into rent and interest-bearing credit and debt. Banking became the steam engine of modern capitalism, anchored in the gold standard, linking money to the price of gold. Since the final decoupling of the US dollar from gold in 1971 and the subsequent establishment of fiat money, that is, government-issued money not backed by a physical commodity, finance has held the steering wheel of neoliberalism.

Conventional economics sees banking and finance as intermediaries between supply (surplus units) and demand (deficit units). Robert Hockett (2019, 492) calls this the 'intermediated scarce private capital orthodoxy'. According to this view, capital is limited to what has previously been accumulated by rentiers in the form of financial assets held in banks and other financial institutions. Banks and capital markets link rentiers of surplus capital with households, firms and governments. Surplus capital is deposited in banks in the form of short-term demand deposits, which are then loaned out on a one-to-one basis in the form of longer-term loans. Interest amounts to money rental rates determined by the law of supply and demand just like all other prices. Deposits, thus, make loans, savings determine investment and interest rates equilibrate private fund supply and demand (Hockett 2019, 500–503).

Hockett (2019, 501) instead makes the case that loans make deposits according to a none-to-many credit-generation model. When a bank receives an application for a loan from a creditworthy business or household, it does not check out how much money is deposited in its vaults. It creates the money *de novo* by simply crediting a borrower account with the given amount and then booking the transaction as an asset and liability of its own and of the borrower. Banks do not merely act as intermediaries between savers and borrowers; they simply type digits on a computer ledger to create money *ab initio* (Mellor 2019, 639). Therefore, the money supply is not scarce. Credit is not limited to privately pre-accumulated capital but endogenously issued. Banks actually borrow depositors' money, keep a percentage to handle daily operations and fictitiously multiply the rest in the form of circulating debt to be invested in the real economy and generate the money that will repay the interest-bearing debt, thus coming full circle ad infinitum. Money is actually interest-bearing debt fuelling the production of future value. In Britain only 3% of total money amounts to tangible currency (notes and coins) in circulation, the remaining 97% being composed of numbers saved in computers. The fear of the central banks that became the money creators of last resort for the banks in the 2008 financial crisis was not the collapse of the money supply, but that ATM machines would run dry (Mellor 2019, 637).

Hockett paints a different picture of finance where the central bank in effect publicly monetises the promissory note privately issued and signed by the borrower in favour of the lending bank. The central bank is placing the full faith and credit of the nation behind the credit of the borrower in the form of the Federal Reserve notes. The private bank is simply assisting the central bank with privately issued promissory notes to swap for spendable, publicly issued promissory notes. The interest it earns on the loan is its payment for serving a public utility. Credit is not based on privately deposited loanable funds, but on the monetised full faith and credit of the state that pays private seigniorage rents with public currency. 'The financial system then looks like a franchise arrangement in which the public is franchiser and the institutions dispensing its full faith and credit are its franchisees' (Hockett 2019, 491). In other words, the capacity of banks to create credit rests on the laws, regulations and guarantees of the state under which they operate. Contemporary financial systems are then best interpreted as public–private franchise arrangements.

The state has been granting monopoly rights to corporations to build infrastructures, energy and telecommunications networks from capitalism's inception, and has been heavily investing in the development of new technologies thereafter (Mazzucato 2013). The Fed and the Treasury department have been directly channelling and managing the flow of monetised public faith and credit through the financial system by backing and often turning private liabilities into public ones. The world's first heavily capitalised securities exchanges, such as those in Amsterdam, London, Paris and New York, were set up as government instrumentalities or sites where government-issued debt could be purchased and sold. Venture capital dates back to 1958 when federal legislation created Small Business Investment Companies that had access to guaranteed financing. 'Capital markets ride on treasury and government agency liabilities just as bank lending markets ride on central bank liabilities' (Hockett 2019, 504). The latter became amply evident with the financial crisis of 2008, when the Fed stepped in to save the bankrupt banks:

> Following the crisis, the very evident public creation of money revealed the inherently political nature of money. When other fiscal and monetary solutions appeared unable to refloat damaged economies, central banks resorted to the explicit creation of money out of thin air. Under what was described rather obscurely as 'quantitative easing', vast amounts of newly created electronic money were used to rescue financial institutions. There was no question of the new money's being borrowed from anywhere. It was a clear demonstration of the sovereign power to create money. Radical voices quickly asked why if the central

> bank could create money out of thin air to rescue the banks they could not create new money to rescue the people. (Mellor 2019, 645)

Mary Mellor (2019, 640–641) argues that bank-created money is socially, ecologically, economically and politically unsustainable. It exacerbates racial inequality by favouring the more creditworthy borrower and locking out the poor and the non-white. Flows of finance at low interest rates are channelled into hedge funds, private equity funds and speculative investments in financial instruments, whereas poor and working-class people are forced to borrow from payday lenders or loan sharks at confiscatory interest rates. Financialisation has created a 'winner-takes-all' economy that has produced the exorbitant concentration of wealth and income documented by Piketty. It drives economic growth and creates ecological damage. It is crisis-ridden, turning private losses into public liabilities. Mellor (2019, 645) stresses the need not just to democratise finance but to reclaim the sovereign power to create money free of debt that could be spent directly into circulation. She calls for a public money system based on a widely democratic, transparent and accountable management of the creation and allocation of money.

Hockett takes this argument to its logical end, suggesting that there are no limits on the state's capacity to generate credit or money. He introduces a tweak to existing institutional arrangements by advocating for the creation of a National Investment Council to coordinate public–private investment at a federal level, accompanied by Federal Reserve reforms such as the creation of Fed Citizen and Residents Accounts, a Fed price stabilisation fund or People's Portfolio and a Fed-administered digital dollar engineered by Blockchain (Hockett 2019, 515–522). These reforms would eventually initiate a 'QE for the people' that would ignite the transition to a full 'People's Fed' steered by a more effective counter-inflationary and counter-deflationary Fed monetary policy.

Fred Block (2019, 529–556) suggests the creation of a national investment bank linked to locally based and non-profit financial institutions such as credit unions, public banks, community banks and non-profit investment banks. Large-scale investment in research and development, infrastructure and clean energy would combine with local investment in affordable housing, small businesses, non-profits and employee cooperatives. The ultimate goal would be the creation of a parallel financial system alongside the existing financial institutions that would gradually replace the private sector with a public one.

Lenore Palladino (2019, 573–591) proposes that the 'parallel credit system' be accompanied by a 'parallel equity system'. He suggests the creation of a Public Investment Platform followed by a 'public investment account' that would offer a 'public option' for investment opportunities to individuals and households locked out of the expensive private sector. Michael McCarthy (2019, 611–633) argues for the creation of state-administered sovereign wealth funds and worker-owned inclusive funds run by firms and corporations.

In short, the aforementioned proposals build on Wright's argument for the creation of a more democratic financial system that would fuel a socialist transition. However, unlike Wright's intention, they tend to address the periphery rather than the core of the problem. To tackle the structural contradictions of capitalism that produce immense inequalities and destroy the planet, it is necessary to alter the mode of capitalist production from within. State-centred, radical democratic rebalances of the capitalist economy need to tilt towards a decentralised, post-capitalist, post-hegemonic, commons-orientated transition geared by the self-management of the economy and society as a whole. As a response to the various crises of capitalism, ecologists, activists, politicians, scholars and citizens gather in all sorts of social movements and communities across the globe to juxtapose capitalist production with commons-based peer production anchored in the principles of democratic self-management, equitable distribution of value, sustainability science and the ethics of collaboration.

1.5 In Defence of the Commons

Following up on the critique of neoliberalism, we now put forward additional arguments to move the terrain of discussion from post-Keynesianism and radical state-centred economics to post-capitalism. The standard neoclassical model of perfect competition, perfect information, perfect risk markets and perfect rationality fails to correctly depict how the economy works. The model of *homo oeconomicus* introduced by marginalism and incarnated thereafter by neoliberalism is challenged today in multiple disciplines, starting with economics itself (Dedeurwaerdere 2013; Keen 2001; Mason 2015; Mazzucato 2018; Vatn 2005). The theory of marginalism that dominates textbook economics is fallacious, superfluous and ideological (Keen 2001; Mason 2015, 162). It reduces humans to calculating 'machines' of pain and pleasure, gain or loss; to mere traders, entrepreneurs or capitalists. It discards an exuberant human psyche replete with heterogeneous emotions, motives and rationales. The model of a rational actor calculating past and present information to maximise future utility is in stark contrast with real-world social dynamics driven by information asymmetries along with diverse motivations (Dedeurwaerdere 2013, 7). Humans are complex animals, fusing monetary with non-monetary motivations in unimaginable ways.

1.5.1 The Digital Economy

The development of ICTs over the last decades poses a number of challenges for neoclassical economics. Information technology transforms norms of consumption, modes of production, commercial transactions, organisational forms, network management, and so on (Brousseau and Curien 2007, 2).

Industry now comes to be organised around a flexible assembly model (dis) intermediated by digital platforms that (dis)connect the place where value is produced from the place where value is collected by decentralising and trans-nationalising economic space, while constituting a mobile global audience that navigates between e-commerce and e-communities; competitiveness relies heavily on technological innovation; products and services bear an increasing information intensity generating a two-way commoditisation and customisation; new business models emerge that adopt a great variety of communication, differentiation and discrimination strategies based on the multimedia character of the Internet (Brousseau and Curien 2007, 3–17).

But instead of information technology becoming the 'lubricant' that removes all friction in commerce and gives reality to a transparent, ultra-competitive market economy, it brings about typical market failures such as club effects, market concentration and monopolisation, while sowing the seeds of a cooperative economy. Markets tend towards greater segmentation rather than greater fluidity; hierarchies become more malleable rather than more efficient; and, most importantly, information becomes a free input into the production of knowledge (Brousseau and Curien 2007, 19).

A number of often disparate authors such as Yochai Benkler (2006), Eric Brynjolfsson and Andrew McAfee (2014), Jeremy Rifkin (2014), Paul Mason (2015) and Michel Bauwens (2019) argue that information technology challenges the basic tenet of marginalism, which is scarcity. Whereas the market economy aims to allocate efficiently scarce resources, information creates an abundance of value owing to its unique characteristics: 1) it is not 'used up'; 2) it can be infinitely reproduced at zero marginal cost; and 3) it produces a number of positive externalities through the creation of network effects. Information 'dematerialisation', that is, the dissociation between information and commodities, produces a knowledge economy built around intellectual commons that constitute a non-rivalrous good, thereby giving rise to a public good within a market economy (Brousseau and Curien 2007, 3, 19–21; Broumas 2020). An agent who transmits information can still keep and consume the same information, granting a very low opportunity cost compared to the utility transferred to the receiver. Therefore, given the limits of saturation effects, a great number of agents can consume the same information simultaneously.

Kenneth Arrow (1962, 609–626), a mainstream economist, pointed out in the 1960s the problem of the optimal allocation of information as a commodity due to its zero marginal cost of reproduction accounting for its incomplete appropriability by a seller. In contrast to tangible commodities such as a car or a chair, the moment information is disclosed, it can be infinitely copied and reproduced almost freely. And since information is abundant by nature and markets exist for allocating scarce resources, there can be no markets for information. Put simply, one cannot easily create a market to sell information. Given that the root of invention and innovation is knowledge, information breeds a contradiction between market economics and the production of knowledge. If firms cannot appropriate the returns of producing knowledge, then they will have little incentive to invest in it. Whence, the notion of knowledge as a public good to be provided by state universities and further advanced through research grants and subsidies. Intellectual property rights protected by the state aim to tackle this contradiction, but they lead to the underutilisation of information and the inefficient use of knowledge.

Ultimately, information technology produces a paradox for conventional economics: it disrupts the function of the price signal and the relevant matching of supply and demand either because richer information than just price is necessary (information-intensive goods) or because it pushes marginal price close to zero (pure information goods) (Brousseau and Curien 2007, 22). The transition to the knowledge economy has led to the increased importance of fixed costs and the diminishing role of competition. The marginal cost, that is, the extra cost in the reproduction of knowledge, is very low. The cost of distributing an ebook on the Internet is close to zero. But the fixed cost of writing a book is still present. Therefore, the existence of large fixed costs upstream compared to the low marginal cost in the reproduction of knowledge downstream undermines the neoclassical ideal of a well-functioning competitive economy.

To recover the increased fixed costs upstream, companies finance them downstream either by rationing demand or applying coarse pricing or shifting revenue towards advertising or, finally, calling for the state to finance infrastructure (Brousseau and Curien 2007, 22). To fill in the gap between supply and demand caused by information overload, they co-opt infomediation among self-organised online consumer communities that spontaneously couple supply with demand, using the zero marginal free supply of tools and content on the Internet to share information. Rather than market operation reaching Arrow-Debreu's neoclassical equilibrium model of perfect information and perfect competition, it resembles a Schumpeterian-Hayekian model wherein suppliers and consumers constantly 'co-invent' the terms of their trade.

Eric Brousseau and Nicolas Curien suggest that the digital economy should become in the long run a 'co-opetition' economy that breeds business to business (B-to-B) marketplaces where companies cooperate upstream as monopolies as well as monopsonies, benefiting from scale effects generated by mass purchases, and compete downstream on the retail markets. Apple is a monopsony in purchasing apps from developers across the globe (Tepper and Hearn 2019). Facebook is the sole 'purchaser' of user-generated content at zero price. It controls almost 80% of mobile social traffic. Airbnb dominates short-term rentals. Amazon bought dozens of e-commerce rivals and online booksellers, acquiring a monopsony position in the book industry. It gets about 75% of ebook sales. Facebook bought Instagram and WhatsApp. Google bought its main competitor, DoubleClick, and vertically integrated online ad markets by buying advertising exchanges. It controls 90% of search advertising. Google's monopsony vision is to become the dominant digital wholesale information broker to the global Internet audience. On the whole, Google, Amazon, Apple, Facebook and Microsoft have together acquired more than 500 companies in the past decade (Tepper and Hearn 2019). Altogether, these companies make up a data-extracting model of platform capitalism to the tune of 3 trillion dollars.

Down the line, Brousseau and Curien (2007, 21–24) anticipate that the digital landscape should experience a 'path-dependent' reconstruction of the value chain where the differentiation of goods and services reduces competition, with infomediation leading to the coexistence of several ecosystems rather than a merciless struggle of the winner-takes-all type. Thus, 'fringe' monopolies allow for a multitude of small businesses or cooperatives to subsist in niche markets. Network interactions will eventually create adaptable relations rather than hierarchical subordination, reconciling stability and flexibility under a repeated game equilibrium.

At present, however, technological change exacerbates the disparity between private and social returns to information (knowledge) (Stiglitz 2016, 48). It enhances rent seeking and the capacity for rent extraction, turning information into an artificially scarce good disproportionally exploited by corporations having differential access to it. Asymmetries of information and concentrated market power create an oligopoly of knowledge production that stifles innovation. The extent to which technological change will reproduce – and even exacerbate – the current concentration of market power or lead to an equilibrium among reticular market powers will be determined by the rules of the game over privacy rights, among others. To the extent that data will be treated as a public good, technological change is likely to produce a game equilibrium and a balance between static and dynamic efficiency rather than an oligopoly of market power.

1.5.2 The Commons

But this depends largely on the future of class struggle. Mainstream information economics focuses on supply and demand dynamics, discarding the potential of online consumer communities actually turning into self-organised prosumer communities that make use of open source technologies on the Internet to create an alternative mode of production that bypasses both firms and managerial hierarchies. They take for granted that capitalist production is the most efficient mode of allocating resources. Yet digital networks, open source technologies, Blockchain and the Internet of Things have the potential to support a new type of social relations anchored in the mutual coordination of common-pool resources, which are not set according to the price mechanism of the market nor the managerial hierarchies of corporations and states.

There are plenty of ideological elements in the Hayekian framework: prices are an accurate and sufficient signal of information to allow for decentralised coordination to produce social welfare; intellectual property rights are necessary and sufficient for the production of knowledge; competition is hard wired into the human species; collective self-management of the economy is destined to failure, and so on. Yochai Benkler (2006) and Elinor Ostrom (1990) consider prices, contracts and strict property rights lossy, sticky and costly. The commons advance, instead, a more refined, flexible and cost-efficient information processing, better attuned to the variability of human creativity than managerial hierarchies (firms, states). The free flow of information among large sets of agents who have cheap access to means of communication produces substantial information gains by better allocating value to preferable courses of action, thereby unleashing creativity and innovation while reducing complexity and uncertainty. The information and allocation gains of the commons could under certain circumstances translate into better, fairer and more sustainable socio-economic outcomes in comparison to price signals and managerial hierarchies. Transparency, openness and sharing could distribute value more equitably than firms that restrict access to knowledge by enclosing information under strict intellectual property rights.

The commons are premised on a simple yet radical idea: great improvements in production could be achieved by reducing barriers to knowledge exchange (Bollier and Helfrich 2015, 145). Collaboration and openness could produce a constantly improving collective repository of best ideas and practices; hence, the open source technologies of the digital commons adding up to rural and urban commons. The commons consist in a shared pool of resources from which everybody can draw or to which everybody can contribute according to their needs and capacities. Collaboration prevents free riding by self-monitoring mechanisms reinforced both online and offline. Cosmolocalism, that is, the local use of global (digital) commons, could democratise the economy and set a new socio-economic paradigm anchored in the self-management of the means of production (Kostakis and Bauwens 2014).

Price signals, property rights and contractual relations are just some elements in an institutional toolkit. Commons-based peer production increases the diversity of actors, motivations and transaction forms (Benkler 2006). It decentralises authority where the capacity to act exists, thereby diffusing power and freedom to the many. Free access to information and the means of production empowers citizens and helps address the sustainability crisis through the ecological control of the economy. Open design, open protocols, open supply chains and open book accounting ensure maximum participation through modularity, and promote strigmergic collaboration by mutual coordination, which can in turn advance democracy, reduce waste and sustain a circular economy (Bauwens et al. 2019).

Further evidence from evolutionary biology and the social sciences illustrates the shift in the scientific understanding of human rationality from the model of the self-interested maximiser, driven by competition and separable motivations, to the model of *homo socialis* featuring cooperation and diverse pro-social motivations (Benkler 2011). The competition hailed by neoliberalism

Table 1.1: Neoclassical vs commons-based economics.

Neoclassical economics	Commons-based economics
scarcity	scarcity (local commons and ethical market entities) ⇔ abundance (global, digital commons) > cosmolocalism, *glocal* commons
self-interest	diverse motivations: self-interest, solidarity, affection, care
competition	cooperation
privacy	open access
strict property rights	relationalised property through sharing
hierarchical management	self-management
planned obsolescence	circular economy
profit maximisation	profit is not central but peripheral > equitable distribution of value and risk
individual labour > capitalist division of labour	collective labour > mutual coordination by stigmergic collaboration, equipotentiality = participation conditioned *a posteriori* by the process of production itself, where skills are verified and communally validated in real time > creativity, self-realisation vs alienation of labour, precariousness, intensification of labour, performance pressure, stress
growth > climate crisis	degrowth > sustainability
collective action > tragedy of the commons	self-monitoring mechanisms for avoiding common-pool resource depletion > comedy of the commons
network effects (Internet) > positive externalities > value crisis > enclosure of the digital commons > surveillance capitalism	the tokenisation/monetisation of positive externalities across the commons value chain > federalism, post-capitalism
finance and credit	community transaction mechanisms such as as internal lending, smart contracts, participatory budgeting, common liquidity fund, resource pooling, microfunding
entrepreneurial innovation	commons-based eco-techno-social innovation
regulatory state, minimum state, capitalist state, social democratic state	commons-centric partner state

as the evolutionary pattern of human society is contradicted on the grounds of cooperation facilitated today by ICTs. Competition is not a zero-sum game between rivals but a win–win game between peer producers collaborating on symmetric terms. Rationality does not always translate into self-interest, since humans often rationally pursue non-self-interested goals. Cooperation rather than competition is the evolutionary drive of human species' survival (Bowles and Gintis 2011).

Today, the decentralised use of the Internet and free software/hardware disrupts centralised capitalist production on the model of commons-based peer production operating in terms of sustainability, openness, sharing and bottom-up techno-social innovation. Commons-based peer production is alive and kicking, as evidenced by the range of the digital commons, the Free and Open Source Software (FOSS) movement, the solidarity economy, platform and open cooperatives, all joining forces with social movements to subvert the neo-liberal hegemony of capitalism. Prominent cases of the digital commons, FOSS, platform and open cooperatives (e.g. Stocksy, Fairmondo, Mozilla Foundation, WikiHouse, Mondragon) will be examined in the course of this book.

1.6 Structure of this Book

Part 1 deals with the liberal argument on the commons. Elinor Ostrom (1990) proved Hardin wrong by illustrating hundreds of cases of common-pool resources self-managed by user communities for centuries according to well-defined rules and norms collectively established. She showed that not only is cooperation possible in hundreds of cases of common-pool resources, but that locally developed institutions and practices occasionally outperform market or state-driven systems governed by private property control and expert regulation respectively. Ostrom's empirical work offers important insights into how formal and informal norms can structure collaboration along the lines of non-property-based schemes.

Lawrence Lessig (2001) and Yochai Benkler (2006) expanded Ostrom's work on the digital commons. Lessig introduced the innovation commons of the Internet. Benkler coined the term 'commons-based peer production' to describe open contributory networks of distributed tasks, set and executed by groups online in a decentralised and autonomous fashion. The proliferation of open/free software in the digital landscape today testifies to a set of collaborative practices not adequately explained in terms of property rights and monetary motivations.

Part 2 examines the reformist argument. David Bollier builds on the work of Ostrom to introduce the model of the green governance of the commons (Bollier and Helfrich 2012). He argues that the state must shift its focus to become a partner of the commons, rather than the market. Along with Silke Helfrich (Bollier and Helfrich 2019), he demonstrates a theoretical framework for the commons based on a common language. Jeremy Rifkin (2014) introduces the model of green capitalism connecting to the Internet of Things infrastructure, fuelled by renewables. He advocates the gradual shift of green capitalism towards the commons, supported by the Internet and free/open source software/hardware.

Trebor Scholz (2016a; 2016b) adds a cooperative twist to the commons by juxtaposing platform cooperativism against platform capitalism (the so-called sharing and gig economy). Platform cooperativism consists of online business models based on democratic self-governance, platform co-ownership and the equitable distribution of value. Kostakis and Bauwens (2014) give a challenging spin to platform cooperativism by introducing the model of open cooperativism between the commons and ethical market entities, operating in terms of open protocols, open supply chains, commons-based licensing and open book accounting. Open cooperativism is backed by a partner state through taxation, funding, regulation, education, and so on. Open cooperativism aims at the creation of a commons-orientated economy based on shared resources from which actors can draw or to which they can contribute according to their needs and capacities. DECODE (Decentralised Citizen Owned Data Ecosystems) is an ambitious research project that seeks to democratise data infrastructures. It has conducted extensive research to apply the principles of platform and open cooperativism in concrete case studies located in Amsterdam and Barcelona (Morell et al. 2017).

Adam Arvidsson and Nicolai Peitersen (2013) illustrate a technologically advanced Habermasian transformation of the public sphere, where collaborative networks of peer producers, supported by the Internet and mobile applications, would open up a more rational and democratic negotiation of economic value, bringing together politics, the commons and a reformed capitalism. Douglas Rushkoff (2016) introduces a model of digital distributism that would reprogramme capitalism into post-capitalism, where the pursuit of growth is subsumed to a sustainable economy based on value creation and the recycling of money.

Erik Olin Wright (2009) portrays a pluralistic socialist transformation, grounded on a centrally coordinated decentralisation of power. His socialist transformation strategy is premised on the radical democratisation of both the state and the economy by civil society.

Part 3 critically engages the anti-capitalist argument. Alexandros Kioupkiolis (2017) attempts to politicise the commons by commoning the political. He calibrates the tension between Ernesto Laclau and Chantal Mouffe's verticalism and Michael Hardt and Antonio Negri's horizontalism in favour of the self-instituting power of the people. Pierre Dardot and Christian Laval (2014) work on a similar line of argument to transform the common into a new type of right anchored in the self-instituting power of the people.

Katherine Gibson and Julie Graham (Gibson-Graham 1996; 2006) embark on a concrete elaboration of the commons into a post-capitalist context. They articulate the creation of a community economy that would gradually transform capitalism into the commons. Dyer-Witheford (1999; 2015) and

De Angelis (2017) formalise the circulation of the commons alongside the circulation of capital with the aim of transforming capitalism into post-capitalism. George Caffentzis (2013) and Silvia Federici (2012) take a more radical stance against capitalism and the state, arguing for the autonomous reproduction of the commons.

Slavoj Žižek (2008; 2010), Jodi Dean (2009), David Harvey (2003; 2010), Paul Mason (2015) and Christian Fuchs (2008; 2011) approach the commons in the context of classical Marxism. Whereas Žižek and Dean adopt a more statist approach, Harvey, Mason and Fuchs seek to strike a balance between the state and the commons.

1.6.1 Thesis

This book makes the case that the liberal argument underestimates the reformist insight that technology has the potential to decentralise production, thereby forcing capitalism to transform into post-capitalism. While the reformists argue for the cooperation of the commons with the state and friendly capital, the anti-capitalists argue for the autonomous development of the commons against and beyond capitalism and the state. Yet the anti-capitalists cannot provide a viable strategy as to how to safeguard the autonomy of the commons under conditions of grave dependency on state and capitalist production. While the reformists attempt to abolish the heteronomy of the commons by means of reverse co-optation via transvestment, they cannot address the precariousness and economic unsustainability that pervades commons-based peer production. They lack concrete strategies to help peers monetise use value and gain public trust and involvement in commons-based peer production. Finally, both the reformists and the anti-capitalists lack adequate strategies to reach a critical mass and transform capitalism into post-capitalism or anti-capitalism.

This is partially due to the contradictions of the commons often replicating the contradictions of capitalism and the state. Localism, gated communities, vested interests, atavism, traditionalism, ideology, conflict, neoconservatism and techno-elitism represent some of the internal contradictions of the commons (Harvey 2003, 169). One of the major problems of the commons is the equilibrium of communities with the fluid, hybrid and mobile identities of individuals in the networked information economy. This is partially coextensive with the tension between the non-commerciality and the commerciality of the commons, that is, the principle of keeping the open character of the commons while securing income for those contributing (Morell et al. 2017, 11). Externally, the commons are facing problems in access to capital and training, lack of entrepreneurial and managerial skills and the absence of institutional support from governments, larger cooperatives and NGOs (Bollier and Helfrich 2015). Both internal and external contradictions can equally result in the tyranny of the commons over the heterogeneity of the individual immanent in the cultural diversity of any collectivity.

Technology has, indeed, the potential to address these issues. It can help feed more people, cure illness, address climate change, create a more equitable economy and enhance democracy. But only a few commons-based applications can currently support such a claim. Human–computer interaction is still in its infancy and relevant research is at a preliminary stage. There are still limited successful cases available to point towards an economically, ecologically and socially sustainable commons-based peer production.

The problem with the information argument is the technological determinism that often comes to downplay the political. It falsely presumes that technological fixes can account for democratic processes. A number of authors such as Trebor Scholz (2016a; 2016b), Bauwens and Kostakis (Bauwens et al. 2019) and Alexandros Kioupkiolis (2019) attempt to address this issue, but still the problem persists: the big challenge lying ahead for the commons is the compatibility of democratic governance with technological efficiency. Participatory democracy, tele-democracy, cyber-democracy, post-democracy, the commons democracy are all terms invented to solve the puzzle. But cyber-optimism is still contradicted by the non-replicability of the digital commons in the rest of the economy, let alone the technical inadequacies in addressing environmental and societal issues along democratic lines. Technology cannot but be subject to the political, that is, the moral ground that forms the rationale behind coding and algorithms. Put simply, technology is necessarily embedded in the broader political institutionalisation of society.

For the commons to avoid both tragedy and/or parody, it is crucial to grow into open, transparent and mutually reinforcing networks that can provide for their members a sustainable livelihood along with the political conditions for democracy, autonomy and justice. To do so, it is essential to transform into multi-way socio-economic circuits of peer production and ethical market operation, supported by relevant state policies. The short-term goal of the commons would be the creation of a commons/private/public economy on the basis of a common pool of resources from which actors can draw and to which they can contribute according to their needs and capacities. The long-term goal would be the gradual adjustment of capitalism to the post-capitalism of the commons.

The commons-based, post-capitalist transition needs to be enacted by a holistic, multidisciplinary strategy aimed at encompassing technology, finance, politics, economics, education, sustainability science and law under commons governance. Proper incentive schemes, well-designed policies, financial mechanisms, law reforms, education are all part and parcel of a post-hegemonic strategy aiming to transform capitalism and liberal democracy into the post-capitalism of the commons, supported by a partner state that represents the interests of the people rather than elites. The comprehensive understanding of a commons-orientated socio-economic transition can potentially lead to the introduction of relevant policies that can mobilise the collective action necessary to embrace a truly collaborative economy premised on principles of sustainability, justice, democratic self-governance and the equitable distribution of value.

PART I

The Liberal Commons

CHAPTER 2

The Liberal Commons

2.1 Introduction

Liberalism is a moral philosophy built on the concept of negative freedom, which dates back to Thomas Hobbes, who defined freedom as the absence of external impediments to the pursuit of one's preferences. Negative freedom does not attribute to freedom a positive content, but is rather synonymous with freedom of individual choice. Negative freedom has thereafter become the backbone of liberal political thought, as demonstrated in the work of John Locke and John Stuart Mill, up until its most contemporary versions such as the work of John Rawls (1971), Robert Nozick (1974) and Friedrich Hayek (1944), to mention some of the most prominent figures. Variations of negative freedom depend on how one defines 'interference', but all agree that to be free is, more or less, to be left alone to do whatever one chooses (Carter et al. 2007, 3). As such, negative freedom encapsulates the core of modernity's legal rights, which demarcate the bounds between the private and public sphere along the lines of property, ethical pluralism and tolerance. Liberalism is associated with the modern state founded on the rule of law and the separation of powers, both constitutive of representative democracy. The fundamental normative principle of liberal democracy is the sovereignty of the people, exercised in the public sphere through the freedoms of speech, assembly and press, and under conditions of transparency and accountability.

In its economic meaning, liberalism champions free trade and market capitalism. The common good identifies with the social welfare generated by the 'invisible hand' of the market regulated by the democratic state. The common good consists in the harmonious coordination of the private and the public sphere for the benefit of the capitalist market, which lays the moral foundation of society. What should be considered private and public is subject to acute political controversy within and beyond liberalism. Very schematically,

---

How to cite this book chapter:
Papadimitropoulos, V. 2020. *The Commons: Economic Alternatives in the Digital Age.* Pp. 33–66. London: University of Westminster Press. DOI: https://doi.org/10.16997/book46.b. License: CC-BY-NC-ND 4.0

liberals and libertarians argue for a minimal state, left-liberals and social democrats argue for increased state intervention, leftists argue for a socialist state and anarchists argue for the abolition of the state.

The last decades have witnessed the emergence of a liberal discourse that seeks to revitalise the concept of the common as the self-instituting power of the people. Whereas the common stands for the collective capacity for self-management, the commons are the concrete instantiations of the common, manifested in local and global (digital) commons. This part covers the liberal argument on the commons, as articulated in the work of Elinor Ostrom, Lawrence Lessig and Yochai Benkler. The criterion by which I classify their work under the term 'liberal' is that all three place the development of the commons in parallel with state and market operation. They advocate for the coexistence of the commons with the public (its associated state and institutions) and private sector. The task of this part is to critically examine the liberal argument and trace out convergences and divergences in the scope of the commons vis-à-vis state and market operation.

Section 2.2 deals with Ostrom's work on local commons. Ostrom addresses the problem of collective action by elaborating the model of polycentrism, whereby the dichotomy between privatisation and/or government regulation is overcome through a combination of state, market and community-based mechanisms governing common-pool resources.

Section 2.3 focuses on the work of Lawrence Lessig and Yochai Benkler who expand Ostrom's work from the local to the global commons of the Internet and free/open source software. They introduce the term 'digital commons' to describe a non-market sector of information, knowledge and cultural production, not treated as private property, but as an ethic of sharing, self-management and cooperation between peers who have free access to online platforms. Similarly to Ostrom, they both consider commons-based peer production as complementary to state and market operation. Benkler often crosses his liberal lines by pointing to the autonomous development of the commons beyond capitalism and the state. Yet this underlying goal generally conforms to the liberal tradition.

The crux of the argument here is that the liberal approach to the commons falls short of connecting local and global commons and, thus, envisioning an autonomous existence of the commons even within the liberal-democratic framework of market capitalism. This shortcoming is coextensive with the broader lack of the political introduced by Alexandros Kioupkiolis to stress the impotence of the liberal commons to address the contradictions of capitalism and the state.

2.2 Local Commons

In his seminal article, Hardin (1968) stressed the problem of the free-rider with regard to the management of common pool resources such as a pasture. The absence of clear property rights results in overgrazing and pasture depletion.

Hardin concludes that the most efficient solution to 'the tragedy of the commons' is either state management or privatisation. When it comes to privatisation, Hardin's argument is consistent with the dominant neoliberalism of our times (Castree 2010, 14). Hardin's metaphor of the grazing commons has been used to explain various situations where the 'tragedy of the commons' is likely to occur, ranging from international relations and state politics to climate change and Internet broadband access.

The 'tragedy of the commons' is commensurate with the problem of collective action posed by Marcun Olson (1965) to describe the action of benefiting from the commons without contributing back (Hess and Ostrom 2007, 10). The 'tragedy of the commons' has also been formalised as a prisoner's dilemma game, in which interdependent decisions by rational agents lacking communication produce irrational outcomes when self-interest prevails (Ostrom 1990, 3). However, all three models are but simplified versions of social dilemmas, the diversity of which surpasses a one-size-fits-all solution (Hess and Ostrom 2007, 11–12). Hardin's argument, in particular, is mistaken for four reasons (Hess and Ostrom 2007, 11). First, he utilises a limited view of private property. Secondly, he presupposes that people act only on self-interest. Thirdly, he identifies common-pool resources with open access commons, taking for granted the absence of rules in the use of the resource in question. Fourthly, he argues that there are only two ways to avoid tragedy: privatisation or government intervention.

But these are not the only options. Ostrom (1990) introduced the analytical distinction between open access and common-pool resources. Whereas open access commons feature the absence of rules in the use of resources, common-pool resources are self-managed according to the norms and rules of the communities involved. Ostrom was awarded the Nobel Prize in Economics in 2009 for having examined numerous successful cases of self-managed natural resources such as forests, fisheries, pastures, groundwater basins and irrigation fields, stretching across the globe from Switzerland to Spain, Nepal to Indonesia (Ostrom 1990). She proved that not only is cooperation possible in hundreds of cases of common-pool resources, but locally developed institutions and practices occasionally outperform market or state-driven systems governed by private property control and expert regulation respectively.

Private property rights have combined with common property regimes for centuries. In the Swiss Alps, for example, plots are individually owned by farmers, while the summer meadows, forests, irrigation systems, paths and roads connecting individually and communally owned plots are managed collectively (Ostrom 1990, 61–65). Mixed regimes of private and common property apply in cases with no clear boundaries, or with a cultural hostility to private property rights. On the other hand, private property rights are most effective in cases where there are clear boundaries to a resource, and the community is highly mobile and heterogeneous.

Hardin neglects several cases where privatisation or government regulation of common-pool resources have had disastrous effects due to rent-seeking mechanisms of the market, combined with government corruption and deficient knowledge of particular circumstances in time and place (Van de Walle 2001; De Alessi 1998). Ostrom has demonstrated that hierarchies, prices and property are 'lossy' in processing information under conditions of uncertainty and complexity. The plethora of limited-access commons thriving across the globe for centuries evince that there is no single model of ideal organisation. There is vast diversity consistent with polycentricity. Redundancy, resilience and experimentation with the freedom to cooperate often produce better practices. Exclusive property, by contrast, limits exploration.

Ostrom's work on the commons breaks the dichotomy between 'privatisation' and/or 'government regulation' by pointing to 'polycentric' systems of governance, where 'a rich mixture of public and private instrumentalities' is employed across a vast diversity of institutions (Ostrom 2012, 60–61). 'We have found that government, private and community-based mechanisms all work in some settings' (Ostrom 2012, 70). Polycentricity refers to a diversity of institutions governing common-pool resources via quasi-autonomous and overlapping decision centres relating to different types and scales of resources. The large scale of climate change, for example, demands the involvement of all three sectors (public, private and the commons) to effectively address the problem, whereas the parcelling out of a meadow in a village for the purpose of grazing involves the villagers and the municipality alone. Ostrom's model of polycentricity manifests today, among other places, in urban commons wherein public-common-private partnerships co-administer common-pool resources such as land, buildings, food, energy, culture and knowledge (Foster and Iaione 2016).

Polycentricity differs from a misconceived sense of anarchism that assumes the total absence of rules, since common-pool resources are governed by well-established rules. After extensive field observations, Ostrom came up with a set of design principles governing the commons, such as the demarcation of clear boundaries, the matching of rules with local needs and conditions, the modification of rules by those directly involved, the monitoring of resources and the imposition of sanctions on free-riders.

2.2.1 A Typology of the Commons

Hess and Ostrom later expanded this research to include intangible goods such as knowledge and information. What followed was a typology of property classified along two axes: exclusion and rivalry (Table 2.1). In neoclassical economics, scarcity produces rivalry and exclusion. A good is scarce and, thus, rivalrous if its use by one person subtracts from the total available, thereby excluding others. Property is the legal form of exclusion rendering a good private. We can distinguish between three types of goods: private, public and common. Private goods are marked by high rivalry and exclusion. An apple or book cannot be used by two people simultaneously and such goods are subject to the economics law of supply and demand. Public goods, on the other hand,

Table 2.1: Typology of property (adapted from Hess and Ostrom 2007; Birkinbine 2018).

		Rivalry	
		Rivalry	
Exclusion	high	high private goods (scarce resources)	low intellectual property (knowledge, language, software)
	low	common-pool resources (forests, irrigation fields, groundwater basins, fisheries, forests, etc.)	public-common goods (defence, highways, parks, airwaves, knowledge, language, free software, etc.)

exhibit low rivalry and exclusion. All citizens can make use of public education, national defence, parks and highways simultaneously. Some common goods, sometimes also referred to as public goods, can be excludable and rivalrous, and others can be non-excludable and non-rivalrous (Kostakis and Bauwens 2014; Benkler 2006; Ostrom 1990). Grazing lands, fisheries and water can be rivalrous and occasionally excludable. But nobody can be excluded from walking on a mountain, swimming in the sea, or breathing the air. Information, language and knowledge – not 'enclosed' by intellectual property rights – are non-rivalrous and anti-rivalrous, meaning respectively that the cost of reproducing an additional unit is near zero, while its use by more people increases its value overall. The more people use a language or software, the more valuable it becomes. Public and common goods thus often blur. The criterion for distinguishing between them is their type of governance. Whereas the former are managed by state governance, the latter are self-managed by communities (Quilligan 2012).

We can further distinguish between two main types of common goods: material/rivalrous (natural resources) and immaterial/non-rivalrous/anti-rivalrous (language, information, knowledge, culture). Depending, then, on the context, the commons can be regulated or unregulated. De Angelis (2017, 62–64) has highlighted the relational/contextual character of the commons. Commons and free access are not always opposed, as Ostrom claims, since they often identify or interrelate. The commons are often open access as in the case of free/open source software and the digital commons (De Angelis 2017, 146).

2.2.2 Institutional Economics vs Neoclassical Economics

Ostrom's work on the commons can be broadly situated within institutional economics, focusing on the impact of incentives on the functioning of institutions and the dissolution of social dilemmas. As such, it adheres to the liberal tradition for a number of reasons. First, she adopts the liberal theory of property rights, albeit in a twisted fashion. Let us recall that John Locke justifies private property on the grounds of individual labour. An apple becomes the private property of the farmer who laboured to produce it. Yet, for Ostrom, property rights do not necessarily equate to individual property rights, but apply to mixed regimes of private and common property rights. Ostrom makes the distinction between exclusive private property rights, and a bundle of rights most pertinent to the use of common-pool resources, such as the right to access and usage (to enter a defined physical area and enjoy non-subtractive benefits), withdrawal (to obtain resource units or products), management (to regulate internal use patterns), and exclusion and alienation (to sell or lease management and exclusion rights) (Hess and Ostrom 2007, 11). In Ostrom's account, property rights define authority over a range of possible actions.

Secondly, she examines common-pool resources through the lens of rational choice theory, employing the methodological individualism of liberalism to solve social dilemmas. In this context, individualism evolves from Hume's and Bentham's utility theory into the self-interested maximiser of neoclassical economics who uses a cost–benefit analysis to maximise her utility by satisfying her preferences. Ostrom, however, challenges the dominant neoclassical model of individual agency in that she considers incentives more complex and varied than a zero-sum game. She rejects the idea that rationality translates solely into selfishness and opportunism. Economic behaviour has always been dependent not only on competition, but also on cooperation in solving day-to-day collective problems (Ostrom 2000, 143). Finally, motivations are often shaped by collective norms and institutional arrangements.

2.2.3 The Critique of Polycentrism

Ostrom's work is attuned to the liberal tradition, given that her polycentrism model situates the commons in parallel with state and market operation. Most importantly, the self-institutionalisation of common-pool resources is foreshadowed by the power of the state and the market, thus limiting the self-instituting power of the people. Dardot and Laval (2014, 143) correctly mention that Ostrom's non-mainstream use of institutional economics and game theory cannot help but conceal the exploitation and power asymmetries inherent in capitalism and the state. In a similar vein, Alexandros Kioupkiolis (2019, 47–48) argues that Ostrom neglects the political as antagonism, struggle and power structures. Within a state-governed polity, any communal autonomy remains at the discretion of the central sovereign authority, while neoliberal capitalism is bent on colonising both the state and the commons. Ostrom fails to see the contradictory logics that bring the commons into conflict with capitalist markets and the modern state.

Benkler (2002b, 378) holds that her studies focus on relatively limited groups of participants, putting her work in tension with large-scale, non-proprietary, open access commons, such as public infrastructures (Frischmann 2012) and the digital commons. Benkler (2013a, 1518–1519) meets De Angelis from the opposite direction: not only do limited access and open access commons depend upon each other, but they often contrast. The asymmetric use (excludability) of common-pool resources – owing to their inherent scarcity – contradicts the open access character of highways and the Internet, for example.

A wide chorus of scholars (Carlsson and Sandström 2008; Dowsley 2008; Harvey 2012; Ostrom and Andersson 2008) have objected that the non-hierarchical self-governance of common-pool resources is politically debilitating at higher levels. It cannot translate into solutions for large-scale problems. Conventional economics considers Ostrom's local commons to be developing at the periphery, thereby not touching the core of the world economy, where the model of the self-interested maximiser reigns supreme (Benkler 2013a).

Nonetheless, Ostrom's empirical work offers significant insights into how formal and informal norms can structure collaboration along the lines of non-property-based schemes. She shifted the discourse on incentives from the methodological individualism of neoclassical economics to the institutional structure of collective agency. In other words, she brought to the fore the concept of the common as the self-instituting power of the people by reinvigorating the democratic elements of participation and inclusion in the collective management of resources. Ostrom inspired a new school of economic thought that works today on applying her design principles to various fields, ranging from rural and urban commons to the digital commons. Yet all these efforts need to integrate into a broader, more coherent political perspective that seeks to move the terrain of discussion from the liberal commons to a post-hegemonic account of the commons. Thus, this book seeks to radicalise the commons and pave the way for a holistic, post-capitalist, commons-orientated transition.

2.3 Global Commons

The notion of the commons was introduced into the contemporary legal debate by Carol Rose with her paper entitled 'The Comedy of the Commons' (1986), spurring a revival of commons scholarship. Rose reversed the so-called tragedy of the commons by highlighting the 'inherently public property' of goods such as roads, navigable waterways and open squares. These sorts of goods are not amenable to private or state management, since they are governed by 'custom' or norms within the relevant communities. Nor can they be classified as limited access commons, since they are open access commons. The unique feature of these goods is that their value is proportional to the increasing number of users. Rose introduced an early version of 'network effects': open access systems that increase their value through the permissionless use of the resource by an indefinite amount of users. This is the case when the value from increased participation outweighs the costs from increased utilisation, thereby reversing the tragedy of the commons into a comedy. Efficiency and welfare would suggest opening relevant resources to public use instead of enclosing them with property rights and state regulation.

Network effects apply today *par excellence* on the Internet and the digital commons, following Metcalfe's law (1995): 'The value of a communications network is proportional to the square of the number of its users.' The more people use a network, the more valuable it becomes. Jodi Dean (2012, 130–131), however, criticises Metcalfe's law with respect to scale (larger networks may be more prone to crashes and delays) and the suppositions between the links. The problem is magnified if one considers the information asymmetries (Grossman and Stiglitz 1980) inherent in networks due to the power asymmetries between corporations, institutions and non-institutional agents. Network effects are exploited today by platform capitalism instead of contributing to a robust and decentralised peer production.

Inversely proportional to the comedy of the commons is the tragedy of the anti-commons, introduced into the legal literature by Michael Heller (1998). In contrast to the tragedy of the commons resulting in the potential overuse of a resource, the tragedy of the anti-commons is a type of coordination breakdown where excessive intellectual property rights and overpatenting (for example, in biomedical research) results in the underuse of a resource. Take the example of AIDS patents preventing the use of drugs by millions of Africans dying of AIDS simply because they cannot afford to buy the medicine. Anti-commons property is the mirror image of commons property. Yet identifying a case of anti-commons does not necessarily induce open access commons or common property regimes, since this could also translate into refined property rights. When the market misallocates resources, the latter can be stuck in low-value uses at either end of the property rights spectrum. Whether this misallocation results in overuse or underuse, the common denominator is waste (Heller 1998, 626). It then depends on the scope and definition of the resource whether this tragedy can be solved by means of better-defined property rights or better-designed commons (Benkler 2013a, 1498–1499).

An intermediary use of the commons lies in Henry Smith's term 'semi-commons' (2000), illustrating well-functioning mixed regimes of private property and commons, as in the case of wheat growing in private allocations within open fields used for animal grazing, the latter having both costs (trampling) and benefits (manure) for the former. A number of scholars have attempted to apply the use of semi-commons to telecommunications regulation, intellectual property and the Internet (Grimmelmann 2010; Heverly 2003; Smith 2005). Relevant policies would demarcate accordingly the private and commons part within the semi-commons, rather than posing the dilemma of either commons or private property. As regards intellectual property, for example, it would deal with the term of coverage or the definition of fair use.

Benkler (2013a, 1523), however, has shown the limits of this approach when it comes to the basic protocols of the Internet such as TCP/IP, HTML and HTTP, which are by default open access commons. Benkler and Lessig extend the legal analysis of the commons to the Internet and the digital commons, which represent a new model of information, knowledge and culture production, anchored in openness, cooperation, mutual coordination and decentralised, bottom-up, techno-social innovation. This new mode of production was first named by Benkler (2006) 'commons-based peer production'. Unlike Ostrom's school of ecological commons, commons-based peer production encapsulates a broader paradigm shift facilitated by new technological development in the networked society (Castells 2000; 2009; 2010). The digital commons are not confined to small-scale communities and local ecosystems, but expand into open and plural shapes of networks that have the potential to occupy centre stage in economic, political and social life.

However, a number of thinkers such as Dardot and Laval (2014), De Angelis (2017) and Kioupkiolis (2019) argue that digital commons are beset with deficiencies similar to those of local commons in their grasp of the political. Additionally, they fail to connect with local commons and counter the contradictory logics of the state and the market. This failure is exacerbated by the current conditions of social fragmentation, exclusion, precarisation, individualism and collective disempowerment.

2.3.1 The Digital Commons

Lawrence Lessig (2001) wraps up the legal debate on the commons in the last decade to focus on the Internet and generalise to the online production of information, knowledge and culture. The Internet originated in the American scientific community and military, sponsored by research fellowships and licensing contracts from the American government. It dates back to the idea of Paul Baran, among others, of digitising communication by translating waves into bits chopped into packets that travel along the wires of a telephone network. Instead of waves transmitting from one line to another via circuits, data could now travel as packets via many lines simultaneously (Lessig 2001, 31). This idea was then implemented in the ARPANET project, funded by the United States Department of Defense, to create a telecommunications network that could withstand a nuclear attack. ARPANET was the first packet-switching network to apply the TCP/IP protocol that would allow computers to communicate with each other, thereby setting the technical foundation for the Internet, which then became the network of networks running in telephone lines (Lessig 2001, 34; Fuchs 2008). The Internet is based on the interoperability between decentralised sub-networks/computers using a generic addressing system (IP numbers and domain names) and technical standards (TCP/IP protocol and HTML) that take the form of open source software (Brousseau and Curien 2007, 5).

Control and freedom on the Internet

Lessig (2001, 23) draws on Benkler to illustrate the architectural design of the Internet. Benkler (2000) divides the Internet into three 'layers': 1) the 'physical' layer consisting of the hardware, wires, cables and the radio frequency spectrum that link computers together on the Internet; 2) the 'logical' layer, that is, the code, the protocols and the software that make the hardware run; 3) the 'content' layer, that is, the data transmitted across the wires, including text, images, music, movies and the like. These three layers together make communication possible on the Internet. Much of these three layers is today either state or privately owned, or both. Yet the code – the instructions inscribed in both software and hardware – that accounts for the core structure of the Internet is still to some extent free. So, too, is much of the content delivered across the network.

Lessig (2001, 177) discovers a tension between control and freedom at all three levels, potentially pregnant with two contrasting tragedies of the commons. On the freedom side, the tragedy derives from potential congestion in the frequency spectrum, resulting in the overuse of the resources on the Internet and beyond (for example, traffic, electricity, etc.) (Lessig 2001, 83–84, 229). On the control side, the tragedy consists in the creation of digital monopolies that limit freedom by causing Internet underuse (Lessig 2001, 175). Lessig (2001, 200–202) argues for a balance between freedom and control on the Internet, tilting towards the protection of the free space across the three layers, which breeds the digital innovation commons, that is, the free and unrestricted production of applications and content by Internet users.

Digital freedom relies basically on the code that regulates the flow of content via the controlled physical layer of the Internet. Code consists in the basic protocols – TCP/IP, HTML, HTTP – that make for the core structure of the Internet, that is, the end-to-end principle, which locates intelligence at the ends of the network rather than at the centre, thereby sustaining a decentralised architecture devoid of central control. On the Internet, each user has the capacity to influence the flow of communication via digital technology's ability to encrypt information. In a digital system all information is coded in a sequence of digits, which can then be easily encrypted. Encryption permits a user to filter information and authorise access to all or part of the information depending on the identity of other users or other criteria (Brousseau and Curien 2007, 7–8). In short, encryption enables all Internet users to lay down 'norms' on the use of information and the subsequent flow of communication.

Internet use, of course, is neither always legitimate nor regulation-free. Given the Internet's effects on commerce, intellectual property, cyber-crime, national security, public freedoms, and so on, non-governmental organisations (NGOs) such as the ICANN (Internet Corporation for Assigned Names and Numbers), the IETF (Internet Engineering Task Force) and the W3C (World Wide Web Consortium), in concert with states, have progressively become involved to co-regulate the network (Brousseau and Curien 2007, 6–8). Thus, the self-organisation of the Internet does not lack an institutional framework completely. Rather, it employs 'framed' self-organisation.

Code is law

Code is law and architecture is politics inasmuch as it enables certain forms of social interaction, while disabling others (Lessig 2001, 35). Code embedded in the technical architecture of the Internet is the social engineering of information, knowledge and cultural production. The underlying political philosophy of the Internet is the liberal ideal of network neutrality that advocates for non-discriminatory traffic management by Internet service providers (ISPs) with regard to the content and applications running in the network. Network neutrality is enforced by the end-to-end principle, which epitomises unconstrained value creation. The Internet was initially designed to remain open and enhance freedom via interconnected networks and flexible applications built on top of basic protocols. Under conditions of uncertainty and complexity, plasticity – the ability of a system to evolve easily in a number of ways – is the optimal method to allow for the broadest range of development and innovation (Lessig 2001, 39). Internet architecture was the key to the explosion of new services and software applications. Cyberspace could, thus, be the dream of the libertarian who envisions the elimination of control.

The hallmark of freedom in the Internet is free and open source software (FOSS) invented in 1984 by Richard Stallman who introduced the GNU General Public License (GPL) as a legal hack in the traditional copyright system, allowing programmers to freely access, copy, modify and distribute software on the same copyright terms. The core defining feature of FOSS is the renouncing of exclusive proprietary control over the software in which one has copyright (Benkler 2013b, 221). FOSS is the collective reversal of the proprietary copyright system through the combination of contract law and copyright (Lessig 2001, 58). Far from meaning the abolition of copyright, FOSS establishes a 'copyleft' system on the basis of the traditional copyright system. While most licences limit the copies one can make, the GPL limits the restrictions on copying. Building on top of the GPL, Linus Torvalds in 1991 developed the Linux operating system, which supports a model of collaborative production of software developers, based on volunteering and sharing (Lessig 2001, 54). GPL/Linux is now the fastest-growing operating system in the world.

Jeremy Rifkin makes the case that the GPL could be considered a digital version of the regulation of the limited access commons, inasmuch as it incorporates many of Ostrom's principles: the conditions of inclusion; the restrictions of exclusion; the rights governing access; withdrawal, enhancement and stewardship of the resources; and so on (Rifkin 2014: 175). The difference here is that FOSS is open access rather than limited access.

Similar efforts are underway to implement Ostrom's principles on Blockchain, which is a decentralised ledger on the Internet, allowing for numerous applications with as yet uncertain potential (Rozas et al. 2018). Blockchain is one of the applications of peer production, which makes use of the end-to-end principle of the Internet, allowing content (file sharing, processing cycles, etc.) to be delivered by equal computers along the network. FOSS, Blockchain and the digital commons are instances of peer production, supported by the architecture of the Internet.

The general idea behind distributed ledgers such as Blockchain is to use peer-to-peer networks to verify the authenticity of a token of value (money), an indicator of personal reputation, a recognised legal agreement among parties or a group encapsulated in smart contracts, or a tool for voting and decision making (Bollier and Helfrich 2019, 326). Distributed ledgers can support the creation of community currencies that enable people to coordinate the terms of their cooperation at scale, without the threat of enclosure. Instead of making decisions through rigid hierarchies with centralised direction and relying on property rights vested in a few people, distributed ledgers can support transparency and democratic decision making.

Holochain is another example of a lighter, far more energy-efficient and versatile set of software applications than Blockchain, since there is no single ledger in Holochain to store data. Holochain is based on an open data, distributed architecture that allows every user to have his or her own secure ledger to store their personal data (Bollier and Helfrich 2019, 326). The core idea of Holochain is to enable the 'renting out' of user-computing capacity in exchange for Holo Fuel currency to circulate within the network and kick-start a new parallel economy of services (Bollier and Helfrich 2019, 328–332). This establishment of Holo Fuel currency basically constitutes a mutual credit system backed by an asset (computing power). As more enterprises join Holochain and back its value with actual assets and services such as food, transport, energy or elderly care services, a commons-based economy will emerge. Holochain can be further used to build decentralised applications for peer governance, social networks, platform cooperatives, open supply chains, community resource management as well as tokenless mutual-credit cryptocurrencies and reputation systems. Thus, Holochain can express the flows of value that market prices cannot represent such as positive (social relationships and contributions to the commons) and negative externalities (waste, pollution).

Cyber-communism, cyber-libertarianism and firm-hosted peer production

Free code builds a digital commons in the production of information, knowledge and culture thanks to the non-rivalrous/anti-rivalrous nature of information. The consumption of one ebook, for example, by one person does not subtract from the total available to others. On the contrary, it produces more information and creates new knowledge. The nature of information combines with the architecture of cyberspace, which, contrary to the physical world, allows users altogether to give away much more information than they can receive alone, thus spontaneously creating a gift economy (Barbrook 1998). One ebook can be uploaded by millions at the same time, while a user can download a limited number of ebooks at a time. Jodi Dean (2012, 146–148) marks this unique feature of the web as a contradiction between the abundance of knowledge production versus the scarcity of human capacity for consumption. This is also the case with scientific research, innovation and culture in the physical world. Information breeds information in the networked social interaction, surpassing individual human limits. The difference with cyberspace is that the proliferation and abundance of information and knowledge can be faster and denser on the Internet, covering simultaneously multiple points in time-space. In purely economic terms, cyberspace carries a ticking time-bomb for the capitalist economy: an abundance of supply versus a scarcity of demand. In contrast with tomatoes which still cannot be cloned indefinitely, information is destined to reproduce information at zero marginal cost.

According to Vasilis Kostakis and Michel Bauwens (2014), FOSS sustains a sort of cyber-communism operating at the very heart of capitalism, where everybody can contribute and share according to their needs and skills. However, the most common political interpretations of FOSS tend to be libertarian rather than communist. Others have pointed to the political agnosticism of FOSS developers (Coleman 2004; Raymond 1999; Stallman 2002).

Richard Barbrook (1998) considers cyberspace a form of high-tech anarcho-communism, which is not only in conflict with digital capitalism, but coexists in symbiosis with the latter. Anarcho-communism is often sponsored by corporate capital. The free circulation of information among users depends upon the capitalist production of computers, software and telecommunications. Anarcho-communism is also symbiotic with the state that subsidises and regulates digital capitalism. Within the digital mixed economy, anarcho-communism blends with state democracy. The Internet user is a consumer in the market, a citizen of a state and an anarcho-communist within a gift economy largely co-opted by finance capital.

Alongside the proliferation of the digital commons, the last decades have witnessed the development of the capitalist commons, with several companies incorporating FOSS development within their operations. For Lessig (2001, 70–72), this offers a win–win partnership for both capitalism and FOSS production. Illustrative is the case of IBM which invested more than \$1 billion to support the development of Linux and Apache. Most recently, IBM bought RedHat, one of the most iconic companies in open source development, for \$34 billion.

The crucial questions here are, first, why does IBM pay for what it could get for free and, second, why does it give its improvements back to the public. IBM profits from the improvements made by millions of developers in the open source movement by incorporating them in the hardware and adding paid services on top of the free software. Instead of IBM paying ten programmers to produce software, it pays significantly lower salaries to a community of peer producers to produce the same software with much better quality. If IBM participates and deflects from the open source movement, it becomes extremely costly to keep its software up to date, since it cannot compete with the work of millions of developers across the globe.

The limitations of the digital commons

Lessig (2001, 9) champions a mixed regime of private property and the digital commons. His core argument is that digital technology could enable more and more people to participate in the creative process, thereby democratising the production of information, knowledge and culture. Following Rose, he holds that FOSS and the digital commons demonstrate that the added value from increased production outweighs the cost from increased utilisation. Therefore, the Internet creates more wealth when held in common than in private (Lessig 2001, 86–88). As Lessig puts it:

> Where a resource has a clear use, then, from a social perspective, our objective is simply to assure that that resource is available for this highest and best use. We can use property systems to achieve this end. By assigning a strong property right to the owners of such resources, we can then rely upon them to maximise their own return from this resource by seeking out those who can best use the resource at issue. But if there is no clear option for using the resource – if we can't tell up front how best to use it – then there is more reason to leave it in common, so that many can experiment with different uses. Not knowing how a resource will be used is a good reason for making it widely available […] Where uncertainty is highest, network designs that embrace end-to-end maximise the value of the network; and where uncertainty is low, then end-to-end is not a particular value. (2001, 89)

Lessig (2001, 72) advocates that intellectual property rights must strike the right balance between free and controlled resources. Control makes sense in the case of scarce and, hence, rivalrous resources suited for commercial appropriation in the market, whereas freedom belongs to the world of ideas held in common. Strict property rights, he claims, burden innovation and creativity (2001, 139–140). Economists have long emphasised the costs of patents to information production, given the public goods nature of information (Arrow 1962). Strong patent protection increases the costs that current innovators have to pay for existing knowledge more than it increases the benefits of appropriating the value of their own contributions (Benkler 2006, 38–39). Strong intellectual property rights lead to commercialisation, concentration and homogenisation of information production rights, thus underutilising information and stifling innovation (Benkler 2002a; Boyle 1996; Samuelson 1990). On the flipside, the more open the access to information goods, the more the value for all.

Today, changes in the architecture of the Internet – both legal and technical – aim at increasing the scope for control of code and content (Lessig 2001, 15). Instead of the Internet promoting innovation, creativity and freedom, it turns into the most efficient censorship and surveillance mechanism, as evidenced in the cases of China and the USA. 'There is no "nature" of the Internet that will assure a continued commons at the code layer, no strong protection limiting the Congress to ensure that adequate resources remain free at the content layer' (Lessig 2001, 139). Some authors claim that we have entered the age of surveillance capitalism (Zuboff 2019). The Internet is not immune to potential gatekeepers and supernodes such as governments and corporations forestalling the openness of the network. Rather, the Internet sustains the political and economic battle of freedom and control, playing out on the interface of software and hardware.

Lessig (2001, 9) is pro-market. He does not question property per se, but only the scope of property. He demonstrates a liberal version of the commons, arguing for the coexistence of the commons with state and market operation across separate but entangled spheres of action. However, such an approach has two major shortcomings: not only does Lessig limit the commons to the digital commons, he also limits the latter with respect to state and market operation. Most importantly, Lessig's version of the commons is undermined by the contradictions of capitalism and the state, that is, the power asymmetries inherent in the core structure of managerial hierarchies, namely the division between directors and executants, managers and workers, representative and citizens, elites and the people. For the commons to provide a sustainable democratic paradigm shift, they need to integrate into a broader political debate that seeks to unify diverse projects under a holistic, post-hegemonic perspective that radically challenges the current neoliberal status quo.

2.3.2 Commons-based Peer Production

Benkler develops a more radical version of the commons compared to Lessig's innovation commons. He builds on Manuel Castells's (2000; 2009; 2010) concept of the networked society – which marks the shift from groups and hierarchies to networks as social and organisational models – with the aim of introducing a novel normative framework for refiguring civil collaboration with respect to the market–state nexus. He demonstrates a model of networked pragmatism/anarchism, based on the decentralised self-management of information, knowledge and cultural production, supported by the Internet and FOSS. The idea of decentralised self-management is not novel in economics and political theory. It is reminiscent of the work of numerous thinkers, related to diverse and often disparate strands, ranging from anarcho-capitalism and anarcho-communism to autonomous Marxism and radical republicanism. What is novel in Benkler's work is the technological substratum of a liberal critique of managerial hierarchies and market limitations on individual freedom, participatory democracy and justice, ameliorated today by the emergence of a new organisational model termed 'commons-based peer production'.

The term 'commons' signifies a particular institutional form of structuring the right to access, use and control resources, which differs significantly from managerial hierarchies and markets. The distinctive features of the commons are: 1) decentralised self-governance through the utilisation of participatory, meritocratic (do-ocracy) and charismatic rather than proprietary or contractual models; 2) the centrality of non-monetary motivations; and 3) the permeation of state and firm boundaries (Benkler et al. 2015, 2–3; Benkler 2016a, 2). Highways, squares, shipping lanes, water, airwaves, scientific knowledge, ideas and the Internet are all commons. The main event for all these systems is open commons, which designate free access, use and control of common-pool resources under symmetric terms (Benkler 2013a, 1500). Open access commons differ from Ostrom's limited access commons in that they are not limited to a restricted number of people who cooperate at a local level, but expand to the global level.

Benkler (2006, 59–90) focuses on the Internet. He defines commons-based peer production as a non-market sector of information, knowledge and cultural production, not treated as private property, but as an ethic of open sharing, self-management and cooperation among peers who have access to fixed capital such as software and hardware. Commons-based peer production consists of open contributory networks of distributed tasks, set and executed online in a decentralised and autonomous fashion.

Benkler mentions that not all peer production qualifies as commons-based production. The term 'commons-based' denotes the absence of exclusive property:

> The salient characteristic of commons, as opposed to property, is that no single person has exclusive control over the use and disposition of any particular resource in the commons. Instead, resources governed by commons may be used or disposed of by anyone among some (more or less well-defined) number of persons, under rules that may range from 'anything goes' to quite crisply articulated formal rules that are effectively enforced. (Benkler 2006, 61)

The term 'peer production' signifies a subset of commons-based production practices, which 'refers to production systems that depend on individual action that is self-selected and decentralised, rather than hierarchically assigned' (Benkler 2006, 62). Similarly to Lessig, Benkler distinguishes between two basic modes of peer production: 1) commons-based peer production (FOSS and the digital commons); and 2) firm-hosted peer production (peer production incorporated into firms such as IBM and Google). The latter refers also to the online business models of the so-called sharing and gig economy (for example, Uber, Airbnb, Kickstarter, TaskRabbit and Upwork), which will be analysed later.

The quintessential instance of commons-based peer production is FOSS, which produces some of the core software utilities running the Web – servers, email, scripting, applications, plug-ins. FOSS accounts for 70% of web servers running on the Apache web server; more than 70% of web browsers (Firefox, Chrome); server-side programming languages (PHP); content management systems (Wordpress, Joomla and Drupal have more than 70% of servers); smartphone operating systems; enterprise software (Google, Amazon and CNN.com run their servers on the GNU/Linux operating system; 40% of firms engaged in software development contribute to FOSS development). In short, roughly half of the Internet runs on FOSS.

FOSS development, however, is not the only instance of commons-based peer production. The commons expand into large-scale collaboration in the networked information environment. They range from the scientific, digital and knowledge commons to non-professional information and cultural production taking place on entertainment sites and in grassroots movements, communities and interpersonal relationships (for example, families and friendships).

The digital commons, in particular, extend beyond FOSS development to distributed content production and sharing of processing, storage and communications platforms. Examples of distributed content production are the Nasa Clickworkers, Wikipedia, Kuro5hin, Multiplayer Online Games, Open Directory Project, Slashdot and Project Gutenberg. Examples of sharing of processing, storage and communications platforms are Napster, Gnutella, SETI@home, Skype, Bitcoin and WiFi. The digital commons have proliferated globally in the last decade to a degree that largely escapes Benkler's own work. Recent research has documented hundreds of cases currently in progress (De Filippi 2015a; 2015b; De Filippi and Tréguer 2015a; 2015b; De Filippi and Troxler 2016). Also, Blockchain technology has arguably the potential to support both online and offline decentralised collaboration (De Filippi and Hassan 2016).

The explanation of commons-based peer production

In explaining the rise of commons-based peer production, Benkler draws on a number of sources. First and foremost, he uses Ronald Coase's transaction costs theory to argue that the rise of commons-based peer production is due to four basic features inherent in the networked information economy: 1) the primary inputs and outputs of production are open access commons – existing information, knowledge and culture; they are non-rivalrous/anti-rivalrous goods, since their marginal cost of reproduction is near zero; 2) there are cheap physical capital costs (cheap processor-based computer networks) coupled with the digitisation of information production; 3) the architecture of the Internet allows for the decentralisation and modularity of human–computer interaction; in addition, human creativity is more central and variable in information production than in other modes of production, meaning that it is more diverse, flexible and, therefore, potentially more effective; and 4) there has been a dramatic decline in communication costs.

However, transaction costs theory alone cannot explain the rise of commons-based peer production. The latter features a diversity of non-monetary motivations, the centrality of which on the digital commons poses a puzzle for neoclassical economics, since it seemingly contradicts its main behavioural model of the self-interested maximiser. Benkler shows that there is no puzzle to solve, since the theoretical framework adopted to explain behaviour by neoclassical economics is simply flawed. The widely held assumption that self-interest motivates behaviour, that managerial hierarchies and markets are the best ways to produce goods, that property rights and contracts are the *sine qua non* for organising production, are not equally applicable to information (Benkler 2006, 41). FOSS forces us to re-evaluate these claims by placing intrinsic and social motivations, rather than material incentives, at the core of innovation; by questioning the centrality of managerial hierarchies and markets to the innovation process; and by challenging the centrality of property, as opposed to the interaction of property and commons (Benkler 2016a, 1).

Lerner and Tirole (2002) have listed a series of intrinsic and social motivations in FOSS production that testify to some combination of hedonic gain and indirect appropriation: the playful joy of creation, reputation, social-psychological rewards and increases in human capital are some of the indirect benefits for those participating in commons-based peer production. Given that two-thirds of the revenues of the software industry are service-based, the skills indirectly appropriated in free software development can be directly redeemed in proprietary projects (Benkler 2002b, 424–425).

Benkler draws on the work of Eric von Hippel (1988; 2005) to further argue that innovation is a collective process of knowledge production and learning. He invokes extensive empirical work to show that humans exhibit diverse pro-social motivations, responding to a range of non-material, non-self-interested motivations, from reciprocity to group identity through, in some cases, altruism (2016a, 8). Experimental and observational data has exhaustively documented that the effects of standard economic incentive tools such as material rewards and punishments are not only inseparable from but, in some cases, detrimental to the sum of motivations across the target population (Bowles and Hwang 2008; Bowles and Polania-Reyes 2012; Frey 1997; Frey and Jegen 2001). One cannot buy friendship and love with money. Not only is there often a tension between material rewards and pro-social motivations, but also between diverse pro-social motivations themselves. Individuals are driven by motivations that differ from each other in mixing motivational drivers.

Beyond neoliberalism

Benkler's goal is not merely to highlight the diversity of pro-social motivations inherent in commons-based peer production, but to question the current dominance of neoliberalism by dispelling the myth of universal selfishness. His main intent is to help transform the commons into an autonomous and sustainable mode of production. His basic argument is that the Internet and FOSS bring to the fore the cooperative element of human nature, occasionally counterweighting self-interested motivations. To further back up this claim, he brings up evidence from evolutionary biology and the social sciences, illustrating the shift in the scientific understanding of human rationality from the model of the self-interested maximiser, driven by competition and separable motivations, to the model of *homo socialis* featuring cooperation and diverse pro-social motivations (Benkler 2011). Rationality does not always translate into self-interest, since humans often rationally pursue non-self-interested goals.

Benkler cites, in particular, Ostrom's work as a landmark in the social sciences, proving that cooperation at a local level occasionally out-competes traditional proprietary and state models. He points, though, to a tension between local commons and the scale at which the digital commons operate in modern complex economies (2013a, 1505). A challenge remains to unite local and global (digital) commons. Conventional economics has noted that Ostrom's work is limited to the periphery, thereby not touching the core of modern economies where the model of the self-interested maximiser still prevails. Yet this does not hold true for the digital commons, which account for a considerable part of the actual economy. FOSS, in particular, is an economically significant institutional and organisational strategy for both corporations and the commons:

> As of January of 2013, Apache held a 55% market share, Microsoft 17%; nginx, an alternative FOSS platform, 13%; Google's servers for its own machines, 4%; and the remainder was held by platforms bunched as 'other' (Netcraft Websurvey 2013). Server-side scripting languages are the primary languages used for programming functions of the Web. PHP, an open source language, is used by 78% of websites, while Microsoft's ASP.Net holds the remaining 20%; most of remaining languages, like Ruby or Python, are also open source (W3Techs 2013). Web Browser statistics are less clearly in favor of open source. Historically, Microsoft's Internet Explorer held over 95% of the market after it squeezed Netscape Navigator out of the market (illegally, according to antitrust adjudications in both the US and EU). Netscape then spun out Navigator to a non-profit, the Mozilla Foundation, as FOSS. Over time, Firefox gradually captured market share over the 2000s, and in 2008 Google released Chrome, and at the same time a parallel, FOSS project, Chromium. As of January 2013, competing methods identify IE as either having 55% of the desktop browser market or 31%; and Chrome and Firefox having either 18% and 20%, respectively, or 36% and 22% respectively (ZDNET 2013). By a different measure, almost 40% of firms engaged in software development reported spending development time on developing and contributing to FOSS software. (Benkler 2016b, 6–7)

The Internet has given the opportunity to individuals, groups and firms to produce a wide range of commercial and non-commercial products and services through a variety of strategies that combine exclusive to non-exclusive property rights applied both to market and non-market models. FOSS testifies to the fact that property (as opposed to a mixed infrastructure of property and commons) is not the sole determinant factor for growth. Commons-based peer production comes in a variety of licences (Ostrom's bundle of rights, GNU, Creative Commons) that do not entail the complete rejection of the property model, but rather the reimagination of it. Property and contractual relations are just elements in an institutional toolkit. Commons-based peer production can be individual or collaborative, commercial and non-commercial. The individual can be both part of and apart from the collective. Commons-based peer production does not dismiss market actors, but increases the diversity of actors, motivations and transaction forms. It decentralises authority where capacity to act exists, thereby diffusing power and freedom to the many.

Like Lessig, Benkler considers commons-based peer production as a third institutional model that offers substantial degrees of freedom and power in addition to state and market operation. The main question then, for him, concerns the scope and role of commons-based peer production in relation to state and market operation. To answer this question, Benkler juxtaposes commons-based peer production with capitalism in terms of information-processing systems. Similarly to Lessig, Benkler illustrates a number of trade-offs between managerial hierarchies (firms and state), markets and the commons, based on the core variables of uncertainty and complexity. His core argument is that commons-based peer production offers some significant information and allocation gains compared to managerial hierarchies and markets. In contrast to capitalism, which tackles uncertainty and complexity with clear property rights and pricing, commons-based peer production introduces more refined, flexible and cost-efficient information processing, better attuned to the variability of human creativity than managerial hierarchies (firms, state) and markets.

The fine-grained, diverse qualities of agents, resources and projects and the subsequent differences in input combinations or user interactions account for the impossibility of reaching managerial decisions or price clearance without significant loss of information, control and, ultimately, effectiveness (Benkler 2016b, 9). The divergence of the existing modes of production – peer production, markets and firms – from the ideal condition of 'perfect information' results in respective information opportunity costs. Human creativity is difficult to qualify/quantify for efficient contracting or management due to the diversity of talent, motivation, experience, availability, and so on. Perfect information is all the more unattainable due to the increased transaction costs inherent in the specification process. Therefore, markets and firms are costly and lossy compared to commons-based peer production. Property and contractual relations render agents and resources 'sticky'. That is, employees are not flexible enough to change information, collaborate and thus co-produce knowledge and innovation. Commons-based peer production aspires to improve on markets and firms by correcting these two failures:

> Where the physical capital costs of information production are low and where existing information resources are freely or cheaply available, the low cost of communication among very large sets of agents allows agents to collect information through extensive communication and feedback instead of using information-compression mechanisms like prices or managerial instructions. (Benkler 2002b, 413)

Commons-based peer production has particular advantages for identifying and allocating human creativity to work on information and cultural resources, since it relies on decentralised information gathering and exchange to reduce uncertainty and complexity in information processing. Information exchange among large sets of agents who use existing information resources cheaply to freely communicate reduces uncertainty as to the likely value of various courses of productive action by creating substantial information and allocation gains. The latter overcome the information exchange costs due to the absence of transaction and coordination costs related to pricing, managerial direction, contractual relations and property rights (Benkler 2002b, 406–412). In short, information production in managerial hierarchies and markets is lossy, sticky and costly.

Given the uncertainty as to the value of various productive activities and the variability of human creativity vis-à-vis any set of production opportunities, decentralised coordination and continuous communication among the pool of potential producers and consumers can generate better information about the most valuable productive actions and the best human agents available at a given time. This way, peer production has the potential to identify who will best produce a specific component of a project.

Yet commons-based peer production will not always be successful or superior to markets and firms. This depends on a complex and varied function playing out in several trade-offs. The primary trade-off is between monetary and non-monetary motivations, and depends on two counterbalancing variables: the degree of information uncertainty and the degree of capital investment necessary for the realisation of a project. The more routine the tasks, and the more capital-intensive a project is, the more appropriate monetary 'incentives' are to motivating contributions, and, therefore, the bigger the role of markets and firms will be in organising production. The more complex and the less costly or capital-intensive a project is, the more likely it is to attract non-monetary motivations, and, therefore, the bigger the space for peer production (Benkler 2002b, 403–404). Benkler perhaps misses out in his hypothesis the superpowers of the corporations that have come to dominate the current economy. The vast majority of people are dependent on capitalism to the extent that they cannot easily leave to enter commons-based peer production.

The success of commons-based peer production depends on four additional variables: 1) the scale of peer production; 2) the degree of modularity and granularity; 3) the trade-off between waste and efficiency; and 4) the cost of integration. Commons-based peer production has an advantage over markets and firms in large-scale collaborations, which are costly to sustain. It would be extremely costly for a firm to produce Wikipedia or Linux. Moreover, large-scale commons-based peer production renders the motivations problem trivial, since monetary and non-monetary motivations coexist in non-exclusive ways (Benkler 2002b, 433–434). As Benkler (2002b, 434–435) puts it: 'The sustainability of any given project depends, therefore, not on the total cost but on how many individuals contribute to it relative to the overall cost.'

The sustainability of commons-based peer production depends also on the degree to which it can reduce the waste produced from duplication of effort. The problem disappears when duplication of effort produces more efficiency than waste. Redundancy, that is, the production of the same component by different people, makes peer production more innovative, robust and resilient.

Commons-based peer production is further limited not by the total cost or complexity of a project, but by its modularity and granularity. Modularity is the degree to which a project can break down into smaller components that can be independently and asynchronously produced and recombined. The higher the degree of modularity, the bigger the autonomy and flexibility of peer production. Granularity refers to the size of each module in terms of the time and effort needed to produce it. The smaller the size, the more people are likely to participate in peer production.

The remaining obstacle to commons-based peer production is the cost of integration, that is, first, the filtering out of incompetent and malign actors and, secondly, the combination of the modules into a whole. One could argue that commons-based peer production could result in various tragedies and Babels of the commons on the Internet and beyond. Benkler (2002b, 436–443) argues that these problems can be solved by a combination of four mechanisms: 1) iterative and modular peer production of the integration function itself (for example, moderation and meta-moderation on Slashdot); 2) technical solutions embedded in the collaboration platform (for example, Slashdot, Nasa Clickworkers project, Kuro5hin); 3) norm-based social organisation (for example, limited access commons, Wikipedia, Kuro5hin); and 4) limited reintroduction of hierarchy or markets to provide the integration function alone without appropriating the full value of the product (for example, IBM, Linux Kernel, Apache). Benkler puts it very succinctly:

> Where the physical capital requirements of a project are either very low, or capable of fulfillment by utilising pre-existing distributed capital endowments, where the project is susceptible to modularisation for incremental production pursued by diverse participants, and where the diversity gain from harnessing a wide range of experience, talent,

insight, and creativity in innovation, quality, speed, or precision of connecting outputs to demand is high, peer production can emerge and outperform markets and hierarchies. (Benkler 2016b, 10–11)

To sum up, commons-based peer production is an information, innovation and knowledge production system that, under certain conditions, bears an organisational advantage over firms, governments and pure market clearance. Its success has additional implications for politics and economics. It requires that we modify our conceptions about motivations and incentives; it recalibrates the role of property and contract in the domains of information-dependent production and innovation; and it requires adaptations to the theory of the firm and organisational management (Benkler 2016b, 2). What would, therefore, be the role of firms, governments and markets in relation to the potential future development of commons-based peer production?

Future scenarios of peer production

One plausible scenario is that firms would continue to prevail under conditions of high capital costs and rent-extraction opportunities that give an advantage over firm-hosted or commons-based peer production. The role of firms in innovation becomes then contingent and path-dependent, rather than efficiency or growth-orientated (Benkler 2016a, 7).

Firms might move also from information product-based business models to information-embedding material products and service-based business models, thereby gradually shifting towards firm-hosted peer production. Jeremiah Owyang argues that, to avoid disruption by peer production, companies must adopt the collaborative economy value chain. He defines the collaborative economy as an economic model where ownership and access are shared between corporations, start-ups and people (Owyang 2013, 4). Given that people are empowered today by digital platforms, companies must change their business models by becoming a company-as-a-service, motivating a marketplace, or providing a platform (Owyang 2013, 1). Rather than sell goods the traditional way, companies can offer products and services to customers on demand or through a subscription model; foster a community around a brand and enable customers to resell or co-purchase products, swap goods or even lend and gift; or transform consumers into partners by enabling them to build products and new services on their platform (Owyang 2013, 10–13). A third scenario would be the transition from firm-hosted peer production to a broader collaborative economy that embraces peer production more openly by adopting a cooperative model rooted in sustainability and reciprocity (Benkler 2016a, 8).

Benkler limits commons-based peer production to information, knowledge and cultural production, arguing that decentralised social production cannot apply to large-scale material goods such as the manufacturing of automobiles, steel or aeroplanes. Commons-based peer production, he claims, is not always the most efficient model even for the production of information, knowledge and culture. It can be prone to failure due to insufficient contributions or to large parts of the population being sceptical about non-market models of provisioning goods (Benkler 2013b, 244). The crux of his argument is that commons-based peer production has certain advantages over the state, markets or firms in identifying and allocating human capital and creativity (Benkler 2002b, 381). Yet commons-based peer production will not replace state and market operation.

Following Jürgen Habermas (1996), Benkler incorporates commons-based peer production into civil society, aiming to broaden the scope of individual and collective autonomy by surpassing the limits of managerial hierarchies and market limitations on freedom, participatory democracy and justice. His core argument is that the commons offer additional degrees of freedom and power for the individual and collectivities. Benkler, thus, abides by the liberal notion of negative freedom inasmuch as he conceives of the commons as an alternative institutional space within the bounds of civil society: 'Freedom inheres in diversity of constraint, not in the optimality of the balance of freedom and constraint represented by any single institutional arrangement' (Benkler 2006, 145–146).

In contrast to positive freedom which gives a meaning to an action, negative freedom consists in a diversity of contextual constraints for actors, opening up more opportunities for action. The role of the law, then, would be to implement policies that diversify the set of options available to all (Benkler 2006, 152). Like Lessig, Benkler expands state neutrality to the digital commons, arguing that the state would do better to enhance commons-based licensing rather than strengthening intellectual property rights (Benkler 2002b, 444–446). Network neutrality would be supported by a liberal state that could play constructive roles in the digital economy through the municipal funding of neutral broadband networks, state funding of basic research, and possible strategic regulatory interventions to negate monopoly control over essential resources in the digital environment (Benkler 2006, 21). In this sense, commons-based peer production is compatible with various theories of democracy and justice in the liberal tradition (Benkler 2006, 184–185; 2003).

Paradoxically, Benkler holds that it is worthwhile to continue building on the successes of commons-based peer production, and trying to control as much of our world as possible with its mutualistic modality of social organisation (Benkler 2013b, 216). However, he points out that the basic problem for a political theory dealing with the emergence of commons-based peer production is the unfeasibility of removing power from even a reasonably well-functioning democratic state and market economy (Benkler 2013b, 242).

But if it is unfeasible to remove power from the state and the market, how can commons-based peer production control as much of our world economy as possible? Benkler himself wonders how generalisable the commons can be beyond constituting a mere hack, beneficial only under particular circumstances and overlaid on the background of a liberal state with a reasonably liberal property and market system (Benkler 2013b, 242). One can, therefore, identify a tension between Benkler's liberal commitments and his anarchistic vision of the commons. On the one hand, he defends the moral values of negative freedom, individual autonomy and pluralism, as embedded in modern capitalist markets and state democracies. On the other hand, he advocates the expansion of propertyless, decentralised and stateless commons-based peer production. Benkler's anarchist side deviates from libertarianism in that the latter acknowledges property rights and a minimum state. Anarchism, instead, rejects property rights, contracts, managerial hierarchies and the state.

Benkler overstates the collective and non-monetary features of commons-based peer production. The work of Lerner and Tirole on FOSS at best shows that extrinsic motivations combine with intrinsic motivations rather than being overshadowed by the latter. Despite Benkler (2002b, 444–446) admitting that commons-based peer production faces a critical design challenge for balancing out motivations, he does not see that monetary motivations still prevail by and large. The need for most parts of society to pay the bills and make a living in a capitalist economy overtakes non-monetary, pro-social motivations. As mentioned earlier, there are no easy exits from capitalism – if any.

A number of authors have identified the co-option of FOSS by capital over the last decades rather than its quasi-autonomous development on the model of the capitalist commons (Bauwens and Kostakis 2014; Birkinbine 2018). Capitalism is capable of adapting and enclosing the commons for its own benefit. Whereas commons-based peer production seems to encapsulate both social and environmental sustainability, it still cannot reproduce itself (Bauwens and Pantazis 2018). Commons-based peer production has difficulty in capturing value creation and providing a steady income for its participants. It is unclear, then, how and to what degree commons-based peer production can sustain a livelihood or create a viable enterprise. Hence, claims about the sustainability of commons-based peer production still rest on thin conceptual and empirical foundations.

Benkler is being realistic when addressing the current premature development of commons-based peer production. He draws attention to the fact that commons-based peer production is still in its infancy and suffers from several imperfections. Further qualitative and quantitative studies are needed to yield better outcomes regarding how central or peripheral a phenomenon this is (Benkler 2002b, 444). At the same time, Benkler is utopian when pushing further the boundaries of commons-based peer production to control as much as possible of the world economy. Alas, he does not illustrate a clear path towards a commons-orientated transition that connects local with global (digital) commons. This is due to the general syndrome that plagues the liberal approach to the commons: the lack of the political.

2.4 The Lack of the Political I

The liberal approach to the commons suggests the quasi-autonomous coexistence of the commons with state and market operation. Ostrom succeeded in shifting the discourse in political science from the methodological individualism of neoclassical economics to polycentric institutions that combine private and public management with collective self-management of common-pool resources, ranging from natural resources to knowledge commons. Lessig introduced the innovation commons of the Internet in the production of information, knowledge and culture, defending the loosening of copyright law in order for the digital commons to unleash freedom and creativity. Along with Benkler, he expanded Ostrom's local commons to global (digital) commons on the model of commons-based peer production, operating in tandem with the state and the market.

All three have contributed to rethinking the common in the singular, meaning the democratic self-instituting power of the people, exercised both on the local and global level. Contrary to local eco-commons, the communities of the digital commons are open, plural, voluntary and dispersed, reaching across social and national boundaries, across geographical space and political divisions. Hierarchies tend to be flat and reversible, with the type of affiliation binding the commons being loose and fluid. The ground of the common is not any ethnic or local identity, but a shared sense of purpose and an ongoing interaction and collaboration along symmetric rules and ethical lines.

Benkler highlights the potential of the digital commons to democratise politics, the economy and culture. The commons can, indeed, bypass the filter of marketability and decentralise the production of information and knowledge. Like Lessig, he stresses the battle over the institutional ecology of a new digital environment:

> The pattern of information flow in such a network is more resistant to the application of control or influence than was the mass media model. But things can change. Google could become so powerful on the desktop, in the email utility, and on the Web, that it will effectively become a supernode that will indeed raise the prospect of a reemergence of a mass-media model. (Benkler 2006, 261)

To avert the corporatism of cyberspace, Lessig and Benkler propose the expansion of commons-supporting licences and copyrights enforced by adequate lobbying, litigation and legal reforms to support the production of open source knowledge and peer-to-peer networks. Rather that clashing head-on with capitalism, commons-based peer production is anticipated as rendering predatory capitalism obsolete through superior working anti-models, running code and a healthy commons that will trump polemics. Historical transformation is projected into a long, incremental, technological development that will establish new social relations of production. Notwithstanding the absence of the revolutionary flame, this immanent transformation of society is actually reminiscent of Marx, who postulated that technological evolution is bound to replace capitalism with communism.

2.4.1 ICTs and Deliberative Democracy

A similar line of argument, drawing often on Habermas, has developed in the last decades to introduce a model of participatory or deliberative democracy anchored in the effective participation of people in decision making (Barber 1984; Bohman 1996; Dryzek 2000; Fishkin 1991; Held 1987; Pateman 1970; Yankelovich 1991). A number of authors have advocated for digital democracy or tele-democracy, supported by ICTs (Arterton 1987; Coleman and Gotze 2001; Grossman 1995; Hague and Loader 1999; Hill and Hughes 1998; van Dijk 2006; Ward 1996). The Internet and mobile applications, it is claimed, can bring about the massification of discourse and prototype the democratisation of media. Push-button voting, tele-referenda, tele-polling, free access to online databases and registers can now provide a higher degree of citizen involvement in political and legislative procedures. Technology can now ensure greater transparency, openness and inclusiveness (Vesnic-Alujevic et al. 2019).

A number of analysts argue that ICTs facilitate the participation of citizen-amateurs in formerly professionalised activities, thus signalling the 'open sourcing' of journalism (Gillmor 2004), politics (Castells 2007; Jenkins 2006), science (Benkler 2002b) and culture (Jenkins 2006; Lessig 2004). The power of 'everybody' (Shirky 2008), the 'crowd' (Surowiecki 2004) or the 'mob' (Rheingold 2003) is giving rise to a new populist renaissance of democratic participation and inclusion.

However, freedom of expression, direct voting and easier access to the media, public services and digital interaction do not automatically translate into a participatory democracy. Lessig and Benkler have warned of the dangers inherent in mass media concentration. With information filtered out by mass media to serve the interests of elites, the manufacturing of consent (Herman and Chomsky 1988) could be even stronger in the case of direct participation in decision making, bringing closer to reality the Orwellian nightmare of Big Brother. The massification of discourse, as manifested on the Internet and social media, can easily result in fake news, delusional narratives and straightforward propaganda.

The pipe dream of a free and 'unbiased' Internet runs the risk of techno-populism, orchestrated by elites for the sake of power, money and dominance. Liberal democracies in concert with capitalism portray the semblance of a pluralistic market democracy. E-populism and fragmentation can be channelled into authoritarian democracies, particularly at times of crisis. Majoritarianism can take various turns: socialism, outright fascism, economic nationalism, social democracy, neoliberalism, and so on. Capitalism has proven resilient enough to accommodate technological change in the ever-expanding cycle of capital accumulation by commodifying even contradictory narratives and lifestyles.

2.4.2 Critique of the Digital Commons

Marinus Ossewaarde and Wessel Reijers (2017) build on a number of authors as diverse as Georg Simmel, Peter Sloterdijk, Martin Heidegger, Katherine Gibson, Julie Graham and Antonio Negri to argue that the digital commons produce an 'illusion of the commons', thereby giving rise to cynicism, which in turn can be interpreted as a contemporary form of false consciousness. The term 'false consciousness' dates back to Friedrich Engels and came to be conceptualised later by the Frankfurt School, Antonio Gramsci and Karl Mannheim, among others, as the compulsive belief that capitalism is an unalterable natural condition based upon widespread consent (Ossewaarde and Reijers 2017, 18). False consciousness resonates today within the widespread belief that there is no alternative to capitalism.

Simmel showed that the monetary economy has the unique capacity to homogenise a diverse order of worth under a single price, thereby reducing particular social values (such as sharing, empathy, solidarity, etc.) into quantitative logic (Ossewaarde and Reijers 2017, 20). Sloterdijk holds that Simmel's analysis reveals the cynicism of money as a particular form of false consciousness that cannot be unmasked through a critique of ideology in the style of Georg Lukács, Gramsci and Mannheim (Ossewaarde and Reijers 2017, 20). It requires, instead, a critique of technology. Jacques Ellul (1967), Herbert Marcuse (1964), Cornelius Castoriadis (1991a) and Andrew Feenberg (2002), among others, expanded the critique of ideology in the field of technology to unmask the so-called neutrality of techne. Contrary to the presumption that technology bears its own autonomous scientific logic, they demonstrated that technology embodies the one-dimensional, calculative logic of capitalism, showing that technology is primarily shaped by sociohistorical values. In contrast to this critique of technology, Sloterdijk targets the modern individual as the incarnation of cynicism in the elevated superstructure of capitalism (Ossewaarde and Reijers 2017, 20).

Ossewaarde and Reijers (2017, 19–20) extrapolate the cynicism of the modern individual into a technologically mutated false consciousness in the digital commons. Digital commons, they claim, depend on implicit and explicit pricing mechanisms that draw the practices of digital communing towards the monetary economy, thus being co-opted finally by capitalism. Digital commoners are actually disillusioned by the power of technology, turning eventually into an undifferentiated swarm of cynical 'embittered loners' and 'mass figures'. They share the same false consciousness as employees, consumers and managers acting in the monetary economy. Rather than resisting the neoliberal hegemony, they internalise the new spirit of capitalism, which has succeeded in dissolving the Marxist ideology critique of industrial capitalism (alienation, domination, the calculative logic of technoscience) into a utility satisfaction deriving from a bunch of commodities. Cynicism manifests itself in conformism to the neoliberal hegemony. Therefore, contrary to the ecological, non-digital commons, there is little emancipatory potential in the digital commons given their apolitical principles. Ossewaarde and Reijers (2017, 26) advocate instead for a free relation with technologies through which the digital commons will supplement emancipatory practices embedded in the ecological, non-digital commons. They consider the digital commons as the 'mirror image' of the ecological commons.

Ossewaarde and Reijers's critique reads like a technological update of the classical ideology critique of capitalism turned against the digital commons. However, they conflate the digital commons with the so-called sharing economy of platform capitalism (for example, Airbnb, Uber, Couchsurfing, etc.). It is a mistake to identify the digital commons with top-down capitalist enterprises operating in terms of profit maximisation. Ossewaarde and Reijers make the same error that the classical ideology critique did: they reproduce a generalised argument that fails to acknowledge a nuanced reality. While it is true that the digital commons have been largely co-opted by platform capitalism today, it is not true that they are apolitical and lack a cooperative ethos. Digital commoners exhibit diverse motivations actualised into hybrid contexts, whether apolitical, libertarian, anarcho-communist, leftist, ecological, hipster, and so on. Ossewaarde and Reijers discard a number of successful cases of platform and open cooperatives which demonstrate the opposite. Vasilis Kostakis (2018) is right to argue that the digital commons have both an immanent and a transcendent aspect vis-à-vis capitalism. In the first scenario, capital and state subsume the commons under a commons-centric, crowdsourced capitalism. In the second scenario, the commons become dominant, forcing capital and the state to adapt to their interests.

2.4.3 Castoriadis and the Political

This book mounts the case that, instead of patiently waiting for post-capitalism to replace capitalism, the paramount political task for the commons would be to form a counter-hegemonic power against and beyond neoliberalism. The current impotence of the liberal commons vis-à-vis capital and the state lies, among other things, in the absence of a link between local and global commons. This absence is indicative of the broader lack of the political that accounts for the failure of the liberal commons to band together dispersed initiatives into a coherent social movement capable of challenging the current neoliberal regime. Dardot and Laval and Kioupkiolis correctly argue that the liberal approach to the commons cannot address the contradictions of capitalism and the state.

Contrary to liberal and illiberal democratic regimes, ICTs today enable the self-instituting power of the people, elaborated in multiple variants of radical democracy. The concept of the common as the self-instituting power of the people put forward in this book stems basically from the work of Cornelius Castoriadis, best recognised for his articles published in the journal *Socialisme ou Barbarie* from 1949 to 1965. In the 40 issues of the journal, Castoriadis developed a radical critique of capitalism and Marxism, resulting in the redefinition of the content of socialism. Castoriadis conceives of socialism as the self-institutionalisation of society by collective management, established first and foremost at the level of production. Socialism presupposes the abolition of the division between directors and executants, penetrating both capitalism and Leninism-Stalinism. It consists instead in the expansion of individual and collective autonomy at all levels of society (Castoriadis 1988, 92–95).

In his later writings, Castoriadis engages in the contemporary discussion over *the political* and *politics* (Marchart, 2007) to enrich his concept of autonomy, which now sets out in two stages: *the instituting* and *the instituted* (Castoriadis 1991b). *The instituted* signifies the radical ground-power, or primordial power, necessary for the self-preservation and self-perpetuation of the human species. It constitutes an explicit power, termed *the political* and manifesting in law, language, religion, and so on. By 'power' Castoriadis (1991b, 149) refers to 'the capacity for a personal or impersonal instance (*Instanz*) to bring someone to do (or to abstain from doing) that which, left to him/herself, s/he would not necessarily have done (or would possibly have done) […]'.

The instituted is nurtured by *the instituting* of the radical and social imaginary. The instituting transcends the instituted by virtue of the autonomy of the anonymous collective to transform the political (Papadimitropoulos 2019). Whereas societies have mostly evolved under conditions of instituted heteronomy, with the essential constituent being the representation of an extra-social source of nomos (whether myth, tradition, religion, class, etc.), autonomy identifies with *politics* that constantly challenges *the political*. Politics conditions the self-institutionalisation of society according to the democratically established rules of the anonymous collective. Democratic politics introduces the concept of the common as the self-instituting power of the people. The common aims at the abolition of heteronomy by establishing the autonomy of the people by/for the people.

Castoriadis's stance on democracy breaks with the liberal separation of politics and the economy by restoring democracy to the roots of the economy. Real democracy cannot exist without economic democracy; without people having an equal say in the production process and planning of the economy; without people regaining their individual and collective autonomy through the self-management of the means of production, the redistribution of surplus value, the division of labour, working conditions and so forth. Real democracy cannot but be direct democracy expanding from production across all spheres of society. Castoriadis, thus, defines the common as the democratic power of the people geared towards the abolition of state capitalism and the establishment of socialism.

It is not, therefore, enough to consider the colonisation of democracy by capitalism as a legitimation crisis, as Habermas (1988) argues. Nor does the contribution of digital commons to an 'ideal' speech situation settle the issue once and for all. The crisis of democracy reflects the structural failure of capitalism to address the real wants and needs of people. The main contradiction of capitalism is not that between owners and non-owners of the means of production, as Marx would have it, but the division between directors (managers) and executants (workers), spreading from the economy to the state and all spheres of society (Castoriadis 1988). Communism is not the final stage of state ownership of the means of production, but the self-management of the commons by people themselves.

In capitalism and the so-called socialism of the Eastern Bloc, workers participate in the production of the enterprise insofar as they do not interfere with the management; citizens participate in state management insofar as they do not govern. The division between directors and workers, representatives and citizens renders power and knowledge inaccessible and secret. The management of the economy and society becomes an affair of experts, a Marxist ideology, a liberal or post-political technocratic consensus, a game theory, a postmodern narrative, a neoliberal competition. Democracy is a sham, a rigged process, a win–win deal, a communication marketing of competing elites in a corporate society. The individual blindly obeys the party or retreats into her private sphere of conformism, becoming a self-interested maximiser and a consumer. Society turns into a cluster of hobbies and lobbies, with populism, nihilism and cynicism representing the new disorder of things.

The division between directors and workers constitutes the core of the rational mastery of capitalism, driving the unlimited expansion of the economy and technology in society and nature (Papadimitropoulos 2018a). Rational mastery echoes the Weberian rationalisation of bureaucracy. But while Castoriadis was calling for the abolition of the division between directors and executants and the establishment of direct democracy at all levels of society, Weber (1978/1922) was arguing for the inevitability of bureaucracy in modern societies and the impracticability of direct democracy. For Weber, direct democracy is functional only locally and among relative equals. The complexity of contemporary societies renders direct democracy inefficient and potentially dangerous in the long term.

2.4.4 The Challenges of Direct Democracy

Daniel Kreiss, Megan Finn and Fred Turner (2011) build on Weber to designate the limits of commons-based peer production. They draw attention to the merits of bureaucracies such as explicit rule making, precision, credentialing, expertise and efficiency that may be undermined by commons-based peer production. They claim that bureaucracies are important in retaining democratic values such as equality, transparency and inclusivity, whereas commons-based peer production is prone to opaqueness, 'benevolent dictators' and gatekeepers. They warn of the danger of commons-based peer production being absorbed by firms and managerial bureaucracies and, finally, extending their mechanisms. In this scenario, the digital commons turn out to intrude into privacy by coercively expanding the workplace into everyday life, thereby technologically reproducing previous forms of social and economic organisation. Rather than offering a revolutionary alternative, they are co-opted by capitalism and the state.

However, the authors are uncritically taking for granted certain bureaucratic values, while omitting the bureaucratic defects that the commons are coming to fix. They abstain from situating bureaucracies in a broader political framework. They dismiss the fact that bureaucracies have been controlled by elites, often lending a helping hand to colonialism, fascism and modern liberal oligarchies. Their argumentation, finally, culminates in fragmented generalisations for both bureaucracies and peer production. A more nuanced and rigorous approach is necessary to unravel the complex dynamics of bureaucracies and peer production. The authors are right to claim that scholars need to examine peer production more thoroughly by posing a new set of research questions regarding the scope of bureaucracies and peer production and their interdependencies. One can begin by asking: Is direct democracy limited solely to locals and equals?

Ostrom proves Weber partially wrong. Lessig and Benkler expand the self-instituting power of the people from local to global (digital) commons. But they cannot offer a holistic alternative for a commons-orientated transition that would clash head-on with neoliberal capitalism. Castoriadis (1988, 121) was one of the first to stress that information technology can support direct democracy on a large scale. He called for the abolition of capitalism and the state through the establishment of the self-instituting power of the people across all spheres of society. Instead of patiently waiting for technology to progressively transform capitalism into post-capitalism, Castoriadis calls for radical social change. The problem with Castoriadis is that he rejected the current political system *in toto*, relying solely on the autonomous activity of individuals and collectivities. However, the commons face today multiple external and internal constraints. They depend largely on financial and technological systems managed by corporate capital and neoliberal state policies. In Castoriadis's terms, the commons are still largely heteronomous rather than autonomous.

For the commons to evolve into a sustainable mode of production, state support is necessary. The state can facilitate the transition to a decentralised and self-managed economy by various means: funding, education, infrastructure, law reform, and so on. Autonomous movements, however, should not resort to any sort of state paternalism to sustain themselves. Heteronomy is not the necessary counterpart of autonomy in order for the latter to abolish the former in the long run. Individual and collective autonomy cannot depend on a flawed representative democracy subject to the neoliberal dictates of capitalism.

Dyer-Witheford (1999; 2015) and Kostakis and Bauwens (2014; 2019), whose work is examined in detail later on, call for the de-statification or commonification of the state. De-statification devolves administrative power to a multiplicity of associations. The role of government is redefined to support collective initiatives rather than substitute for them; diffuse rather than concentrate power; and nurture social transformation from the bottom up rather than engineer it from the top down.

The state should transform into mini-states of commons-based peer production ecosystems that implement direct democratic procedures and practices. This political task requires the institutional reconfiguration of the separation of powers. Post-hegemony is the vision to create a holistic political alternative to neoliberal state capitalism out of self-perpetuating, autonomous, commons-based enterprises and organisations, supported by reticular market and institutional mechanisms aligned around the commons. To this end, Ostrom's polycentric model needs to transform into the post-hegemony of the commons. The main challenges for post-hegemonic politics today are how to connect local with global commons; how to bring together and coordinate dispersed, small-scale civic initiatives; how to confront established social systems and power relations in the market and the state; and how to create a counter-hegemonic power that fosters a commons-orientated, sociopolitical transition against and beyond neoliberalism.

PART 2

The Reformist Commons

CHAPTER 3

The Reformist Commons

3.1 Introduction

As discussed in Part 1, Benkler sets out three basic future scenarios for the commons: 1) the capitalist commons on the model of firm-hosted peer production; 2) the transition from firm-hosted peer production into a broader collaborative economy that embraces commons-based peer production more openly; and 3) the autonomisation of commons-based peer production. Part 2 critically engages with the work of a number of thinkers who have built on the second scenario with the intent of pushing for the third. From a political viewpoint, the reformist approach to the commons combines liberal, social democratic, socialist and revolutionary elements in multiple variants.

David Bollier (2003; 2008) recalibrates the liberal state towards the support of the commons rather than the capitalist market. He introduces a green governance model aiming to tackle climate change and protect the natural commons. Along with Silke Helfrich (Bollier and Helfrich 2019), he provides an analytical roadmap towards a radical commons-orientated transition. Jeremy Rifkin (2014) introduces the model of green capitalism, connecting to the Internet of Things infrastructure, fuelled by renewables. He advocates the gradual shift of green capitalism towards the collaborative commons, supported by the Internet and free/open source software/hardware.

Trebor Scholz (2016a; 2016b) adds a cooperative twist to the collaborative commons by juxtaposing platform cooperativism against platform capitalism (the so-called sharing and gig economy). Platform cooperativism consists of online business models based on democratic self-governance, platform co-ownership and equitable distribution of value. Kostakis and Bauwens (2014) give a challenging spin to platform cooperativism by introducing the model of open cooperativism between the commons and ethical market entities, operating in terms of open protocols, open supply chains, commons-based

How to cite this book chapter:
Papadimitropoulos, V. 2020. *The Commons: Economic Alternatives in the Digital Age.* Pp. 69–136. London: University of Westminster Press. DOI: https://doi.org/10.16997 /book46.c. License: CC-BY-NC-ND 4.0

licensing and open book accounting. They attempt to bridge local and global (digital) commons by incorporating the ecological model of Design Global–Manufacture Local (DG–ML) into open cooperativism, backed by a partner state through taxation, funding, regulation, education, and so on. DECODE (Decentralised Citizen Owned Data Ecosystems) is an ambitious EU-funded research project that attempts to push forward platform and open cooperativism by building the technological tools necessary to sustain decentralisation, democratic e-governance and alternative business models.

Adam Arvidsson and Nicolai Peitersen (2013) illustrate an ethical economy of productive publics, consisting of collaborative networks of peer producers, supported by the Internet and mobile applications. Commons-based peer production could be a model of economic democracy in which the universal measure of value would be the general sentiment. Arvidsson and Peitersen demonstrate a technologically advanced Habermasian transformation of the public sphere, which would open up a more rational and democratic negotiation of economic value, bringing together politics, the commons and a reformed capitalism.

Douglas Rushkoff (2016) suggests a hybrid business model of cooperation between corporations and the commons in the form of a 'benefit corporation' where the pursuit of growth is subsumed to a sustainable economy based on value creation and the equitable recycling of money among the commons. The 'benefit corporation' model would be framed by non-profit and social enterprises, crowdfunding, local currencies, time banks and platform cooperatives built on Blockchain protocols.

Erik Olin Wright (2009) posits a pluralistic and heterogeneous socialist transformation, grounded on a centrally coordinated decentralisation of power. His socialist transformation strategy is premised on the radical democratisation of both the state and the economy by civil society.

Overall, the reformist camp contributes to the discussion on the commons by offering a concrete link between the local and the global commons, embedded in a broader societal transformation steered towards a commons-orientated transition. But still, there is a considerable lack of the political with regard to the formation of a coherent counter-hegemonic block of the commons against and beyond neoliberalism. This lack translates into the absence of a set of concrete policies that would provide a clear path towards a broader commons-orientated social change.

3.2 The Green Governance Commons

David Bollier has offered one of the most widely accepted definitions of the commons as shared resources self-managed according to the rules and norms of the community (Bollier and Weston 2012, 343–352). His early work mostly relates to the preservation of the traditional commons of nature against the current tragedy of the commons caused by a predatory capitalism eating up the earth's resources for the sake of profit maximisation and unlimited growth (Bollier 2001; 2003). He addresses the commons from the viewpoint of the human right to a healthy and clean environment, encapsulated in the long tradition of the 'commons law' that aims at securing the conservation of natural resources, while keeping them open for public use (Bollier and Weston 2012, 347). Bollier and Helfrich's later work encompasses all fields of the commons, from Ostrom's traditional commons, arts and cultural commons, neighbourhood commons, exchange and credit commons to the digital commons (Bollier and Helfrich 2015).

Bollier introduces a new policy and law architecture on the model of 'green governance'. On a local level, he adheres to Ostrom's design principles. On a macro-policy level, like Ostrom, Lessig and Benkler, he places the development of the commons in parallel with state and market operation:

> The overall goal must be to reconceptualise the neoliberal State/Market/ Commons – to realign authority and provisioning in new, more beneficial ways. The State would maintain its commitments to representative governance and management of public property just as private enterprise would continue to own capital to produce saleable goods and services in the Market sector. (Bollier and Weston 2012, 350)

At first sight, Bollier's model of green governance seems to follow the liberal tradition. Yet Bollier holds that the state must shift its focus to become a partner not only of the market sector but mainly of the commons sector (Bollier and Weston 2012, 349–350). The state must assume a more active role in establishing and overseeing large-scale common-pool resources such as the atmosphere, the oceans, hard and soft minerals, timber, public land, national parks and wilderness areas, rivers, lakes and other bodies of water (Bollier and Weston 2012, 349–350). Like Lessig and Benkler, he goes along with wealthy corporations becoming business partners of the digital commoners (2008, 15–16, 20, 229). His perspective, however, extends well beyond the state and capital by envisioning the autonomous development of the commons.

In accordance with the General Public License (GPL) invented by Stallmann, Bollier points to the inversion of private contract and property to serve collective goals. New property regimes could combine with 'stakeholder trusts' and digital networking technologies for the purpose of sustaining a more transparent, participatory and accountable commons (Bollier and Weston 2012, 350–351). Bollier has also proposed a variety of measures for the democratic finance of the commons: social and ethical lending by credit unions and public banks, crowd-funding (for example, Goteo), complementary currencies, time banks, and so on (Conaty and Bollier 2015).

Bollier and Helfrich (2012; 2015) document dozens of notable commons. In their most recent book (2019), they put forth the socio-ontological dimension of the commons to stress the deep interrelationality of the commons. They formulate a language for the commons that contrasts the terminology of mainstream economics and neoliberalism. The commons language moves beyond misleading binaries such as collective/individual, cooperation/competition, consumer/producer, public/private by introducing terms such as the capping of common wealth instead of scarcity, care-wealth instead of wealth, affective labour instead of labour, collaborative finance instead of finance, commons-public partnership instead of public–private partnership, DIT (do it together) instead of DIY (do it yourself), reciprocity instead of trade, heterarchy instead of hierarchy, provisioning instead of production, semi-permeable membranes instead of closed boundaries, sharing and pooling instead of resource allocation, value sovereignty instead of price sovereignty, relationalised property instead of public–private–collective property (Bollier and Helfrich 2019, 51–73).

Under these terms, Bollier and Helfrich construct a theoretical 'umbrella' for numerous already existing commons-based patterns. By 'pattern' they mean a kernel idea for solving problems that shows up again and again in different contexts that require different solutions. For example, a co-op in a German city and in an American city may face similar problems but in different legal, economic and cultural contexts. Bollier and Helfrich demarcate a triad of commoning that consists of three interconnected spheres: 1) social life (the social sphere), 2) peer governance (the institutional sphere) and 3) provisioning (the economic sphere). All three spheres are penetrated by various patterns that transgress Ostrom's design principles: the cultivation of shared purpose and values, free contribution, gentle reciprocity, deep communion with nature, cultural diversity, the creation of semi-permeable membranes between the commons and the state/market, transparency, conviviality, consent in decision making, the relationalisation of property, monitoring and graduated sanctions, the distinction between commons and commerce, the support of care and decommodified work, the reliance on federated/distributed structures, and so on (Bollier and Helfrich 2019, 93–193).

Bollier and Helfrich (2019, 290) illustrate a relational approach to state power through which the state could support the commons in various ways. The state could provide infrastructure, technical advice and funding to help people acquire land and buildings for community-supported agriculture and housing commons, offer neighbourhood services such as care for the elderly, and launch maker-spaces, energy cooperatives, tool-sharing commons, repair cafés and time-banking exchanges. The state could serve as clearing house for technical, legal and financial issues concerning the commons in diverse contexts (agriculture, social services, energy, alternative currencies, etc.). The state could install open platforms inviting citizens to assist city councils in urban planning, government websites encouraging citizen feedback about public services, participatory budgeting programmes to allow citizens to co-determine spending decisions. The state could also support co-housing, volunteer networks for the elderly, food cooperatives, and so on. Free and open source software could become the default infrastructure in public administration and education.

Instead of schools turning into the quasi-captive extensions of large software corporations' marketing departments, they could educate students in the use of open source software, which would then have spin-off effects for higher education, municipal government and the general public. State-endorsed open design protocols for information services, housing, ride-hailing services and energy grids could foster open source innovation and benefit local communities, preventing proprietary lock-ins by larger companies (Bollier and Helfrich 2019, 307–311). Bollier and Helfrich call on us to imagine a town:

> in which supermarkets are run as cooperatives, helping residents to buy higher-quality, local food produced under fair and eco-responsible conditions. The local taxi service and tourist lodgings are managed by platform cooperatives, letting households and the community share the benefits. Nursing services are run by a neighborhood home care venture such as Buurtzorg [...] Electricity generated by rooftop solar panels is pooled and shared via distributed ledger technology software, which is reducing high electricity bills and allowing public divestment from fossil fuels and nuclear power. (2019, 305–306)

Ultimately, the state would facilitate a commons-orientated, post-capitalist transition by shifting power from the market to the commons. This would be supplemented by three distinct strategies by/for the commons: 1) the development of community charters as tools for constituting commoning; 2) the creation and use of distributed ledger platforms that can advance cooperation on digital networks; and 3) the design of commons–public partnerships, as outlined above, that could leverage state power for the commons (Bollier and Helfrich 2019, 310–311).

Overall, Bollier and Helfrich offer both a theoretical framework and an analytical roadmap for a commons-orientated, post-capitalist transition, aiming to bring together local and global (digital) commons under commons governance. Perhaps this scattered transition could be accelerated by a holistic political strategy seeking to bootstrap the spontaneous coalescence of the commons around a coherent post-hegemonic socio-economic paradigm moving beyond and against neoliberalism.

3.3 The Collaborative Commons

Jeremy Rifkin (2014, 1) makes the case that we have witnessed over the last decades a paradigm shift from market capitalism to the collaborative commons on the model of a hybrid economy, part capitalist and part commons. The term 'collaborative commons' is a contradiction in terms, since by definition there are no non-collaborative commons. Rifkin perhaps seeks to emphasise by that term the collaborative element inherent in the commons.

Rifkin (2014, 30) reads modern history through the lens of technological evolution, embedded in different business models and social norms. The commons date back to feudalism, when agricultural life was communally structured. The landlords leased their land to peasants who combined the individual plots into open fields and farmed them collectively. The birth of capitalism originated in the enclosure of the commons for the purpose of wool production. Capitalism began in the textile industry, powered by hydraulic energy. The synergies created by the print revolution and wind/water power democratised both literacy and energy, challenging the hierarchical organisation of feudalism (Rifkin 2014, 36). Later, the convergence of coal-powered printing and coal-powered rail transport, combined with the invention of the telegraph, created the communications/energy matrix of the First Industrial Revolution (Rifkin 2014, 46). The discovery of oil, the harnessing of electricity, the telephone and the internal combustion engine gave rise to the communications/energy matrix of the Second Industrial Revolution. Colonial capitalism, backed by government funding, was the business model for both the First and Second Industrial Revolutions, consolidating production and distribution under centralised, top-down management (Rifkin 2014, 46). Rifkin binds the rise of the commons in the last decades to a Third Industrial Revolution, fostered by the interlinking of renewables with ICTs.

3.3.1 The Third Industrial Revolution

The Third Industrial Revolution disrupts the centralised capitalist model through the decentralised use of data analytics, artificial intelligence, 3D printers and FOSS, all sustaining the communications/energy matrix of the Internet of Things. Hundreds of start-up businesses infofacture their products using 3D printers in FabLabs powered by their own energy (Rifkin 2014, 70). The Internet is gradually becoming a neural network, transforming homes and businesses into micropower plants, harvesting renewable energy on site. Alvin Toffler (1980) coined the term 'prosumers' to describe the class of consumers who have evolved beyond passive consumption. Prosumers now produce their own energy across the net; manufacture almost everything using 3D printers and open source software; advertise their products for free on hundreds of websites; acquire education for free through massive open online courses (MOOCs); exchange products and services in the sharing economy, and so on (Rifkin 2014, 19).

The Internet and free software already disrupt several media industries in software production, web services, entertainment, communications and publishing (Rifkin 2014, 65). Blockchain may also have a significant impact on the finance sector, among others, insofar as it could support various sorts of micro-finance based on cryptocurrencies such as Bitcoin, enabling peer-to-peer transactions to take place instantaneously anywhere in the world with no intermediaries (banks, governments) or transaction fees (Rifkin 2014,

255–260). Alongside cryptocurrencies, community currencies and micro-currencies could also produce an alternative currency system (Rifkin 2014, 261). The democratisation of communication, energy and logistics could bring back the commons by distributing finance and the means of production to the people, thereby empowering individuals and collectivities. The commons, thus, emerge as the self-instituting power of the people on the web and beyond.

In the future, ICTs are expected to integrate into life sciences on the model of bioinformatics, which has the potential to convert the ones and zeros of digital information into the letters that make up the alphabet of DNA, thereby virtually unleashing unlimited information capacity and storage (Rifkin 2014, 86). Rifkin's core argument is that the coming together of the Communications Internet with the Energy Internet and the Logistics Internet in the intelligent infrastructure of the Internet of Things (IoT) is giving rise to a Third Industrial Revolution, fuelled by the renewables that will increase thermodynamic efficiencies in the marshalling of resources and the recycling of waste, thereby driving down the costs of production and distribution of goods to near-zero marginal levels:

> The Internet of Things will connect everything with everyone in an integrated global network. People, machines, natural resources, production lines, logistics networks, consumption habits, recycling flows, and virtually every aspect of economic and social life will be linked via sensors and software to the IoT platform, continually feeding Big Data to every node – businesses, homes, vehicles – moment to moment, in real time. Big Data, in turn, will be processed with advanced analytics, transformed into predictive algorithms, and programmed into automated systems to improve thermodynamic efficiencies, dramatically increase productivity, and reduce the marginal cost of producing and delivering a full range of goods and services to near zero across the entire economy. (Rifkin 2014, 11)

The end of capitalism and the rise of the collaborative commons

Rifkin repeats Marx's and Keynes's claim that capitalist competition will bring about new technologies that will increase productivity, decrease prices and replace human labour with machines. Automation will produce technological unemployment that will eclipse capitalism in the long run due to the absence of consumers to buy the cheaper products. Given the near-zero marginal cost of production, scarcity will give way to abundance that will deplete exchange value in favour of shareable use value, thus rendering the 'invisible hand' of the market obsolete. Put simply, nobody will be willing to pay for products if they can get them for free or produce them on their own.

Capitalism will then shrink to niche markets, clearing the ground for the rise of the collaborative commons, that is, a broad movement of civil society, comprising NGOs, charities, organisations, arts and cultural groups, social enterprises, cooperatives, scattered communities, Transition Towns, ecovillages, FabLabs and other formal and informal institutions that generate social capital. Thus, Rifkin simply reproduces the argument that dates back to Marx and is taken up by often disparate contemporary authors such as Barbrook and Benkler, arguing that technology will help create an abundance of the commons that will eventually replace capitalism with another socio-economic model, be it anarcho-communism or post-capitalism.

Capitalism's internal contradictions not only undermine its own survival, they also threaten the sustainability of the planet itself. Hyper-productivity accounts for the entropic bill of the capitalist machine in the Industrial Age, that is, the massive energy waste shown in the carbon emission rates and climate change. The collaborative commons, instead, champion the transition from carbon-based fuels to renewable energies and the use of fewer natural resources more efficiently on the model of a circular economy, supported by the Internet of Things. In contrast to the centralised, proprietary and profit-driven capitalist business model, the collaborative commons represents an alternative business model based on a communication/energy/logistics matrix that sustains a 'smart' infrastructure designed to be open, collaborative, decentralised and distributed. The end-to-end principle of the Internet provides autonomy for the users, enhancing commons innovation and creativity. The collaborative commons advance sustainability, open source innovation, access, transparency and the search for community. As Rifkin (2014, 18) eloquently puts it: 'The IoT is the technological "soul mate" of an emerging Collaborative Commons.'

Rifkin brings up the work of Brett M. Frischmann (2012) to criticise Benkler. Frischmann conceives of the commons as infrastructures rather than open access commons, addressing demand-side market failures that stem from positive externalities widespread in natural resources, roads, electricity systems, telecommunications and knowledge. Rifkin (2014, 194) claims that Benkler neglects the critical role that energy plays in infrastructure. The course of modern history is marked by the convergence of new communications media with new energy regimes that sustained the infrastructure of the First and Second Industrial Revolutions. Rifkin goes along with the liberal commons by introducing a three-stakeholder model in the Third Industrial Revolution, comprising the commons, the state and the market (Rifkin 2014, 196). But he takes a leap forward by linking local and global commons via the Internet of Things infrastructure, the operating logic of which is best served by commons management (Rifkin 2014, 195). He therefore introduces a commons-based business model as an alternative to capitalism, envisaging the gradual adjustment of the latter to the former.

Like Lessig and Benkler, Rifkin acknowledges that the adjustment of capitalism to the commons is not going to be a smooth one: 'The struggle over governance of the three interlocking Internets that make up the Internet of Things is being aggressively waged among governments, capitalist enterprises, and champions of the nascent social economy on the Commons, each with ambitions to define the coming era' (2014, 195). Rifkin (2014, 202) invokes studies showing that the Communication Internet increasingly looks like a Monopoly board, where a handful of corporations compete for dominance: Google rules search; Facebook social networking; eBay auctions; Apple online content delivery; Amazon retail, and so on. Global media are concentrated in the hands of a few giant corporations that decide what is news (Rifkin 2014, 213).

'Algorithmic manipulation' is the name of the game for actors who have a commercial interest in tampering with the data and producing fake news, predatory advertising and corporate propaganda (Rifkin 2014, 203). Surveillance capitalism is engineered by the power of algorithms to create toxic feedback loops of class and ethnic racism, transforming into weapons of math destruction. Software used in job recruitment, college admission processes, criminal justice and crime prediction often encodes racial prejudices and biases into sloppy statistical models, reproducing unfairness and inequality (O'Neil 2016). Yet, for Rifkin, free software, creative commons licensing and free wi-fi are still islands of freedom in the capitalist ocean of control (Rifkin 2014, 147–151, 173–192).

On the Energy Internet, global energy companies aim to centralise the smart electricity grid and enable the commercial enclosure of new renewable energies (Rifkin 2014, 205). Countries, on the other hand, are introducing green feed-in tariffs to motivate users to produce their own electricity and share it across the net. In response, companies are changing their business model to accommodate decentralised energy production. They are focusing on the management of energy use rather than solely on sales (Rifkin 2014, 206).

Reality check

The struggle between prosumer collaborators and investor capitalists has only just begun, with the state calibrating corporate centralisation versus commons decentralisation. The main question is whether the digital oligarchy of surveillance capitalism can control the billions of prosumers who will have access to the means of production in the decades to come. The answer, obviously, depends on the future of class struggle in global politics.

At the moment, however, despite the fact that more and more people produce their energy locally, the EU follows the US in the adoption of a series of neoliberal policies well suited to large energy companies. Most EU policies and regulations have abstained from introducing community-based feed-in tariffs or micro-grid infrastructures to support local renewable energy production. Instead, the EU has been granting massive subsidies to large gas, coal and nuclear companies, promoting gas pipelines, enormous energy infrastructures and modest CO_2 reductions (Hammerstein 2019, 29–30).

Rifkin overstates the current status of the collaborative commons. He mentions that community currencies are proliferating in Greece and Spain (2014, 262). But this is not the case. While it is true that there are 1,100 cooperatives in Greece at the time of writing, most of them are struggling to survive and facing considerable financial strains. This holds true for most commons-based peer production across the globe. The major problem of the commons is their economic sustenance due to the lack of access to resources and capital. The commons depend almost exclusively on state funding and the volunteering of activists who can afford to contribute. However, most of society cannot exit capitalism, even if they aspired to. Additional barriers relate to the significant gap in managerial and technical skills, sectoral and operational isolation in a number of subsectors, and a lack of public policy and institutional support from both the state and larger cooperatives (Papadimitropoulos 2018b; Scholz 2016b). More than 90% of co-ops are consumer co-ops, with the main owners not being workers themselves. Even in worker-owned cooperatives, workers are often not co-op members. Therefore, many co-ops are co-ops in name only. They are basically market entities that have adopted capitalist practices, as their main interest is to get a higher selling price or lower buying price in the market (Gindin 2016).

3.3.2 Platform Capitalism, aka the Sharing Economy

Rifkin includes the so-called sharing economy in the collaborative commons. The term 'sharing economy' arises from the early development of a number of non-profit, peer-to-peer initiatives inspired by the moral values of a gift economy supported by ICTs (for example, Couchsurfing). Nowadays, the term sharing economy has evolved to refer to a collaborative economy where individuals are coordinated through online software platforms for the production, distribution, trade and consumption of goods and services, typically in a peer-to-peer fashion.

Yet not only does the online commercialisation of the gift economy in the last decade render the sharing economy a fallacy, it also misclassifies true aspects of the gift economy – manifested in commons-based peer production – under the wrong term. The term sharing economy is a greatly misleading marketing buzzword that deliberately confuses two different economic modes: sharing and commercial exchange (Lee 2015; Olma 2015; Schor 2015; Slee 2015; Walker 2015). Sharing is a feature of a gift economy that has been prevalent among communities (families, friends and colleagues) from society's inception (Mauss 1967). Sharing means giving something away as a gift, allowing someone to use something you own temporarily or having something in common with somebody else. Sharing can be an act of distribution, co-belonging and communication, as in the cases of sharing a chocolate, a room or thoughts and emotions (John 2012, 169–170). Sharing became widespread as a term particularly with the advent of Web 2.0, which gave Internet users the opportunity to generate content online on platforms such as Facebook, YouTube, Flickr, Twitter, in wikis, on blogs and on several other websites (John 2012, 167). Sharing has transformed into a form of prosumption, that is, the blending of consumption with production that has served the creation of big data, fuelling marketing and advertising during the last decades (John 2012, 168).

The sharing economy is, then, a euphemism for the emergence of a neoliberal model of platform capitalism that creates value by facilitating exchange between consumers and producers. Platform capitalism is a vast digital ecosystem that interconnects cloud computing, big data and mobile apps (Norton 2018). Digitisation and networking on the Internet has helped expand the monetisation of goods and services, thus rendering on-demand commercial exchange of all kinds more viable and efficient.

Platform capitalism relies on the intersection of three economic laws: 1) Metcalfe's law of network effects, 2) the Pioneer Advantage Law and 3) the winner-takes-all law (Vercellone et al. 2019, 8–13). Whereas industrial capitalism is supply-side economics of scale, platform capitalism depends on demand-side economies based on network effects on the Internet, that is, social networking and demand aggregation enhanced by applications and algorithms controlling big data (Van Alstyne et al. 2016). Platform capitalism is actually a data-extractivism model generated by network effects.

In contrast to 'pipeline' businesses creating value by controlling a production line where inputs at one end of the chain transform into outputs at the other end, platform capitalism incorporates the classic value-chain model into a digital landscape marked by three major shifts: 1) from resource control to the orchestration of the network of producers and consumers; 2) from internal optimisation to network interaction; and 3) from a focus on customer value to a focus on ecosystem value (Van Alstyne et al. 2016). In short, platform capitalism is set up by the algorithmic top-down orchestration of the bottom-up networking between producers and consumers on the Internet.

Network effects reinforce the competitive advantage that a pioneering platform gains in a market thanks to a technical innovation or commercial intuition. Pioneering platforms 'lock in' consumers and producers, thereby preventing potential competitors from penetrating. This progression leads to the establishment of a monopoly, with a few players capturing the largest share of a market.

Platform capitalism employs several business models (Torregrossa 2018). A key one is the multi-sided platform model based on intermediaries (companies) acting as matchmakers in multi-sided platforms that create value primarily by enabling direct interactions between two or more customer or participant groups. Prominent examples of multi-sided platforms and the participants they connect include Alibaba.com, eBay (buyers and sellers); Airbnb (dwelling owners and renters); the Uber app (professional drivers and passengers); Facebook (users, advertisers, third-party game or content developers and affiliated third-party sites); Upwork, Freelancer (professionals and companies).

Online platforms help companies to realise monopoly rents on big data, advertising space and cloud-based computing (Facebook, Google, Amazon); to sell products and services (Amazon); to extract fees by enabling peer-to-peer and peer-to-business transactions (eBay, Alibaba.com, Airbnb, Uber, Upwork, Freelancer); or a combination of the above (Amazon) (Kenney 2014; Lobo 2014; Pasquale 2017, 312; Srnicek 2017).

The illusion of economic freedom

Platform capitalism is considered to transform consumers into micro-entre-preneurs, trading, sharing, swapping and renting products and services, thus unlocking the untapped value or excess capacity of underutilised assets and services (cars, rooms, consumer goods, labour, capital, wi-fi, etc.). The online on-demand economy creates a 24-hour global marketplace, supposed to reduce waste and transaction costs, deepen human capital specialisation and increase efficiency in labour markets, employment, asset management and pricing, thus resulting in higher levels of productivity, innovation, environmental sustaina-bility and inclusive growth (Codagnone et al. 2016a; 2016b; Sundararajan 2016).

Rifkin's inclusion of the so-called sharing economy in the collaborative com-mons reflects a neoliberal economic account, represented by some thought leaders in Silicon Valley such as Tad Friend (2015) and Nicholas Lemann (2015), who conceive of the emergence of platform capitalism as a natural transition towards a more autonomous, deregulated and flexible market where both companies and independent contractors are now freer to work outside the conventional time and place framework (Codagnone et al. 2016a, 13; Pas-quale 2017, 309–311). Freelancers can now have a more creative, autonomous and flexible work life, thus leading to a more balanced private life. Platform capitalism can bolster a decentralisation of power that would translate into an economic democracy and participatory culture, thus leading to the highest possible freedom for firms, households and individuals (Bruns 2008, 227–228; Jenkins 2006, 275; Tapscott and Williams 2006, 267).

Silicon Valley's techno-populist tales of 'user empowerment' and 'digital socialism' are made of promises to bridge the gap in consumption and income inequality (Morozov 2014; 2015). However, equalising access to communication services and digitising disintermediation between idle capital and consumers via online platforms do not automatically eliminate or weaken inequalities. On the contrary, they can augment existing inequalities concentrating the new markets of platform capitalism into the hands of a few corporations (Morozov 2018).

Arun Sundararajan (2016) mistakenly claims that the so-called sharing econ-omy consists of crowd-based 'networks' rather than centralised institutions or 'hierarchies'. While it is true that platform capitalism has decentralised economic activity, by no means does this point to a truly decentralised economy. Online platforms are available to front-end users who are controlled by back-end centralised server infrastructures, managed hierarchically by decisions made in Silicon Valley and executed by black box algorithms (Scholz 2016a, 26). Consumers, providers and producers pay a fee to exchange products and services online, thereby bringing enormous profits to platform owners. The big money goes to the oligarchy of the shareholders, and the scraps to on-demand workers. In short, platform capitalism represents a digital oligarchy that leverages market power via network effects to extract rents from participants.

In Marxian terms, platform capitalism captures the use value of the general intellect, produced by the sociality of Internet users in social media, online platforms, search engines, blogs and mobile applications. It leverages the network effects generated by user interaction on the Internet, thereby sustaining a digital oligarchy that commodifies the social imaginary (Fuchs 2014). Trebor Scholz has termed the commodification of network effects 'crowd fleecing', meaning a new form of exploitation, put in place by four or five upstarts, to draw on a global pool of millions of workers in real time (Scholz 2016a, 4). Platform capitalism is a technologically advanced form of exploitation, resulting – on average – in a 'race to the bottom' with regard to workers' wages and living standards. Earnings in platform capitalism range from very low to modest, with only a small minority of workers making above middle-level incomes (Codagnone et al. 2016a, 6).

What is at stake in platform capitalism is the meaning of work per se. A number of authors have built on the Marxian notion of the proletariat, arguing that digitisation has created a new, diverse type of proletariat. Already in the 1980s, Andre Gorz (1980, 69) argued that automation and computerisation had rendered the underemployed, probationary, contracted, casual, temporary and part-time worker a 'post-industrial neo-proletariat'. This tendency is even more pronounced today in the context of digitisation. Ursula Huws (2003; 2014) speaks of a new class of information-processing workers – the cybertariat. Guy Standing (2011) and Nick Dyer-Witheford (1999, 88, 96) claim that poorly paid, insecure and deskilled service workers constitute the new type of precariat. Castells (2000, 244) considers low-paid service workers as a new 'white collar proletariat'.

However attractive the prospect of transforming workers into microentrepreneurs or flexible freelance workers, platform capitalism puts – on average – the worker at a disadvantage, as it transforms labour into an auction, creating a disproportionate supply and demand feedback. On the one side, it favours the 'haves' over the 'have-nots' – as every auction does – while, on the other, it obliges the exploited amateurs to push professional prices down by selling their services cheaper. In the name of entrepreneurship, labour flexibility, autonomy and freedom of choice, platform capitalism shifts the burdens of risk (unemployment, illness, old age) on to the workers' shoulders. It offers no minimum wage, no security, no health insurance, no pension, no unemployment insurance, no paid holiday or paid sick days (Scholz 2016a). The elimination of workers' rights and democratic values such as accountability and consent indicate the lack of dignity for workers who are in a position of unfavourable information and power asymmetry (Newlands et al. 2016, 9, 14).

Platform capitalism has colonised the public and private sphere to such an extent that it has integrated communication and information technologies into a global cyber-market, blurring the boundaries between 'virtual' and 'real', 'work' and 'play', 'production' and 'consumption', 'private' and 'public'. Dallas Smythe speaks of the 'audience commodity', which portrays the media audience as a commodity sold to advertisers. Especially today, social media on the Internet commodify the sociality of users by converting the latter into data sold to advertisers. Personal data are used in the creation of targeted advertisements, and the user's click and buy process generates profit for the advertising company. Off-the-job time becomes a marketing playground, serving the reproduction of commodities. Everything, including leisure, play, friendship, love and sexuality, becomes a 24-hour commodity market. Consumers of social media become prosumers, producing commodities in the form of personal data (Fuchs 2014, 89–95).

Christian Fuchs (2014) holds that the use value generated in social networking and search engines is part of digital labour that produces surplus value for the social media corporations, thus creating a new form of exploitation. Not only do digitisation and automation result in unemployment and precarious labour, they also render *produsers* and *prosumers* part of the working class, transforming society into a cyber-factory. Digital labour splits into waged and unwaged online labour. Whereas waged online labour consists in labour performed on crowdsourcing platforms, unwaged online labour includes almost any social activity on the Internet, from chatting, posting and searching to reviewing, commenting, and so on (Fuchs 2014; Scholz 2012).

Micro-tasking, that is, the decomposition of work into small parts, on platforms such as Amazon Mechanical Turk is a further expansion of Taylorist logic in the field of digital labour that disconnects the worker from the overall product of his work, thereby rendering her a mere cog in the machine of a faceless production. Labour alienation, exploitation, precarity and insecurity are the outcomes of the strategic nullification of federal law in platform capitalism by corporations making use of legal grey zones to misclassify employees as independent contractors, avoid taxes, and violate local laws, labour laws, privacy and anti-discrimination laws (Codagnone et al. 2016a; Huws 2014, 26–39; Scholz 2016a; Standing 2011). There is also strong evidence that insecure employment and precariousness result in psychological morbidity (Virtanen et al. 2005).

Beyond social democracy

Rifkin's optimism is only partially supported by the facts. The expansion of neoliberalism across the globe has been accompanied by the rise of neo-fascist far right-wing populism in the United States and Europe. Neoliberal neocolonialism spreads from public assets, real estate and agriculture to big data and biotechnology, privatising the very genes of nature. On the Internet, platform capitalism is making billions by exploiting FOSS development and the digital commons to the extent that a number of open source software companies are now adopting a more closed approach with regard to their copyright licences (Krazit 2018). Hence, rather than the so-called sharing economy paving the way for the collaborative commons, it signals a new era of cyber-exploitation. Koen Frenken (2017) anticipates three possible futures for the sharing economy: 1) the neoliberal development of platform capitalism, where several micro-platforms integrate into super-platforms; 2) the social democratic development of platforms where the state intervenes to tax and redistribute rents from winners to losers; and 3) the citizen-led democratic control of platforms in the form of platform cooperativism.

Rifkin advocates a social democratic, commons-orientated transition, in which the developed nations in concert with big corporations would be the leaders of the Third Industrial Revolution, which is projected to gradually align around the collaborative commons. Rifkin has succeeded in linking local with global commons via the Internet of Things infrastructure, best served by self-management. Yet he overstates the role of technology while underplaying the role of democracy. Similar to the liberal approach to the commons, he abstains from addressing the contradictions of capitalism and the state, thus reproducing the lack of the political in the reformist approach to the commons.

The transition to the commons is not merely a technical issue of algorithms programming win–win partnerships between capitalism, the state and the commons. It requires a shift to another model of society, anchored in the abolition of the division between directors and executants; hence the need for the creation of a novel anthropological type. Rifkin (2014, 274–286) touches on this issue by considering humans equipped with empathy, affection, reciprocity and companionship rather than self-interest alone. He downplays, though, the right to have a direct say in the economic and societal affairs that determine one's life. Instead of assigning politics to technocratic elites, supposed to represent the people, freedom as autonomy consists in the equality of participation in the formation of the law governing society. Freedom translates into the self-instituting power of the people. Therefore, the key to the commons transition is the establishment of direct democratic procedures on a post-hegemonic political level that encompass the reconfiguration of power in the direction of the commons.

3.4 Platform Cooperativism

Trebor Scholz (2016a; 2016b, 23–24) juxtaposes platform cooperativism against platform capitalism in a mission to bring together the roughly 170 years of the cooperative movement with commons-based peer production. The idea is to use the algorithmic design of apps such as Uber in the service of a cooperative business model premised on communal ownership, democratic governance, sustainability and equitable distribution of value (Scholz 2016a; 2016b). Instead of workers earning paltry fees from precarious labour that makes investors rich, they would design, manage and own apps themselves. Platform cooperativism operates on the model of a multi-stakeholder cooperative of consumers, providers, investors and producers. It aims to reunite existing cooperatives and labour unions under digital self-governance.

Platform cooperativism spans the economic landscape. Since 2015, platform co-ops have emerged across a broad range of sectors, including e-commerce, cleaning services, culture, finance, software development, transportation and more. Over 300 case studies of platform cooperativism have been documented thus far.[1] A non-exhaustive typology classifies cooperatives as follows: cooperatively owned online labour brokerages and market places (for example, Loconomics, Fairmondo); city-owned platform cooperatives (for example, Fairbnb); producer-owned platforms (for example, Stocksy, Resonate); union-backed labour platforms (for example, National Domestic Workers Alliance); data co-ops (for example, MIDATA); and protocolary co-ops enabling peer-to-peer interaction (for example, Backfeed, La'Zooz). These innovative organisations are increasing in numbers and testing a range of operating models. In the following, I illustrate the cases of Stocksy and Fairmondo to exemplify the organisational principles of platform cooperativism.

3.4.1 The Stocksy Case

Stocksy is a platform cooperative that accepts and provides royalty-free stock photography and video via an online marketplace that provides sustainable careers to artists through co-ownership, profit sharing and transparent business practices (Scholz 2016b, 78). Stocksy was started by iStockphoto co-founders Bruce Livingstone and Brianna Wettlaufer, who in 2000 pioneered the idea of selling stock photos online in exchange for small fees (Cortese 2016). iStock caught the attention of Getty Images, which acquired it in 2006 for $50 million. Livingstone and Wettlaufer grew dismayed as the community spirit they had cultivated and the royalties photographers received began to erode under the new ownership. Photographers grumbled that they were being underpaid and exploited by online sites, thereby feeling disenfranchised. This is a general trend in the creative industry where workers are likely to have no control over their artistic work, experience precarity and are poorly paid.

For this reason, using money from the sale of iStock to Getty, Livingstone and Wettlaufer founded Stocksy in 2013 with the aim of putting power back into the hands of the artists. Stocksy pays photographers 50–75% of sales.[2] This is well above the going rate of 15–45% that is typical in the stock photography field. The company also distributes 90% of its profits at the end of each year among its photographers. Contributing Stocksy photographers receive 50% of a Standard Licence Purchase and 75% of an Extended Licence Purchase. Every Stocksy contributor receives a share of the company, with voting rights.

At the time of launch, Stocksy had about 220 contributing photographers, with plans to grow to approximately 500 photographers in its first year. Stocksy now has over 900 contributing members, selected from over 10,000 applications. Its revenue doubled from 2014 to 2015 to $7.9 million. For 2015, Stocksy paid out over half of its revenue as royalties to its contributors, totalling $4.3 million. Revenue for 2016 grew to $10.7 million, with $4.9 million paid out to contributors. In total over its first four years of business from 2013 to 2017, Stocksy paid out over $20 million to its nearly 1,000 artists. After starting with six founding members, Stocksy's staff numbers reached 50 in early 2018.

Stocksy is a multi-stakeholder cooperative divided into three membership classes: founders, staff and artists (Gordon-Farleigh 2017); 90% of the dividends are awarded to Class C (artists), and 5% each goes to Class A (founders) and Class B (staff). Every member has an equal voting share. The governance does not follow a vote-by-committee approach, but a transparent, flat decision-making process, with members participating through an online system. The board includes directors from each class and any member can propose resolutions. An exhaustive resolution and voting process is considered bureaucratic and costly. Having open conversations on a simple platform is more effective.

3.4.2 The Fairmondo Case

Fairmondo is an online marketplace that aims to challenge the big players in e-commerce such as Amazon and eBay (Scholz 2016b, 79). Founded in Germany in 2012, Fairmondo is a multi-stakeholder cooperative open both to professional and private sellers. The products on offer have no general restrictions unless they are illegal or run counter to Fairmondo's core values such as fairness and sustainable consumption. The fairness of the products is assessed by shared criteria, which remain open to discussion and improvement by the members and the more than 12,000 users. Currently, Fairmondo offers over 2 million products, the majority being books and media articles.

Its governance model is based on a legally binding commitment to uncompromising transparency and democratic accountability.[3] Democratic control is guaranteed through the one-member-one-vote principle. The managing board is elected by employees. Decision making is based on a majority consensus; 90% of Fairmondo constituents must agree prior any modification to the general principles. Fairmondo's inclusive and transparent principles actively build on members' trust by avoiding the deceptive information that plagues traditional marketplaces, such as false externalities or hidden costs. The Fairmondo crowd receives real information about what they are buying.

Fairmondo was financed through crowdfunding, with over 2,000 members investing over €600,000 in shares. There is a cap of €25,000 for the number of shares that anybody can hold. Thus, disproportionate financial investment or investment by non-cooperative associations are prohibited. Dividends are distributed as broadly as possible: 25% is distributed to co-op members through shares; 25% is distributed through 'Fair Funding Points' (voluntary work is rewarded by points that legally stake a claim on future surpluses); 25% is donated to a number of non-profits chosen by Fairmondo members. The last 25% is pooled into a common fund used for the development of the wider Fairmondo project. Internal stakeholders (partners, staff, etc.) operate under a defined salary range ratio of 1 to 7 from lowest to highest paid.

Fairmondo co-ops are committed to open source and innovation. The code used for its online marketplace platforms must be published under a licence that ensures full openness regarding developments or forks. The code can be found on Github. By contributing to the digital commons, Fairmondo represents a model of open cooperativism, the operating principles of which will be detailed in the following section.

3.4.3 The Challenges of Platform Cooperativism

The two cases illustrated above adhere to the seven principles of platform cooperativism defined by Scholz (2016a, 18–21; Platform Coops Infographic 2017) as follows: 1) voluntary and open membership; 2) democratic member control; 3) members' economic participation; 4) autonomy and independence; 5) education, training and information; 6) cooperation among cooperatives; 7) concern for community. Platform co-ops respond to the market failures of platform capitalism by lowering transaction and retention costs, transferring surplus revenue to members, protecting workers from exploitation, disincentivising short-termism and offering a prospect of data democracy.

Scholz identifies a number of challenges for platform cooperativism. He touches upon the main obstacles that the cooperative movement has faced from its inception, such as competition, financing, regulation, education, member involvement and identity. Some scholars (Frenken 2017; Van Doorn 2017) have argued that platform cooperativism needs to address three major problems regarding: 1) self-government, 2) financing and 3) market competition/value proposition.

Platform co-ops seeking to scale up in the digital landscape need to accommodate a wider range of member identities with divergent needs and interests that tend to produce conflicts and ideological oppositions (Frenken 2017, 12). Blockchain could perhaps offer solutions to the problems inherent in digital decision making. It might enable decentralised trust-creation mechanisms and provide automatic and secure coordination of network interactions through smart contracts (Morell et al. 2017, 60). The present discourse on Blockchain, however, is rather libertarian and conceals the danger of replacing the current oligarchies with new oligarchies in the name of democracy, decentralisation, and so on. Attention, therefore, should be drawn to shifting the discourse from libertarianism to cooperativism.

Platform co-ops also have difficulty in raising venture capital, and embark on R&D on their own, which is significantly detrimental to their capacity to innovate and produce new lines of products and services (Frenken 2017, 12). New funding structures (crowdfunding, cooperative banks and credit unions, Blockchain and alternative currencies) and locally focused commissioning from the public sector could provide vital revenue to platform co-ops (McCann and Yazici 2018, 4). Attracting funding relates directly to the need of platform co-ops to offer a convincing value proposition if they are to survive market competition (Van Doorn 2017). If platform co-ops are to move beyond 'luxury cooperativism', they must address the needs and limited resources of low-income workers, their households and their neighbourhoods. To do so, they need to serve a specific need better than competing platforms, while embodying a concrete set of values for specific consumer categories.

One central problem that potentially undermines platform cooperativism is the pitiless competition it faces from traditional and platform capitalism. In light of the 20–30% that companies such as Uber are taking as profit, one solution put forward by Scholz is for platform cooperatives to run on 10% profit, which could then be partially translated into social benefit for workers (Scholz 2016a, 13). Indeed, this is one of the competitive advantages of platform co-ops compared to capitalist platforms. Yet Scholz is aware that the competitiveness problem of platform cooperativism cannot be dealt with solely through a pricing strategy. A broader regulatory framework is a *sine qua non* for the advancement of platform cooperativism (Smorto 2017).

Scholz founded the Platform Cooperativism Consortium (PCC) in 2016, which has received funding to support the cooperative platform economy through research, experimentation, education, advocacy, documentation of best practices, technical support and the coordination of funding and events.[4] In 2018, the PCC received an additional Google.org grant of $1 million to further enhance the economic development of cooperatives in the digital economy.[5] The PCC focuses specifically on creating a critical analysis of the digital economy, and designing open source tools for education, governance and finance, among others. The goal is to create a platform ecosystem that can be variously supportive for local co-op initiatives. Several other incubators and accelerators have emerged in recent years such as CoopVenture (France), Start.Coop (US) and incubator.COOP (Australia), aiming to finance the development of co-ops across the globe. Resonate, a platform co-op made by and for musicians, recently received $1 million from Reflective Venture Partners, which funds Blockchain technology-related start-ups and organisations (Hurst 2018).

Scholz has also been involved in lobbying to introduce regulation on cooperatives. The Platform Cooperativism Consortium Policy Group recently submitted an agenda to promote and build support for platform cooperatives through a new bill of rights for American workers to US Senator Kirsten Gillibrand.[6] Andrea Nahles, head of the Social Democratic Party of Germany, committed to support platform cooperativism in Germany. Jeremy Corbyn's Labour Party in the UK included platform cooperativism in its Digital Democracy Manifesto.[7]

Scholz has met critiques from the far left that, especially with the Google. org co-signing, platform cooperativism still mimics the gig economy, a capitalistic structure (Anzilotti 2018). To truly dismantle capitalism, those critics argue, fundamental changes are needed at the national political level to regulate against monopolies such as Google, and to provide for equity-creating, distributive resources such as Universal Basic Income and universal healthcare. Scholz counter-argues there can still be reforms that work within capitalism and that really change power relationships. He contends that it is unrealistic to think that platform co-ops will dominate capitalist markets. Rather, he envisions a more diversified economy. Therefore, there is a tension here between his radical pretensions and his projecting a mixed economy. A more radical line of argument holds that platform cooperativism should integrate into a broader model of open cooperativism.

3.5 Open Cooperativism

Bauwens and Kostakis (2017a) argue that cooperatives in general and platform cooperatives in particular usually function under the patent and copyright system, and they are, consequently, not creating, protecting or producing commons. They are limited to local or national membership, thereby leaving the global field open to be dominated by capitalist enterprises. As a result, traditional and platform cooperatives are closed market entities, bending over time to the competitive pressure of capitalist enterprises. To address these issues, Bauwens and Kostakis advocate for the incorporation of platform cooperativism into a broader model of open cooperativism grounded on the principles of commons-based peer production. Before delving deep into this argument, it is essential first to examine its broader normative premises.

3.5.1 Extractive Peer Production

Bauwens and Kostakis (2014; 2019) build on the work of Ostrom, Lessig and Benkler, but they differ from them in that they seek to transform capitalism into the commons. From this angle, they are closer to Bollier who follows Michel Bauwens in his argument that the state should support the commons instead of market capitalism. As with Rifkin, Bauwens and Kostakis's general argument echoes Marx's claim that capitalism is doomed to failure as the evolution of technology reduces the costs of production to the degree that capitalism can no longer sustain itself. The evolution of technology undermines capitalism inasmuch as it makes workers redundant for the reproduction of production. Bauwens and Kostakis's core argument is that the digital commons can merge with local cooperatives and replace capitalism from within, just as capitalism did with feudalism. *Pace* Rifkin, they take a radical stance, introducing a post-capitalist model that will force capitalism to adjust to the commons in the long run with the aid of a commons-orientated partner state.

Instead of a Marxist revolutionary party capturing state power and implementing central planning of production in a long-term mission to establish communism, Bauwens and Kostakis concentrate power *ab initio* on commons-based peer production. They demonstrate a post-capitalist version of the commons on the model of Design Global–Manufacture Local (DG–ML) or 'cosmolocalism', which connects local with global commons via the Internet and free and open source software/hardware. The commons advance a simple yet radical idea: great improvements in production could be achieved by reducing barriers to knowledge exchange. Collaboration and openness could result in a constantly improving collective repository of best ideas and practices; hence, the significance of the digital commons adding up to the rural and urban commons. Cosmolocalism, that is, the localised use of the digital commons, can help people reappropriate the means of production across the globe and secure their sustainability against capitalism and statism.

At the crossroads of traditional capitalism, cognitive capitalism and peer production

Bauwens and Kostakis's political economy of post-capitalism is predicated on a philosophy of history premised on a mix of Schumpeterian and Marxian insights. In *Network Society and Future Scenarios for a Collaborative Economy*, they adhere to a somewhat teleological account of history, determined by successive techno-economic shifts in the modes of production and exchange (2014, 2–14). They integrate their analysis of peer production into a neo-Schumpeterian narrative, developed in particular by Carlota Perez, in which economic crises, triggered by technological innovation, are an inherent characteristic of capitalism, forcing the latter to progress over time. Technological innovation drives capitalism's development into a spiral of upswings and downswings, lasting approximately 40–60 years, until the next one 'takes off' (Perez 2002, 15). Following Andrew Feenberg (2002), they do not conceive of technology as neutral, deterministic or univocal in its effects, but rather as a terrain of social struggle between alternative norms, values and social imaginaries (Bauwens et al. 2019, 33).

Kostakis and Bauwens (2014, 10–14; Bauwens 2014) hold that the global economy is now at the turning point of a novel technological revolution, with three different value models competing for dominance: traditional capitalism, neo-feudal cognitive capitalism and peer production. Like Benkler, they identify two modes of peer production: 1) an extractive peer production with a for-profit orientation, developing on the model of neo-feudal cognitive capitalism; and 2) a generative peer production with a for-benefit orientation, emerging in the form of local and global commons.

Traditional proprietary capitalism is in decline, since it suffers from an irreversible contradiction: it aims at infinite growth on a finite planet, causing both economic and ecological crisis. Industrial capitalism evolves into a neo-feudal cognitive capitalism, in which strong intellectual property rights are in the process of being replaced by centralised networks of peer production, dominated by finance capital (Bauwens 2005; Benkler 2006; Castells 2000; 2009; 2010). Cognitive capitalism is considered a new type of capitalism in which the control of information has replaced traditional material production and distribution, becoming, therefore, the basic source of value (Bell 1973; Boutang 2012; Drucker 1968; Webster 2006). As such, cognitive capitalism splits into two modes: 1) netarchical capitalism; and 2) anarcho-capitalism (Kostakis and Bauwens 2014, 25–27).

Netarchical capitalism is another name for platform capitalism. It refers to front-end digital platforms centrally controlled by back-end server infrastructures, whose primary function is the extraction of value from peer production and crowdsourcing (Kostakis and Bauwens 2014, 23–29). One prevalent business model of netarchical capitalism is the monetisation of attention capital and Internet user data through advertising. Netarchical capitalism lives on the positive externalities produced by Internet users, transforming into a parasitic and rent-seeking capital (Bauwens et al. 2019, 37). Some of the most prominent companies of netarchical capitalism are Google, Facebook, Amazon, Airbnb and Uber. Jeff Howe defines crowdsourcing as follows:

> Simply defined, crowdsourcing represents the act of a company or institution taking a function once performed by employees and outsourcing it to an undefined (and generally large) network of people in the form of an open call. This can take the form of peer-production (when the job is performed collaboratively) but is also often undertaken by sole individuals. The crucial prerequisite is the use of the open call format and the large network of potential labourers. (Howe 2006)

Crowdsourcing is part of outsourcing, that is, a business practice of one company hiring another company or individuals to perform tasks, handle operations or provide services previously done by the company's own employees. Digitisation has propelled outsourcing and the concomitant globalisation of neoliberalism from 1980 onwards. The Internet, software technology and telecommunication devices have allowed corporations to outsource production with the aim of becoming more competitive. Online platforms helped decrease their costs and increase productivity by buying cheap and temporary labour from precarious freelancers or peer producers across the globe (Howe 2008).

The 2008 financial crisis exacerbated the low-wage crisis of the last decades and, combined with the expansion of neoliberalism and digitisation, gave rise to the platform capitalism of the so-called sharing and gig economy. Whereas the 'sharing economy' consists in the online renting or exchange of idle assets such as cars, bikes, rooms, and so on, the 'gig economy' refers to the buying and selling of freelance labour online. Both the gig and the sharing economy are crowdsourcing models, enabled by digital platforms (Bock et al. 2016; Codagnone et al. 2016a; 2016b; Sundararajan 2016).

Crowdsourcing is centralised inasmuch as companies control production and profit from freelancers and peer producers, and distributed inasmuch as freelancers and peer producers across the globe can earn a living. As mentioned earlier, prominent examples are digital platforms such as Amazon Mechanical Turk, Upwork and Freelancer where businesses and freelancers (designers, developers, copywriters, translators and so forth) connect and collaborate remotely. TaskRabbit is a 'skills' marketplace, which matches freelancers with local demand, allowing consumers to buy labour for everyday tasks, including cleaning, moving, delivery and handyman work. Kickstarter is a case of crowdfunding enabling people to go to the marketplace itself to fund their projects instead of depending on banks. What is interesting to consider here, according to Bulajewski (2012), is that Kickstarter charges '60 times the actual cost of providing a service by skimming a percentage off financial transactions'. Thus, Kickstarter is but a parasitic form of netarchical capitalism.

The second mode of cognitive capitalism is digital anarcho-capitalism, which echoes the Austrian school of economics (Schulak and Unterköfler 2011) in the sense that it approximates its theoretical models. 'While netarchical capitalism mainly exploits human cooperation, distributed capitalism is premised on the idea that everybody can trade and exchange; or, to put it bluntly, that "everyone can become an independent capitalist"' (Kostakis and Bauwens 2014, 31). Anarcho-capitalism differs from anarchism in that it is still based on property law and a minimum state, whereas the latter rejects property and state altogether.

In digital anarcho-capitalism, the Internet sustains the infrastructure for a decentralised peer network of for-profit entrepreneurs. The most profound example is the Bitcoin project, which relies on the distributed database – public ledger – of Blockchain which maintains a continuously growing list of records called blocks. Bitcoin is a digital currency based on the open source software of Blockchain, which enables decentralised peer-to-peer transactions without the need for intermediaries such as banks, states, and so on. It is deliberately scarce (21 million bitcoins), which makes it highly speculative and competitive. As a result, Bitcoin is prone to producing oligarchies and crises (Kostakis and Bauwens 2014, 32–33). In this sense, not only does it reproduce already existing inequalities by excluding the penniless, it also creates new ones.

Kostakis and Bauwens (2014, 27–28) claim that neo-feudal cognitive capitalism produces an increased contradiction between decentralised peer production and centralised profit accumulation. Technology enhances the production of a decentralised use value, which cannot fully translate into exchange value, thus undermining the very foundation of capitalism, that is, profit maximisation. Innovation becomes social, diffusing via peer-to-peer networks, and capital becomes an *a posteriori* parasitical intervention rather than the *a priori* condition of innovation (Kostakis and Bauwens 2014, 28–29).

> In capitalism, value is mostly related to things, that is, commodities, and is expressed in their exchange for one another based on a nominal representation of money. In the realm of P2P, value is attributed to contributions as a shared effort among peers, and is reflected in the shared significance of those contributions as recognised by those peers […] In a transition period, there is value competition: a dominant form of value operates under the capitalist logic, and a new social logic of value is emerging in seed forms. (Bauwens et al. 2019, 15)

Paradoxically, neo-feudal cognitive capitalism produces non-capitalist and post-capitalist forms of value creation. Users and communities utilise digital platforms to connect themselves for multiple purposes, as in the case of the revolutions of the Arab Spring and the various groups active in social media (Bauwens et al. 2019, 38). Bitcoin illustrates that digital currencies could provide a viable alternative to banks, financial institutions and state monetary policies. It remains to be seen whether and to what degree Bitcoin can scale up and decentralise the economy. Irrespective of that, Blockchain technologies have the potential to help communities reach consensus and self-organise, among other things.

Ultimately, neo-feudal cognitive capitalism creates a value crisis, reintroducing the Marxian argument that technological progress is antagonistic to profit rates. The response of neo-feudal cognitive capitalism is the enclosure as much as possible of the digital commons into the confines of surveillance capitalism. Yet Bauwens et al. (2019) stress that the basic underlying freedom of the Internet has not yet been brought fully under corporate control. The commons use the Internet as much as capital and governments do. The unsustainability of contemporary value flows can be counteracted by the innovative social relations of generative commons-based peer production. Bauwens et al.'s (2019, 4–5) core argument is that commons-based peer production contains both an immanent and transcendent aspect. It is immanent to the extent that commons-based peer production is essential to allowing capitalism to reproduce itself. It is transcendent to the degree that it can progress into an autonomous mode of production that can subsume both capitalism and the state.

> At this stage, commons-based peer production is a prefigurative prototype of what could become an entirely new mode of production and

a new form of society. It is currently a prototype since it cannot as yet fully reproduce itself outside of mutual dependence with capitalism. This emerging modality of peer production is not only productive and innovative 'within capitalism', but also in its capacity to solve some of the structural problems that have been generated by the capitalist mode of production. In other words, it represents a potential transcendence of capitalism. (Bauwens et al. 2019, 6)

3.5.2 Generative Peer Production

Bauwens, Kostakis and Pazaitis (2019, 3) adhere to Bollier's definition of the commons as shared resources self-managed by user communities according to the rules and norms of the community. Commons-based peer production is further inspired by the principles of free software. It is characterised by equipotentiality, holoptism and stigmergy (Bauwens et al. 2019, 12). Equipotentiality opens up equal opportunities for everyone to participate according to their skills. Participation is conditioned *a posteriori* by the process of production itself, where skills are verified and communally validated in real time. Holoptism contrasts with the panopticism that penetrates modern systems of power (Foucault 1977) in that it grants access to all information necessary irrespective of participants' position or power. Holoptism allows, thus, for stigmergic processes of mutual coordination wherein participants can match their contributions to the needs of the system (Bauwens 2005). Stigmergy is a form of self-organisation based on indirect coordination (Marsh and Onof 2007). As in the cases of Wikipedia and FOSS development, an action leaves a trace which stimulates another action, and so on. Hence, commons-based peer production favours mutual coordination over central control, self-management over hierarchy, access over ownership and transparency over privacy.

Commons-based peer production develops in two basic modes: local and global (digital) commons (Kostakis and Bauwens 2014, 45–58; Bauwens et al. 2019, 39–46). Some examples of local commons are community land trusts, degrowth and permaculture movements, Transition Towns, the Bologna project, the Quebec economy, interest-free banks, autonomous energy production, and plenty of other collective projects scrutinised by Ostrom (1990).

Global commons, on the other hand, develop on the basis of the Internet and FOSS. The architecture of the Internet has facilitated decentralised and quasi-autonomous communication between multiple computer users, while the applications of FOSS have disrupted capitalism by supporting hybrid modes of ownership, value distribution and governance.[8] Commons-based peer production is neither hierarchyless nor structureless.

Further, CBPP projects do have systems of quality control that represent a kind of benevolent hierarchy or heterarchy. These 'maintainers' or 'editors' protect the integrity of the system as a whole and can refuse contributions that endanger the integrity of the system. However, and this is crucial, they do not coerce work. (Bauwens et al. 2019, 12)

For example, Wikipedia's governance is a mixture of democracy, aristocracy and monarchy. Democratic voting with regard to the content is accompanied by the aristocracy of the most reliable users and the monarchy of the founder/leader in cases where neither solely democracy nor aristocracy works.

Cosmolocalism: the Design Global–Manufacture Local model

Despite the ever-growing potential of the digital commons and the optimisation of local assets and infrastructures by local commons, Bauwens and Kostakis admit that both local and global commons are more like centripetal lifeboat strategies that cannot but conform in the long run to the mainstream of capitalism. To address this issue, they attempt to connect local with global commons on the model of Design Global–Manufacture Local (DG–ML), which has been enabled by the conjunction of modern ICTs with desktop manufacturing technologies (such as 3D printing and computer numerical machines) (Bauwens et al. 2019, 39–46; Kostakis and Bauwens 2014). Open coding connects to design and manufacturing via the Internet, free software and 3D printers. In a nutshell, the DG–ML model follows the logic that what is not scarce becomes global (for example, global commons of knowledge, design, software) and what is scarce (for example, hardware) is local. Global commons connect to local commons via Transition Towns, decentralised communities and FabLabs/maker-spaces based on FOSS and renewable energy systems distributed through microgrids on Blockchain and the Internet of Things. Blockchain technology has the potential to 'plug' into the DG–ML model on the principles of self-governance, decentralisation, transparency and equitable distribution of value (Pazaitis et al. 2017a). The DG–ML model also links to the degrowth movement which signals a radical political and economic reorganisation leading to reduced resource and energy use (Kallis et al. 2018).

The DG–ML model represents an on-demand distributed mode of production that differs from mass production in scale, location, operation and consumer–producer relationship. As such, it bears significant advantages: 1) it lowers production and transaction costs (no patent costs, no transportation and maintenance costs, no planned obsolescence); 2) it democratises production by unleashing new bottom-up forms of value creation, collaboration and techno-social innovation; 3) it blurs production and consumption, thus empowering *prosumers*; 4) it equitably distributes value to community members; 5) it has the potential to enhance gender balance and non-discriminatory practices via customisation and open access; and 6) it contributes to a sustainable and resilient society and economy (Kostakis et al. 2015, 126). The literature has documented thus far several case studies in the fields of agriculture, manufacturing and biotechnology (Kostakis et al. 2015; 2016; Giotitsas and Ramos 2017; Papadimitropoulos 2017). However, these do not currently pose a threat to capitalism. The DG–ML model is still at a preliminary stage and is premised on hypotheses that need to be tested empirically before it crystallises into a sustainable economic model. Bauwens and Kostakis are aware that the DG–ML model alone cannot challenge capitalism.

The principles of open cooperativism

For this reason, they endeavour (Scholz 2016b, 163–166) to address the challenges of the cooperative movement. Cooperatives tend to self-enclose around local or national membership, thereby losing their broader political identity and gradually adopting competitive mentalities. They thus risk being outperformed and, finally, absorbed by the large corporations that dominate the global arena. Cooperatives also do not create, protect or produce commons, since they usually function under the copyright and patent system. Platform cooperativism improves on these deficiencies by linking to commons-based peer production and furthering international alliances both on the economic and political level. Fairmondo, for example, contributes to the commons by publishing its code on Github, while expanding its operating model in the UK.

Bauwens and Kostakis (Scholz 2016b, 164) recognise that this practice needs to radicalise and integrate into a generalised commons-orientated transition. They therefore embark on merging traditional and platform co-ops with the commons on the model of open cooperativism. Their goal is to infuse traditional and platform co-ops with the principles of commons-based peer production. To this end, they approach commons-based peer production as 'a new logic of collaboration between networks of people who freely organise around a common goal using shared resources, and market orientated entities that add value on top of or alongside them' (Scholz 2016b, 163). Open cooperatives internalise negative externalities; adopt multi-stakeholder governance models; contribute to the creation of material and immaterial commons; and are orientated towards a global socio-economic and political transformation, albeit locally based.

In contrast to the corporate strategy of planned obsolescence that renders resources artificially scarce, open cooperatives function under conditions of natural abundance where what can be shared is shared as commons. Market value is created from scarce resources, adding value on top of or alongside the abundance of the commons. Open cooperatives employ market strategies that recognise natural abundance and refuse to generate income and profits by extracting rents from artificially limited resources.

Abundance and scarcity combine communism and reciprocity respectively. Under conditions of abundance, peer production satisfies the communist principle: from each according to their ability, to each according to their need.

Under conditions of scarcity, peer production adopts the reciprocity principle: to each according to their contribution (Bauwens et al. 2019). Peer production often involves distributed tasks rather than fixed jobs. Compensation, thus, in the form of salaries may not always be the most adequate means of reward for those contributing to the commons. For this reason, open co-ops should practise open value accounting or contributory accounting in which incomes are distributed according to one's contribution. In the case of Sensorica, a co-op that produces scientific instruments, each contributor is assigned 'karma points' (Scholz 2016b, 165).

In addition to paid wage labour for members and contributors, value is also distributed via tokens of reputation that can be variously redeemed. Tokens may count for equity, decision-making power, property ownership or labour certificates (Rozas et al. 2018). 'Tokenisation' of reputation prevents the co-optation of commons value by a few well-placed contributors, as in the case of platform capitalism. It creates a fair immaterial value flow alongside wage labour rather than an unjust capitalist co-optation. Blockchain could be employed here to register reputation in a transparent way. One should, however, notice the dangers of economism and data fetishism – even robotism and automation – lurking behind the intent to translate everything into algorithms, numbers or tokens registered on Blockchain. A balance, therefore, should be kept between quantifiable and non-quantifiable variables.

In contrast to imperfect market price signals and overproduction, open cooperatives can enhance sustainability and reduce waste by adopting open supply chains and open book accounting, thereby achieving greater coordination between supply and demand, which can in turn sustain a circular economy wherein outputs of one production process are used as inputs for another. 'What market pricing is to capitalism and planning is to state-based production, mutual coordination is to peer production' (Bauwens et al. 2019, 5). Open knowledge and open design ensure further optimum participation through modularity and granularity.

Open co-ops adopt Copyfair licences that allow for the commercial use of the commons and ensure a level playing field for ethical enterprises willing to contribute to the commons (Bauwens et al. 2019). In contrast to Benkler's optimism about the prospects of commons-based licensing, Bauwens and Kostakis are vigilant against the actual co-optation of cyber-communism by platform capitalism. They argue that the more communist the sharing licence, the more capitalist the practice (Bauwens and Kostakis 2014). And this is, indeed, what the last two decades have seen occurring in FOSS production (Birkinbine 2018). Existing copyleft licences (GPL, Creative Commons) are not sufficient for the reproduction of the commons, since they do not require reciprocity (contributions in the form of money or know-how, resources, and so on). To reverse this, Bauwens and Kostakis suggest a Peer Production/Copyfair Licence (PPL), first designed and proposed by Kleiner (2010). Copyfair differs from copyleft licences in that it allows for the commercialisation of commons knowledge in exchange for rent or analogous contributions. This way, the commons could secure their economic sustainability and autonomy vis-à-vis capitalist enterprises.

The ecosystem of open cooperativism

Let us imagine, therefore, two overlapping platforms: the commons platform and (platform) capitalism. The former is based on an abundance of resources whereas the latter counts on scarce resources and draws on the commons on condition that it uses Copyfair licences, thereby establishing an open cooperativism between the commons and a friendly capitalism. Bauwens and Kostakis's (Bauwens et al. 2019, 6) core argument is that firms that cooperate with the digital commons and, therefore, have access to a vast pool of knowledge, as in the case of IBM, obtain a competitive advantage over proprietary firms that rely solely on their private R&D. The hybrid of post-capitalist commons can beat capitalism on its own ground: that is, competition.

Let us take one step further and imagine the gradual consolidation of friendly capitalism with the commons, of scarcity with abundance. Corporations gradually merge with open cooperatives built on the commons. Open cooperatives expand from digital infrastructures to physical ones – phygital – and achieve a more efficient resource use through the creation of a genuine sharing economy based on co-ownership, transparency, distribution of value and co-governance. The ideal gift economy would then be a simple mathematical function of abundance and scarcity, democratically programmed to reproduce the sustainability of the commons. Planned grassroots socialism comes into play in the form of open cooperativism engineered by a mix of institutional and technological reforms. This new ecosystem of open cooperativism comprises three institutions/partners: 1) the productive community, 2) the entrepreneurial coalition and 3) the for-benefit association (Figure 3.1).

The productive community consists of all members, users and contributors of *glocal* commons who produce the shareable resource, either for payment or as volunteers. The commons-orientated entrepreneurial coalition consists of generative enterprises that add value to the scarce common resources. Generative enterprises contrast with extractive enterprises in that they do not seek to maximise profits without sufficiently reinvesting surplus in the maintenance of the productive communities (Figure 3.2). They integrate values such as sustainability, knowledge sharing, the mutualisation of infrastructure and a more inclusive distribution of value (Bauwens and Niaros 2017, 21). Profit is not central but peripheral to the social and environmental goals of the community. The best example of the difference between extractive and generative enterprises is industrial agriculture and permaculture. Whereas in the first case the soil becomes poorer and less healthy, in the latter the soil becomes richer and healthier. Some striking examples of extractive corporations are Facebook,

Productive community	Linux	Mozilla	GNU	Wikipedia	Wordpress
Entrepreneurial coalition	e.g. Linux Professional Institute, Canonical	e.g. Mozilla corporation	e.g. Red Hat, Endless, SUSE	e.g. Wikia company	e.g. Automatic company
For-benefit association	Linux Foundation	Mozilla Foundation	Free Software Foundation	Wikimedia Foundation	Wordpress Foundation

Figure 3.1: The three institutions that shape the model of open cooperativism (Bauwens et al. 2017, 13).

EXTRACTIVE OWNERSHIP	GENERATIVE OWNERSHIP
1. Financial Purpose: maximizing profits in the short term	**1. Living Purpose:** creating the conditions for life over the long term
2. Absentee Membership: ownership disconnected from the life of the enterprise	**2. Rooted Membership:** ownership in human hands
3. Governance by Markets: control by capital markets on autopilot	**3. Mission-Controlled Governance:** control by those dedicated to social mission
4. Casino Finance: capital as master	**4. Stakeholder Finance:** capital as friend
5. Commodity Networks: trading focused solely on price and profits	**5. Ethical Networks:** collective support for ecological and social norms

Figure 3.2: The differences between extractive and generative ownership (Bauwens et al. 2017, 13).

Uber and Airbnb, which do not share any profits with the co-creating communities they depend on for their value creation and sustenance (Bauwens et al. 2017, 13–14).

In the best of cases, generative enterprises identify with the productive community, which forms a meta-economic network rooted in the transition from community-orientated business to business-enhanced communities. Some prominent examples are the Catalonian Integral Cooperative or CIC (Catalonia Spain), the Mutual Aid Network (Madison, Wisconsin USA) and Enspiral (New Zealand) (Bauwens et al. 2017, 14–15).

The third institution that binds together productive communities and commons-orientated enterprises is the for-benefit association, which supports the infrastructure of commons-based peer production. In contrast to traditional non-governmental and non-profit organisations which operate under conditions of scarcity, for-benefit associations operate under conditions of abundance. Whereas the former identify a problem and provide a solution, the latter maintain an infrastructure of cooperation between productive communities and commons-orientated enterprises, protect the commons through licences, manage conflicts, fundraise, etc. (Bauwens et al. 2017, 15). For example the Wikimedia Foundation collects the funds to support the server space without which access to Wikipedia would become impossible.

The WikiHouse case

In the following, I illustrate the case of WikiHouse for the purpose of exemplifying the model of open cooperativism. WikiHouse is an open source project that allows anyone to design, share, fabricate and assemble their own house (Priavolou 2018, 75–76). The idea is simple: globally crowdsourced and freely downloadable designs are used to manufacture building components locally. WikiHouse enables users to download Creative Commons-licensed building plans from its online library and customise them to create jigsaw puzzle-like pieces out of plywood with a CNC router. The WikiHouse project is, thus, a distinct example of the DG–ML model: what is light (the design templates, blueprints, help manuals and support) is shared globally, while what is heavy (cutting the wood, assembling the house) takes place locally, with improvements on the design then fed back into the common-resource global pool.

WikiHouse takes levels of energy performance, quality, precision and user customisation that were previously prohibitively expensive, and dramatically lowers the factors of time, cost and difficulty. WikiHouse components can be digitally manufactured not just in large centralised factories, but by a distributed network of small businesses and maker-spaces using widely available tools and materials. This allows many companies to combine their innovations and create the most sustainable, low-cost building systems, based on interoperable standards and design principles.

The design principles of WikiHouse can be summarised as follows:[9]

1. Share global, manufacture local. Take something that works, copy, adapt, give credit and share.
2. Design for cheap, abundant, standardised, sustainable and, if possible, 'circular' materials. Release small, iterate and 'fork'.
3. Design to lower thresholds of time, cost, skill, energy and resources in manufacturing, assembly and use.
4. Maximise the safety, security, health and well-being (physical and mental) of users at all stages of a product's life.

5. Design software and hardware that is modular and inclusive, whereby elements can be independently altered, substituted, mended or improved.
6. Knowledge should always be free but professionals should be paid.
7. Democracy is a good design principle that superpowers citizens.
8. All companies can participate in the WikiHouse commons, but no one ever gets a monopoly or lock-in.

WikiHouse's early development was supported by an entrepreneurial coalition bringing together a structural engineering company (Momentum Engineering Ltd), an architectural studio (Architecture00), a multidisciplinary firm (Arup Associates Ltd) and a social housing company (Space Craft Systems Ltd) (Priavolou 2018, 76). WikiHouse is now being developed by a passionate R&D community of thousands of designers, engineers, inventors, coders and social entrepreneurs. In 2014 the WikiHouse foundation was established as a non-profit legal entity to maintain the commons infrastructure and open source licences, fundraise and coordinate cooperation between the productive community and the entrepreneurial coalition.

WikiHouse prototypes have been adopted by various communities across the globe (for example, Farmhouse, WikiStand and WikiTower) (Priavolou 2018, 76). The first WikiHouse in Latin America was built in 2015 to spark interest in innovation in the favelas of the city of Rio de Janeiro, while the WikiLab project in São Paulo aims to adapt the WikiHouse technology to mild climates. In Europe, it is worth noting the adaptation of the WikiHouse system by an ongoing programme in the city of Almere in the Netherlands, where 20 pilot prototypes are to be built by non-professionals. The project is financed by the city of Almere, the national government and the province of Flevoland.

WikiHouse is a response to the failures of centralised systems and markets since the industrial revolution. It aims to address unsustainable, undemocratic and unaffordable housing by breaking our dependence on fossil fuels and debt, empowering smarter citizens and building resilient communities and healthy, sustainable, economically productive, liveable cities. The goal is to build digital tools to support a new social and economic infrastructure for democratic development by diffusing sustainable housing tools to every citizen and company on earth.

The partner state and the challenges to post-capitalism

The replication of the WikiHouse model across other sectors of the economy could enhance the future of open cooperativism. Kostakis and Bauwens (2014; Bauwens et al. 2019) hold that the model of open cooperativism should scale up from regional to national and transnational level to establish a hegemonic counter-power against and beyond predatory capitalism and neoliberalism. At the macro-level, the three institutions of productive communities, entrepreneurial coalitions and for-benefit associations could apply to the evolution of civil society, market entities and the state respectively. They portray a post-democratic model of power distributed in a meritocratic, stigmergic and negotiated coordination that thrashes out differences and designs away 'unnecessary' conflict by allowing for the maximum human freedom compatible with the object of cooperation (Bauwens 2012). The for-benefit association, in particular, could be considered a snapshot of a future partner state, which could facilitate commons-orientated production. A number of 'partner cities' such as Barcelona, Ghent, Bologna and Napoli already support and guide various urban commons in the fields of mobility, shelter, food, energy and culture through public–common partnerships (Bauwens and Niaros 2017). The ultimate goal would be the transition from urban commons to the city as commons (Foster and Iaione 2016).

The role of the partner state is of paramount importance, since it could boost the transition from capitalism to the commons through a de-bureaucratisation and commonification of the public sector with the aim of sustaining an open cooperativism between the commons and ethical market entities willing to minimise negative social and environmental externalities. To this end, taxation of social/environmental entrepreneurship, ethical investing and productive labour should be minimised, whereas taxation of speculative, unproductive investments, unproductive rental income and negative social and environmental externalities should be increased (Bauwens 2014; Bauwens et al. 2016; Kostakis and Bauwens 2014, 66–67). In addition, education and publicly funded research and innovation could be aligned with the commons-orientated economic model (Kostakis and Bauwens 2014, 68).

The last decades have witnessed the dominance of a neoliberal narrative limiting the state to the role of regulator. When this is not the case, political discussion revolves around a liberal or social democratic narrative focusing on issues of fair competition, new labour regulation, lifelong learning and training, the green economy, work security, trade unions, minimum wages, and so on.

Bauwens and Kostakis, on the other hand, argue that it is necessary to move away both from a distributionist welfare state and a neoliberal state by establishing mini-states of commons-based peer production ecosystems steered by a commons-centric partner state that implements direct democratic procedures and practices (Bauwens and Kostakis 2017b). Likewise, leftist or post-Keynesian versions of the state focusing solely on taxation, public investment, public ownership and capital controls should be 'updated' according to the principles of the commons.

To sum up, Bauwens and Kostakis's model constitutes a strategy, which is both reformist and revolutionary, aiming to transform the current politico-economic system towards the creation of a commons-orientated ethical economy based on a democratic self-institutionalisation of society. It champions a post-capitalist model of open cooperation with a friendly capital willing to adjust in the long run to a commons-centric society.

Jacob Rigi (2014) has argued that by embracing a sort of 'corporate commons', as in the case of IBM investing in open source software, Bauwens and Kostakis reproduce capitalist exploitation inasmuch as they adhere to the capitalist categories of the market, commodity, surplus value, profit and capital. The commons exploit their contributors by renting their surplus value to capitalism. But this argument is not valid, given that profit is redistributed within the commons. Bauwens and Kostakis conceive of the commons as entrepreneurial projects operating in terms of the medieval guilds or the Enspiral project (Pazaitis et al. 2017b), which externally trade their goods in the marketplace, while acting internally as solidarity systems redistributing their income in new projects through a collaborative funding process.

Bauwens and Kostakis admit that capital flows towards peer production might distort the commons. However, friendly capital provides the means for undermining capitalism itself. Capital investment is a necessary condition for commons sustainability. One should also notice that Bauwens and Kostakis are introducing Copyfair with the aim not of selling but of renting commons knowledge. Instead of predatory capital free-riding on the commons, friendly capital would circulate within the commons with the aim of securing the reproduction of the latter. In any case, the transvestment of value (Kleiner 2010) from capitalism to the commons is unavoidable in any scenario involving a future transition to the commons, whether reformist, revolutionary or state-driven. Expropriated surplus value returns to the 'production source'.

Bauwens and Kostakis's model of open cooperativism echoes in a sense Cornelius Castoriadis's project of individual and collective autonomy. Like Bauwens and Kostakis, Castoriadis was arguing for the democratic self-institutionalisation of society via the establishment of regimes of direct democracy, implemented first and foremost at the level of production and expanding accordingly to all levels of society (Castoriadis 1988). But whereas Castoriadis was against any sort of state- or market-driven reformism, Bauwens and Kostakis aim to reform capitalism into a commons-orientated civil society through the establishment of a post-capitalist economy built around the commons, ethical market entities and a partner state. Bauwens and Kostakis's less radical stance makes sense, since capitalism and the state are not going to wither away any time soon – if at all. Occasional deals with capitalism and the state are unavoidable even in the most radical and revolutionary options for a commons transition. Bauwens and Kostakis's project could read as a technological 'update' of Habermas's model of deliberative democracy. Yet, contrary to the liberal premises of Habermas's theory, commons-based peer production is not a third institutional force merely adding up to state and market operation, but a quasi-autonomous socio-economic model aiming to gradually absorb both the state and the market in its operation.

Bauwens and Kostakis have succeeded in connecting local and global commons via digital platforms that bear the potential to promote self-governance, cooperation, innovation, sustainability and distribution of value. The virtue of their work is that they have introduced a model of self-institutionalisation of civil society, comprising both state and market mechanisms along democratic, ethical and ecological lines. They advocate a global, decentralised and mutually coordinated open cooperativism facilitated by ICTs. They thus intend to beat capitalism on its own ground by competing in terms of self-management fostered by eco-technological and economic hacks, which seems, indeed, a plausible strategy. Bauwens and Kostakis employ a high-tech rationale to produce a concrete plan of transforming capitalism from within. Yet this is not enough. The commons are still in their infancy and face numerous barriers and contradictions owing to the global dominance of surveillance capitalism (Papadimitropoulos 2018b). It is reasonable to assume that the commons cannot compete with the behemoths of capitalism on various grounds: economic and political power, know-how, infrastructure, skills, etc. Bauwens and Kostakis's model needs a more vibrant political spin to propel a post-hegemonic strategy aimed at politically combatting capitalism and reaching a critical mass. It requires centrally coordinated macro-policies to apply the principles of the commons at a local, regional, national and international level in a mission to reverse the current tide of neoliberalism towards a commons-orientated transition. This could be achieved by a partner state embracing the principles of the commons more openly.

3.6 DECODE: A Multidisciplinary Framework for the Commons

It is worth mentioning here a groundbreaking research project that has contributed to the creation of a multidisciplinary framework for the commons from the perspective of open data. DECODE (Decentralised Citizen Owned Data Ecosystems) was funded by the European Union's Horizon 2020 research and innovation programme during the period 2017–19 to develop technology (applications of Blockchain and the Internet of Things) that puts people in control of their personal data and paves the way for the creation of a 'data commons'.[10] DECODE has introduced an alternative to surveillance capitalism by building privacy-enhancing and rights-preserving data infrastructures in Barcelona and Amsterdam with the aim of giving back data sovereignty to citizens and creating public value with data. One could read the DECODE project as an attempt to expand Ostrom's 'bundle of rights' on or to the digital landscape by designing a set of economic, eco-social, legal and technical tools to support new decentralised technologies, democratic e-governance and alternative business models, which treat data as a common good (Morell et al. 2017, 8).

Part of the DECODE project was to conduct research (literature review, digital ethnography, co-creation sessions, interviews) on the commons with the aim of checking the applicability of the commons principles (democratic governance, openness, transparency, sustainability) through a sample of one hundred cases located in the city of Barcelona (Morell et al. 2017, 16). The sample reflected the heterogeneity of the commons, taking into account cases involving different types of actors (public administration, companies, cooperatives, communities without legal format), in diverse areas (cultural, tourism, mobility), with different goals (knowledge co-creation, community engagement, business) and economic models (profit and non-profit orientated). By mapping a vast number of cases, DECODE has offered one of the most systematic classifications of the commons, thereby:

1. expanding the geographical and empirical base of the literature;
2. providing insights into the design and performance of the commons from the perspective of their economic, social and environmental sustainability;
3. helping advance commons-based peer production on the models of platform and open cooperativism.

DECODE has articulated the commons principles along four dimensions: governance, economic model, knowledge/technology policy and sustainability (Table 3.1). The ways in which the commons principles combine with the above four dimensions create a variety of open commons-based business models classified into four families of digital content commons or data commons (Table 3.2) and five families of open data (Table 3.3). The term 'family' indicates the proximity and interrelation of different business models. A business model 'describes the distinctive and fundamental principles and mechanisms by which an organisation deploys a strategy to create, sell and use values (of use and exchange) in order to fulfil its primary goals' (Harracá 2017, 9). Open business models can be understood as those models that encourage sharing of knowledge under open licences, whether free or with some rights reserved (Tebbens 2017). Open data and the commons are not always identical. Open data and the commons have in common that anyone can access, use or share the data/content under certain licences. Open data are a subset of the commons most of the time. However, there are cases where not all open data is produced as a common (i.e. private firms), and some data can be common but not open to all (i.e. Good Data) (Morell et al. 2017, 52).

Table 3.1: Dimensions of commons principles (adapted from Morell et al. 2017, 16).

Dimensions	Principles
governance model	cooperative, foundation, openness in participation
economic model	non-profit, transparency
knowledge/technology policy	open content, open data, FOSS, decentralised
sustainability	inclusion, gender policy, green

Table 3.2: Open commons-based business models (adapted from Morell et al. 2017, 62).

	DIGITAL CONTENT COMMONS design, information, music, videogames, publishing, audiovisual, photography	FOSS	OPEN HARDWARE	PLATFORM COOPERATIVES
Mode of production	Commons-based peer production (e.g. Wikipedia) Centralised (individual or firm-hosted peer production)	Commons-based peer production Firm-hosted peer production (e.g. IBM)	Commons-based peer production (e.g. Open Source Ecology, Farm Hack, L'Atelier Paysan) Firm-hosted peer production	Commons-based peer production (e.g. Loconomics, Fairmondo)
Governance	Community governance (Wikipedia) Centralised (e.g. Flickr)	Community governance usually through a foundation (e.g. Firefox led by Mozilla Foundation, Debian led by Software in the Public Interest, Linux led by the Linux Foundation) Centralised (e.g. WordPress led by Automatic, Open Office led by Sun)	Community governance (e.g. Open Source Ecology, Farmhack) Centralised Multi-firm governance along the value chain (with lead firms)	Community governance
Licensing	Creative Commons or/and FOSS Restrictions on commercial use	Open licence Proprietary licence Dual licensing	Open licensing of at least the core design Restrictions on commercial use (NC clause, dual licensing, protected extensions)	Open licensing of at least one of the platform assets (software, databases and brand) No open licences

(Continued)

Table 3.2: (*Continued*)

	DIGITAL CONTENT COMMONS **design, information, music, videogames, publishing, audiovisual, photography**	**FOSS**	**OPEN HARDWARE**	**PLATFORM COOPERATIVES**
Revenue model	Charging for a physical copy of the content (e.g. a book or a record) Selling merchandise related to the content (e.g. a band's T-shirt) Charging for a related service (e.g. a live performance, a seminar, a webinar) Charging for licensing if the content is used for commercial purposes Charging advertisers or sponsors Membership, donations Pay-what-you-want Third-party funding (firms, state funding, grants, organisations)	Freemium (free to download and use) and Premium (selling an extended version of the software) Charging for a complementary service (e.g. training, technical assistance) Charging for licensing if the software is used for commercial purposes Dual licensing Advertising Donations Pay-what-you-want Crowdfunding Third-party funding (mainly software firms)	Selling the physical product Charging for a complementary service (e.g. training, technical assistance, expertise) Selling an accessory Dual licensing Donations Crowdfunding Third-party funding (state funding, grants, firms, organisations)	Freemium and Premium (charging for a version that offers more functionality to the user) Transaction fee Subscription Selling personal data Advertisement Sponsorship Third-party funding (firms, state funding, grants, organisations)

Table 3.3: Open data business models (adaptation from Morell et al. 2017, 68).

	Government open data	Private standalone open data	Non-commercial centralised open data production	Multi-stakeholder data pooling	Commons-based data crowdsourcing
Mode of production	State-produced or collected by the state from third parties	Intra-firm data production and/or crowdsourcing	Expertise applied to open and/or crowdsourced data (e.g. Wikileaks)	Pooling expertise	Community crowdsourcing Open data obtained from third parties
Governance	Centralised	Centralised (the firm provides the baseline dataset) Decentralised	Centralised (individual or entity)	Shared (with a leading entity)	Collective governance usually coordinated by a foundation (e.g. OpenStreetMap Foundation)
Licensing	Permissive	Permissive, open and proprietary licences combined	Open licensing allowing commercial use	Open licensing allowing commercial use	Open licensing allowing commercial use
Revenue model	State funding	Data-related services Gaining knowledge, experience Creating business opportunities	Donations Notoriety	Contributions from stakeholders Data-related services Gaining knowledge and experience Public funding	Freemium and Premium Selling related products or services Donations Public funding

The tables shown here demonstrate that the commons experience a variety of business models, with some cases fully adhering to the commons principles, and others combining commons-based peer production with firm-hosted peer production, community governance with centralised governance, open licences with proprietary licences, and so on. Different types of commons – from digitally supported natural commons and platform cooperatives to open data and the digital commons – have particularities, thus bearing some intrinsic possibilities with regard to the business models that can be developed to ensure their sustainability. Different business models apply to different types of commons. To mention some examples:

- In general, digital commons and/or digitally supported commons have created new logics of value creation and business model possibilities that are not present in the natural-resources-based commons such as gardens or summer meadows. Digital commons cannot sell their content, but they can leverage it to create revenue or they can sell advertising space and sponsorship.
- Crowdsourcing and donations, as sources of revenue, may be more successful when a project is supported by a broader community as in the case of Wikipedia and Mozilla Firefox.
- Unlike FOSS, open hardware commons can sell hardware. But open hardware commons face non-negligible marginal costs included in the production and distribution of physical goods. The materiality of hardware does not allow for the freemium and premium strategy that FOSS has recourse to. Some firms can, instead, produce a product with a free licence and another product with a proprietary licence. In terms of the mode of production and governance, commons-based peer production is often only possible at the design stage. The complexity of the manufacturing, delivery and quality-control phases may require managerial coordination by firms.
- Subscriptions and transaction fees are the most common ways of obtaining revenue for platform cooperatives due to their crucial role in coordinating diverse activities such as the selling of products and the renting of different professional services (for example, Stocksy, Fairmondo, Loconomics).
- When a platform is under an open licence it can easily be replicated, which poses a threat to the community, since its value-creation tool can be co-opted by other communities or profit-orientated firms. On the flipside, when the common produced is platform-based and material, licensing can be less of restriction with regard to potential revenue models (Morell et al. 2017, 51).

Overall, the above tables help systematise the main features that define the compatibility of open business models with the commons and identify further the right choices regarding the sustainability of the common in question. They help envisage a model of open cooperativism that deploys a number of business models and incorporates a multitude of communities and organisations in a mission to further expand commons-based peer production. Yet the sustainability of the commons relies on other factors apart from the business model such as democratic governance, social and gender inclusion and the environmental impact of the commons. Access to finance, legal regulation and competitive dynamics with capitalist firms can also profoundly affect the sustainability of a common. Whence, the need for a holistic, multidisciplinary framework that integrates commons sustainability into a post-hegemonic political strategy capable of encompassing the various dimensions of the commons under commons governance.

3.7 Productive Publics

Arvidsson and Peitersen draw on Benkler's conceptualisation of the digital commons as a decentralised mode of social production to develop in tune with Bauwens and Kostakis a post-capitalist theory of value. Similarly to Bauwens and Kostakis, they hold that the suicidal contradictions of capitalism, countervailed by the commons, can pave the way for the creation of an ethical economy immanent in the technological evolution of the factors (means and relations) of production, as Marx would have it (Arvidsson and Peitersen 2013, viii). They suggest that the necessary precondition for the realisation of an ethical economy is the construction of a new public sphere articulated on the productive publics built around the commons.

> Productive publics, a fundamental building block of the ethical economy, are voluntary associations of strangers, who are united by their devotion to a common project or pursuit, like open source software, urban agriculture or Ducati motorcycles. In recent years such productive publics have become an important source of value creation, both inside and outside corporate organisations. (Arvidsson and Peitersen 2013, 49)

Arvidsson and Peitersen depart from Gabriel Tarde's concept of 'publics' to distinguish between publics and communities. Whereas the term 'community' signifies a social structure consisting of dense webs of interpersonal interaction and a durable attachment to a shared identity, the term 'public' refers to an association of strangers, united by an affective attachment to a common thing or representation, be it a brand, an artist or an idea (Arvidsson and Peitersen 2013, 66–71; Arvidsson 2013, 374). Publics are temporary and transitory forms of association and, therefore, weaker and less enduring than communities. They are self-organised entities governed by a particular discourse centred around a common set of values. Publics sustain communalities without communities. They are held together by what Cornelius Castoriadis and Charles

Taylor call a social imaginary, that is, a general affective representation corresponding to a symbolic signification, be it socialism, capitalism, Christianity, a brand, a group, and so on.

The term 'publics' resembles the term 'multitude' introduced by Hardt and Negri (2004) to denote the spontaneous coalescence of dispersed subjectivities, collectivities and movements around the creation of common wealth. Arvidsson and Peitersen use both terms interchangeably to refer to the socialisation of production from the 1970s onwards, marking the era of post-Fordism. Information and communication technologies have permitted the displacement of large factories and vertically integrated corporations by networks of small producers scattered across the globe, and the subsequent diffusion of social capital, blurring productive and non-productive activities both inside and outside the corporation (Arvidsson and Peitersen 2013, 29, 49).

Inside the corporation, social media and mobile devices have supported the creation of inter- or intra-firm networks of productive publics that facilitate knowledge sharing and collective innovation processes among employees. The key to gaining competitive advantage has shifted from merely increasing productivity to facilitating the flow of knowledge within organisations. Accordingly, a brand is not only a symbol of a product, but also a common ethos, uniting employees, consumers, managers and investors around a common purpose. Companies such as Apple, Google and IBM depend on socialised innovation communities for their business models. The strategic source of profits and competitive advantage moves from material production per se to the capacity for brand innovation and flexibility (Arvidsson and Peitersen 2013, 31–32).

At the intersection of corporations and civil society, the rise of productive publics is driven by the delinking of identity from rigid structures and hierarchies, as evidenced in the so-called participatory culture: consumer tribes or 'brand communities'; fan culture, mods, hippies, hipsters, artists and bohemians introducing street fashion and new artistic styles; prosumer practices and a DIY movement leading on the hackers of the open source movement; the expansion and intensification of political activism and new social movements; an emerging social entrepreneurship and global solidarity movement; new forms of spirituality and body practices such as yoga, jogging, macrobiotic foods and a host of alternative lifestyles. In short, the rise of social production is a reactivation of civil society, sparked by networked media along with higher rates of education that generates a multitude of expressions, competencies and knowledge skills (Arvidsson and Peitersen 2013, 72).

The ontological relativism of postmodernism combined with the outsourcing of capitalist production across the globe has resulted in the individualisation of 'produsage' and the fragmentation of ethical horizons, both hailed by neoliberalism as hallmarks of freedom, pointing in the direction of more autonomous markets, in which everybody could become an entrepreneur. Digitisation has transformed traditional capitalism into cognitive capitalism, where information and knowledge have become the primary resources of value. Financialisation, finally, is supposed to democratise investment and, therefore, boost productivity and inclusive growth.

However, like Bauwens and Kostakis, Arvidsson and Peitersen argue that productive publics create a diverse order of worth, a multitude of values, which cannot be monetised as such, thus causing a crisis of value for both capitalism and the commons. Corporations attempt to accommodate this diverse order of worth by turning ethics, sustainability and social responsibility into marketing opportunities, while investing in user-led innovation projects that directly include consumer creativity in the corporate value chain. Yet finance lacks a common standard to measure this diverse order of worth.

Arvidsson and Peitersen interpret this lack as an irrationality featuring both in Marxist and neoclassical economics, since neither the labour theory of value nor the subsumption of value under price can account for an objective measure of value. A surplus of value permeating both capitalism and the commons constantly escapes monetisation. The value crisis is not only economic, but ethical and political. Following Habermas, Arvidsson and Peitersen (2013, 5–6) describe a legitimisation crisis, which reduces economics, ethics and politics into a more or less corrupt bargaining between particular interests or the naked exercise of raw power.

3.7.1 Revisioning Value in Terms of the General Sentiment

Let us take a step back and consider first what is value. In economics, there are two basic answers: the Marxist/classical and the neoclassical. Classical economists such as Ricardo, Marx and Smith defined value in terms of the time spent in the production of one unit. A car is more expensive than a chair, because of the larger amount of time invested in its production. On the other hand, neoclassical economics subsumes value under price on the grounds that any attempt to assign an objective measure to value is metaphysical (Arvidsson and Peitersen 2013, 10–12). Market prices by definition reflect all the information necessary, transforming uncertainty into calculable risk.

Arvidsson and Peitersen consider both approaches outdated. The classical theory is today obsolete for two basic reasons: first, labour costs are a small share of total production costs (for example, machinery, logistics, patents, intangibles) and, second, the production of intangible assets, that is, brand innovation and flexibility, does not exhibit a linear relation to the amount of time invested in production per unit. Non-linearity translates into the autonomisation of finance compared to real production (Arvidsson and Peitersen 2013, 37–38). The becoming complex of labour is evident even within Marxist thought, where the so-called 'transformation problem' remains unresolved, namely how socially abstract labour, that is, the average labour time needed to produce a commodity, corresponds to empirically observable prices. The neoclassical definition of value is also misleading, since the calculative frames of finance, employed to project the future performance of brands, products, corporations and states, are to some extent speculative and corrupt.

Arvidsson and Peitersen combine key concepts from various thinkers to introduce a new value regime inherent in productive publics. To begin with, the evolution of collective intelligence corresponds to what Marx called the 'general intellect', that is, publicly available knowledge and skills, which surpass the factory's borders, undermining the very existence of capitalism by rendering traditional labour obsolete (Arvidsson and Peitersen 2013, 35). Hardt and Negri argue that this is the case now in cognitive/information capitalism. They claim that the labour theory of value does not hold today. They reintroduce the transformation problem by the back door of Spinoza's *Ethics*, to argue that value is the 'power to act', that is, the power to utilise all the resources available to the multitude for its own ends. Hardt and Negri (2000, 29) incorporate into their analysis the Foucaultian notion of biopolitics, according to which power expands from the factory into *psyche*, the body and the entirety of social relations. Biopolitics combine with Deleuze and Guattari's poststructuralist notion of biopower to stress the social reproduction of bodies, values, relations and affects beyond the factory setting (Hardt and Negri 2000, 28).

Hardt and Negri build on the concept of 'immaterial labour' introduced by Maurizio Lazzarato and Paolo Virno to argue that value is immeasurable. Immaterial labour breaks down into two basic components: 1) the production and manipulation of affects, requiring (virtual or actual) human contact, labour in the bodily mode; and 2) the automation and commoditisation of cognitive knowledge by ICTs (Hardt and Negri 2000, 293). In short, immaterial labour consists in an affective/cognitive dimension expanding from material labour employed in the factory setting into society as a whole. As such, immaterial labour cannot be measured in time units, since it introduces a creative/subjective/qualitative dimension capitalised *par excellence* by finance.

Tiziana Terranova (2004) draws on the tradition of Italian 'autonomist' Marxism to coin the term 'free labour', which represents the most extreme development of the capitalist 'subsumption of life', along with being the most promising candidate for the negation of the capitalist order overall. To address the inadequacy of the labour theory of value to account for the capitalist 'subsumption of life', a number of Marxist and post-Marxist observers call for the cyber-communism of a value-free system of production and distribution, imagining a 'circulation of commons' of non-proprietary resources that are freely and openly available for appropriation (Dyer-Witheford 2006; Bauwens 2005). Bauwens and Kostakis's work could be considered an exemplary version of the circulation of the commons alongside post-capitalist production.

Arvidsson (2009) holds that the value crisis of contemporary capitalism does not entail the 'end of value' and the miraculous transition to cyber-communism, but, more likely, it opens up the possibility of alternative standards of value, since immaterial and free labour circulate in productive publics. Arvidsson and Peitersen consider the term 'labour' outdated, given the non-linearity between productivity measured in time units and prosumer practices in productive publics. They do not suggest that labour has 'disappeared' or 'no longer counts', but that it insignificantly relates to quanta of time, since most profit is generated in finance.

To further demonstrate their theory, Arvidsson and Peitersen (2013) combine Aristotle's 'ethics' with Hannah Arendt's concept of 'action'. Arendt (1958) distinguishes between labour, work and action. Labour is the human activity motivated by necessity, whereas work is action driven by self-expression and will. Action, finally, is the construction of a common world together. Therefore, participation in productive publics should be understood as a combination of work and action. Whereas the value of labour is set according to the fixed external parameters of time or productivity, the value of work and action is set according to the reputation of the participants in a particular public. 'Reputation is an inter-subjective measure of excellence, the criteria of which are themselves inter-subjectively elaborated: they depend on the "orders of worth" that are contained in the ethos of a particular public' (Arvidsson and Peitersen 2013, 88). For Aristotle, on whose thought Arendt builds, action relates to virtue, that is, the ability to adapt and live well with others. It is not enough, therefore, for a craftsman to perform excellent work, but she needs also to exhibit the virtuous character of the social individual, always seeking moderation between two extremes of action (Arvidsson and Peitersen 2013, 90). Ethics is not primarily about choosing 'good' or 'bad' in terms of a Kantian universal moral standard. Rather it is about finding ways for free men to construct a viable community (*polis*).

Accordingly, Arvidsson and Peitersen (2013, 91) conceive of reputation in productive publics as combining both the excellent skills of the participants and their virtue to act in ways that reproduce the vitality of the public. For example, in FOSS development, software developers are judged not only by their ability to write 'beautiful code', but also to solve conflicts, socialise new members and contribute to the reproduction of the public in general. Similarly, participation in productive publics is not conditioned exclusively by self-interest, but by the desire to create meaningful ties with others. With Aristotle in mind, Arvidsson and Peitersen use the term 'philia' to refer to the socially recognised self-realisation of the participants in productive publics. Reputation, thus, builds upon an ethical capital that can be redeemed in a variety of ways (Arvidsson and Peitersen 2013, 106). But still there is a lack of a common standard to measure reputations circulating in different publics and compare them against each other.

Arvidsson and Peitersen draw on Negri (1999) to argue that the universal measure of value in the new reputation economy of productive publics could be the affect circulating through social media and monetised by finance. Social media introduce an objectification of 'networked' subjectivity by measuring public affect and providing reputation metrics through data-mining techniques such as network and sentiment analysis. Finance produces value by transforming affect into a convention based on an interpretation that reduces complexity. Value is the affective investment of the public (employees, prosumers, investors, activists, citizens) in the intersubjective creation of 'truth, beauty and utility', as embedded in the economy. Thus, affect could become the new general equivalent of value in the form of the 'general sentiment', which consists in aggregations of subjective affective investments that derive from a multitude of different actors. 'A new standard like the general sentiment would further contribute to connecting such diverse publics into a "networked multitude," able to set its own values and, as a consequence, make the process more rational' (Arvidsson and Peitersen 2013, 127–128).

3.7.2 The Politics of Productive Publics

Arvidsson and Peitersen do not expect the prices of assets simply to reflect the general sentiment. The relation of pricing decisions and the general sentiment depends on the political design of the technological infrastructures that are to sustain the productive publics. The general sentiment is merely a bottom-up sensor of civil society's ethical pluralism that presumably contains the seeds of a new rationality, culminating in a new ideal speech-act situation, as Habermas would have it. Following Habermas, Arvidsson and Peitersen demonstrate a technologically updated affective transformation of the public sphere, which aims to bring together politics, civil society and capitalism under a more rational, ethical and democratic negotiation of value.

Arvidsson, Bauwens and Peitersen (2008, 17–18) envision three different scenarios for the future development of the ethical economy, which could be considered either separately or in tandem. The first scenario comes in two versions. The first is pretty much the perpetuation of the present state of affairs, where the ethical economy represents a niche within a predominantly capitalist economy. The second version corresponds to a form of 'information feudalism', where corporations use all legal and technical means to reinforce their rights to immaterial production and data usage. In this version, the ethical economy is used as a source of free or cheap labour, as in the case of platform capitalism.

In the second scenario, the ethical economy would have become sustainable perhaps through a basic income scheme, extended public funding, friendly capital or through the proliferation of collaborative practices. But still, the ethical economy would be subordinate to a dominant capitalist economy.

In the third scenario, the ethical economy becomes the dominant system. Ethical-market formats such as social entrepreneurship, platform cooperativism and global–local cyber-collectives have moved to centre stage and capitalism shrinks to the production of mostly scarce material goods. This scenario presupposes that the ethical economy has obtained a competitive advantage over capitalism, having transformed into a more sustainable socio-economic model compared with for-profit enterprises.

This transition, however, requires the establishment of an institutional infrastructure that could support a more ethical, rational and democratic way of reconnecting the economy to society. To this end, Arvidsson and Peitersen (2013, 125–131) introduce the politics of standards whereby the widespread capacity to construct technological interfaces would be anchored in the transparent representation of the dynamic and universal expression of the 'networked' multitude of publics who contribute to the formation of the general sentiment. They take a stand for an open and neutral Internet to be defended by traditional parliamentary politics that can secure the kinds of legal frameworks necessary to facilitate the construction of the new public sphere. Like Bauwens and Kostakis, they call for the adoption of open protocols, open supply chains and open book accounting. Yet Arvidsson and Peitersen acknowledge the fact that the neutrality of the Internet is currently under threat from political and commercial forces that are planning to impose biased standards in favour of their commercial interests. Besides, social media platforms such as Facebook and Twitter have little interest in providing open access to data on their traffic. Furthermore, current plans for the next generation of the Internet of Things tend to privilege closed standards. To prevent this, Arvidsson and Peitersen advocate for traditional political lobbying and activism to safeguard network neutrality and regulate social media companies. Their ultimate goal would be a global New Deal around sustainability and social responsibility.

3.7.3 Critique of Productive Publics

This reformist approach is not enough, however, to support the commons. Civil society is by and large colonised by the system, as Habermas would have it, or mesmerised by the rational mastery of capitalism, in the words of Castoriadis. The romantic reconciliation of affect with the Enlightenment commitment to rationality and measurement bears little resemblance to the current status of the commons, which are largely co-opted by capitalism. Platform capitalism revolves around a group of corporations that control information and have gained disproportionate market power, with the economy as a whole experiencing a gaping inequality in the last decades, exacerbated during the post-crisis period by state policies such as fiscal retrenchment and quantitative easing (Stiglitz 2016). And while it is perfectly reasonable to level the playing field by distributing value among economic actors, Arvidsson and Peitersen cannot rely on a vague mix of lobbying, activism, grassroots spontaneity and corporate social responsibility. By blindly integrating the commons into the hybrid of productive publics, the latter encompassing 'corporate communities' with civil society initiatives, not only do Arvidsson and Peitersen neglect the immense power asymmetries and income inequalities prevalent in capitalism, they also hide the exploitation inherent in both waged and unwaged offline and online activity. By advocating the financialisation of affect through the use of social media, they expand economism across the social factory. Rather than rendering affect the primary sensor of society, they render quantification the primary indicator of affect, thereby perpetuating the alienation of humankind via the calculative logic of capitalism. Put simply, they reproduce the neoclassical dictum that value equals numbers.

Arvidsson and Peitersen bypass the fact that we are already experiencing a state of 'information feudalism', where firms and corporations make billions out of monetising users' personal data and online activity. As mentioned earlier, Fuchs holds that the use value produced in social networking and search engines transforms into a surplus value for the social media corporations, sustaining new forms of exploitation in the contemporary information economy. Exploitation expands from social media companies to capitalism as a whole, since digital labour comprises waged and unwaged labour, spanning across the globe (Fuchs 2014). From slave mineral workers working at gunpoint in Africa and workers at Foxconn working long hours and unpaid overtime, to assemblers in Silicon Valley who are exposed to toxic substances and software engineers at Google who are highly stressed and overworked, proletarians evolve into cybertarians, precariats, underpaid workers and prosumers, subordinated to the few highly paid executives and freelancers benefiting from skills-biased technological change. The contemporary proletarianisation of the global workforce is encapsulated in Dyer-Witheford's (2015) concept of the global cyber-proletariat.

Rigi and Prey (2015) engage in the discussion to criticise both Arvidsson and Fuchs. Following Marx, they argue that information, knowledge and affect, when not exchanged with capital (as in the case of software, services, teaching, nursing, etc.), do not produce exchange value, since they can be reproduced at near-zero cost. Therefore, information, knowledge and affect have only use value, which can be commoditised in the form of monopoly rent as in the case of personal data extracted by corporations from social media and search engines. When Fuchs states that Internet users produce surplus value exploited by corporations, this is due to a misunderstanding of Marx. The same holds true for Arvidsson who claims that labour time is irrelevant in the case of social media, since most of their value derives from the production of affective relations – the so-called philia – commoditised in the form of rent and finance capital. But profit in the form of rent, Rigi and Prey argue, is a transformation of surplus value from other sectors of the economy and, therefore, labour time. Marx's labour theory of value is indispensable for understanding digital labour, given that surplus value transforms into profit, rent and interest. Therefore, the immaterial labour of the multitude upon which both Fuchs and Arvidsson build their arguments cannot but produce measurable common wealth either in the form of direct exchange value or rent extraction.

Rigi and Prey, however, do not clearly see that the Marxian concept of labour as commodity underestimates the basic contradiction of capitalism, that is, the division between directors and executants. Bowles and Gintis (1980) and Castoriadis (1988, 242–258) have shown that labour is a field of class struggle structured by the social relations of capitalist production. Neither labour power nor prices can be determined by an 'objective' economic law. Capitalism is not a strictly rational economic system, since there can be no rigorous economic science. The determination of capital and labour costs is a complex function of numerous indeterminate variables such as ideology, speculation, technical change, consumer choice, politics, and so on. Capitalism is the realm of continuous bargaining and power games between buyers, sellers, companies and governments. Thus, the development of the capitalist economy is pretty much unaffected by production costs, market equilibria or perfect information, since price signals reflect uneven supply and demand. In other words, power, as the force to make people do or not do what they otherwise would not do or do, is the primary determinant of value produced by labour and exploited by capital. The political, thus, comes into play in terms of class struggle, conflict, antagonism and power structures.

Capitalism is an evolving system whose main factor of transformation is class struggle. While Arvidsson and Peitersen recognise the potential of the commons to subvert the capitalist order, they hesitate to do so. Affection, grassroots democracy, transparency and self-realisation remain empty shells if not accompanied by the abolition of the distinction between directors and executants and the establishment of the self-instituting power of the people exercised beyond the bureaucratic hierarchies of corporations and states. If the main issue at stake is the elimination of the repressive reality of capitalism, the reduction of necessary working time to a minimum and the maximisation of 'free' time, the eroticisation of society and the body and the shaping of society and humans by Eros, and the emergence of affective social relations, then politics should rather integrate economic value into the social imaginary of peer-to-peer relations. To this end, concrete policies need to build on best collaborative practices to subsume the economy under democratic self-management.

3.8 Digital Distributism

Douglas Rushkoff's work could be read both as a critique and an optimisation of Arvidsson and Peitersen's productive publics, as he provides a more nuanced illustration of the interlinking between technology and economy. He concurs with Bauwens and Kostakis's thesis that corporatism is caught up in a growth trap inasmuch as it aims at infinite growth on a finite planet. Rushkoff reiterates the claim that we are today on the verge of a structural breakdown, as corporatism – backed by digital industrialism – runs out of places from which to extract value for growth. This last statement reasserts Harvey's (2010, 30) observation that 3% growth in perpetuity is running into serious environmental, market, spatial and profitability constraints. At the same time, financialisation has led to a significant disconnect between capital and real value. As a result, Schumpeter's creative destruction process may turn into a *destructive* destruction, pushing corporatism towards hybrid business models that favour a more sustainable and social approach to enterprise (Rushkoff 2016, 100). Rushkoff (2016, 98) wonders whether this is a cycle repeating itself or a unique and unprecedented challenge to our economic operating system. This consideration is all the more important in the case of digital industrialism, which aims at putting humans out of the equation, with the danger of a permanent consumer shortage.

Industrialism dates back to the end of feudalism and the birth of capitalism, which was financed by the aristocracy to usurp the power of the bourgeoisie (Rushkoff 2016, 18–22). By 'bourgeoisie' Rushkoff refers to the middle class of merchants, craftsmen and the petty bourgeois of small peasant proprietors, who sprang up in the medieval burgesses. Industrialism's primary intent was to subvert the rise of the middle class, the guilds and their peer-to-peer market system through the introduction of mass production, which disempowers craftsmen by disconnecting them from their skills and value creation. Capitalism is the product of the revolution of the rich against the rising middle class.

3.8.1 Digital Industrialism and Artificial Intelligence

Digital industrialism is to some extent the continuing proletarianisation of large segments of society by new technological means. The digital marketplace works on a power-law dynamic, creating a winner-takes-all disparity. The rule is that roughly 80% of sales come from 20% of products. When a bricks-and-mortar CD store plays a particular song that also takes the form of an online recommendation on a website, this recommendation leads to increased sales, which reproduces a feedback loop of the same or similar songs. People tend to choose what other people have chosen first, and this consumer behaviour is then amplified by machines at the expense of all other choices. This is not merely a distortion promoted by the biggest distribution platforms, from Amazon and iTunes to Spotify and Netflix, as Rushkoff (2016, 28–30) suggests, but is a masterfully orchestrated manipulation of taste by the marketing departments of corporations, aiming to reproduce the likes of the 'mainstream' commercial platforms, which in turn sell 'mainstream' consumers to advertising agencies. It is the self-perpetuating spiral of mass culture serving the interests of a liberal oligarchy, masked by the illusion of pluralism and freedom of choice. By this I do not intend to diminish the rapid expansion of creativity during the last decades, supported by the Internet. I merely want to stress its unfair distribution by mass media. The Internet follows suit by training people to accept the two or three choices at the top of popularity lists. The 80/20 ratio applies to every creative industry, from books, music and movies to smartphone apps.

Digital industrialism is crowdsourced to prosumers who produce an economy of likes by surfing the Internet, pushing buttons, and creating reviews, comments and the like. Big data turns the Internet into an advertising real estate. Big data fuels the customisation of demand by advertisers and marketers, who count on analytics to successfully predict buying intentions. The Internet and social media serve as agencies of attention and reputation. But only celebrities and superstars can handsomely redeem their accumulated reputational currency through social branding. Everyone else is a mere appendage of big data production, benefiting from the services provided by search engines and social media in exchange for giving up their privacy. Not only does digital industrialism replicate the core division of industrial capitalism between directors and executants, it further colonises time and space by turning human data into a commodity reproduced by users themselves. As a result, people are reduced to a manageable mainstream set of trends, categories and numbers, unwittingly contributing to the dehumanisation of artificial intelligence.

Artificial intelligence is a branch of computer science that produces technological advances in machine learning, pattern recognition, image classification, speech recognition, problem solving and knowledge engineering, with a vast range of applications in the fields of robotics, Internet searching, online advertising, e-commerce, fraud detection, medical diagnosis and implants, financial advice, tax preparation, customer service and genomic sequencing, among other things (Brynjolfsson and McAfee 2014, xii, xiii, 91). Digital industrialism's next stage is full automation engineered by the merging of big data with artificial intelligence on the Internet of Things infrastructure. The neocolonisation of big data is accompanied by the education of artificial intelligence by the crowd itself through machine learning. Corporations use crowdsourcing to constantly feed the algorithms with self-perpetuating learning patterns. Precarious freelance workers across the globe unknowingly contribute to their substitution by machines. Rushkoff (2016, 51) argues that most of the technologies we are currently employing replace far more jobs than they create. The reason is that jobs not yet subject to automation – that is, jobs requiring human maintenance, affection and creativity such as art, education, healthcare and social services – are not supported by venture capital, since they are considered costly and unscalable.

3.8.2 Technological Unemployment

Based on economic theory and two hundred years of historical evidence, mainstream economics holds that technological unemployment is only temporary and not a serious problem, since it creates in aggregate more jobs that those it destroys (Brynjolfsson and McAfee 2014, 173–175). Technological advances increase labour productivity, profits, wages and demand for labour, especially for workers whose labour complements technology. Technology also reduces the costs of production and, by extension, the prices of products and services, thus increasing the purchasing power of workers (Brynjolfsson and McAfee 2014, 143).

Whether or not this will be the case in the near future depends on what economists call 'elasticity of demand', that is, the percentage increase in demand for each percentage decline in price. For example, halving the price of artificial light did not double the demand for electricity, resulting in a fall in the total revenues for the lighting industry. Also, the increase of productivity in agriculture and manufacturing via technological innovation led to lower prices and improved quality, but did not increase employment and the demand for agricultural and manufacturing products. The general rule of the economy is that elasticity equals exactly 1%: an increase of 1% in productivity will be matched by an identical increase in demand. Occasional inelasticity is offset by the freeing up of money to be spent elsewhere in the economy so that overall employment is maintained.

Eric Brynjolfsson and Andrew McAfee (2014, 131–146) have shown that automation results in the decoupling of productivity from employment, thus exacerbating unemployment in the late 1990s. Algorithmic machines tend all the more to replace routine jobs in services, software, media, manufacturing, finance, music, retailing, trade, and so on. Skills-biased technological change, that is, the increasing demand for IT skills, decreases the demand for low-skilled labour, pushing wages lower, thus increasing the gap between highly and less educated workers. Physical capital (machinery) substitutes for labour, thus increasing the gap between the profits of capital-owners and the share of income going to labour.

Talent-biased technological change produces 'winner-takes-all' markets for the 0.1% of CEOs and superstars, widening income inequalities all the more (Brynjolfsson and McAfee 2014, 134–162). The CEO-to-worker pay ratio in the US rose from 46:1 to 331:1 between 1983 and 2013, while median income has stagnated for the last four decades and the minimum wage is lower than it was sixty years ago (Stiglitz 2013). The question then is which history's data should we take into account: the two centuries ending in the late 1990s showing that technological unemployment is temporary, or the twenty years since then?

Skills-biased technological change cannot explain either why highly skilled workers have moved into lower-skilled jobs nor why even highly skilled workers are not paid well (Stiglitz 2016, 9). Thomas Piketty's *Capital in the 21st Century* alludes to an inherent flaw of capitalism that favours a small minority at the top. He demonstrates that the return on capital is greater than economic growth, thus leading to ever-increasing inequality. Wealth grows faster than income. This is confirmed by a recent report by Oxfam, illustrating that the wealth of the richest 62 people on the planet rose by 45% in the five years between 2010 and 2015, while the wealth of the bottom half fell by 38% (Oxfam 2015). Stiglitz (2016, 12–13) suggests that the explanation for economic inequality is more nuanced due to the complex dynamics of financialisation, demographics, globalisation, technological change and urbanisation.

From a neoclassical economics viewpoint, unemployment and income inequalities are considered a structural indicator of meritocracy and an additional incentive for the overall improvement of the economy. But so far the experiment of neoliberalism has failed. Low interest rates and quantitative easing have poured more money into the economy in the last decade, but this is not trickling down into the real economy through investment or loans to small and middle-sized businesses that could create employment and increase wages. Money instead circulates in the form of rent at the top of the finance sector via share buybacks, stocks, commodities, private equity and derivatives, inflating asset bubbles while deflating the economy at the bottom (Stiglitz 2013).

3.8.3 Digitisation, Finance and the Start-up Economy

Digitisation was supposed to democratise finance (Rushkoff 2016, 169–183). The Internet would spread financial information and make markets more transparent and resilient, empowering individual investors to cut out the middlemen (the banker and the broker) and keep more autonomy and cash for themselves. Yet studies show that increased access to trading tools and market data often creates the illusion of market competency and encourages poor decision making (Rushkoff 2016, 177). Do-it-yourself traders simply cannot compete with market specialists and analysts, who have, among other things, access to inside information. The game is to some extent rigged. The digitised marketplace does not rely so much nowadays on brokers or specialists, but on high-frequency trading executed by highly sophisticated algorithms, often employing several price manipulation schemes such as 'pump and dump', 'front-running', 'wash trading', 'spoofing', and so on. Investing has turned into a game between algorithms exploiting trading protocols. While long-term investors intend to grow money by assessing the true value of companies, algorithms seek to profit from volatility. The mix of rational and speculative high-tech investing creates a non-linear, chaotic system that often propels unpredictable anomalies called 'bubbles', like the one of 2008. Ruskoff (2016, 184) rightly argues that instead of integrating the marketplace, digitisation generates derivative systems that create synthetic growth through recycling sheer churn.

Finance's synthetic growth integrates the hypergrowth logic of the start-up economy, expanding winner-takes-all markets, where early-stage technology investors are the rare big winners who offset the dozen or more losers (Rushkoff 2016, 184–195). The goal is a multi-million dollar exit through acquisition or IPO, which can then be reproduced ad infinitum. Start-ups ignite a vicious cycle where previous years' assets are converted into stockpiles of dead assets. Rather than engineering a new technology, they are actually reallocating capital. Digital entrepreneurs end up becoming the next generation of venture capitalists. Companies that have grown too wealthy and unwieldy follow suit by turning to the acquisition of start-ups. Thus, value has been converted into an enormous amount of waste in the casino capitalism of short-termism. The seeming democratisation of investment through crowdfunding parasitic platforms such as Kickstarter simply exacerbates winner-takes-all extremes. Pouring more money into the bottom of the pyramid does not result in more successful start-ups. It simply adds to the value extracted by those on top of the pyramid (Rushkoff 2016, 196–202). One could argue in a Schumpeterian fashion that innovation is a process of trial and error benefiting the few lucky and competent ones. But still, the social darwinism of innovation feeds on a loop of inequality, short-termism and waste.

3.8.4 Installing Digital Distributism

Rushkoff stresses that technology is not a bug in the system. Capitalism is not succumbing to automation. The latter simply adds to the initial programming of capitalism by early bankers to make more money through debt-based, interest-bearing, bank-issued central currency, which evolves nowadays into fiat money biased towards perpetual growth. Digitisation is an algorithmic multiplier embedded within the gigantic ledger of finance. Profit begs for more, bubbles burst and the boom–bust operating system reboots the next creative destruction.

Rushkoff (2016, 77–81) warns that the next time will not be a cyclical downturn, with corporations attempting to compensate for the disruptive impact of digital technology. This is not another creative destruction but a structural breakdown, as corporatism – backed by digitisation – runs out of places from which to extract value for growth. Big data capitalism is not going to save the day, since marketing and advertising accounts for less than 5% of gross domestic product (GDP). 'Eventually, social branding has to run out of fodder. As more and more markets lose all revenue potential except what they can make as social media marketing platforms, who is left to buy all this marketing and consumer data?' (Rushkoff 2016, 37). Rushkoff's (2016, 105) core argument is that the equivalence between growth and progress is not only artificial but unsustainable in a contracting marketplace and on a planet with limited resources. He projects that automation is likely to produce a consumer shortage that may force corporations to recode their operating systems and learn to scale down by adopting hybrid business models such as open sharing and collaboration models, 'inclusive capitalism', the 'benefit corporation', the 'flexible purpose corporation' and the 'low-profit limited liability company' (2016, 106–121). Rushkoff considers the not-for-profit model as the fittest for the future of an enterprise in a digital landscape.

The Mozilla Foundation is the best example of a digital not-for-profit company (Rushkoff 2016, 127–128). The success of the company is based on its widely used open source technologies supporting the Firefox web browser in a field dominated by platform monopolies such as Microsoft and Google. Mozilla is made up of two entities: Mozilla Foundation, a non-profit, and Mozilla Corporation. Mozilla Foundation oversees the corporation, which is responsible for Mozilla's software development, marketing and distribution. The corporation also collects the revenue generated by Firefox, but it has no publicly traded stock, no dividends and no shareholders. All profits are redirected back to the Foundation's social mission to promote the development of public access to and adoption of the open source Mozilla web browsing and Internet application software. By distributing profits within the non-profit instead of delivering them to shareholders as capital gains, Mozilla is able to maintain its network of volunteers and 500–1,000 paid employees. Capital is, thus, in the service of its employees and customers, not vice versa.

The ultimate goal of capitalism's structural adjustments towards more sustainable and socially responsible business models would be the prioritisation of value creation and money circulation by distributing currency to more people and enterprises. Blockchain, local and cooperative currencies, credit and time banks are all formats that could facilitate recycling rather than hoarding (Rushkoff 2016, 124–167). Investors would then turn to bounded investing such as union pension funds, affordable housing investment funds, communities, interest groups and a mutually supportive range of businesses, where money ends up circulating rather than being sucked up by a company foreign to the ecosystem. Bounded investment is less dependent on growth than it is on sustainability.

Rushkoff identifies direct public offering (DPO) as the most promising financial structure that allows small and medium-sized businesses to raise investment capital from any number of accredited or unaccredited investors as long as they align with the social mission of the business. Unlike an IPO, a DPO takes effect on the state level, meaning that it is not subject to an expensive and arduous vetting process; and unlike crowdfunding, a DPO offers equity and dividends instead of a payout on exit. A DPO provides the legal framework through which a business can raise money from investors, suppliers, employees and consumers, constituting a multi-stakeholder cooperative serving the goals of the community instead of capital.

The coalescence of traditional cooperatives with platform cooperatives under the digital commons would be both a response to predatory capitalism and an attempt to tackle the sustainability crisis and technological unemployment. The objective would be to transform work from waged slavery to self-realisation, self-investment and co-ownership of the means of production (Rushkoff 2016, 212). Resistance to digital industrialism may look like reclaiming communism, but it merely points to the reclamation of the commons on the model of digital distributism, which utilises technology to create self-sustaining, highly reciprocal, peer-to-peer, worker-owned and community-defined marketplaces. As Rushkoff puts it:

> Digital industrialism sought to extract value from the system using new, digital means: digital distributism seeks to use those technologies to distribute new capabilities to small businesses and real communities. Digital industrialism accepts growth as a condition of nature; digital distributism strives towards a dynamic steady state. Where digital industrialism pushes corporations even further from value creation, a more distributed approach to digital business embraces and enriches broader constituencies of stakeholders. Where an industrial approach to networking yields the platform monopolies of Uber and Amazon, a distributed one yields worker-owned cooperatives at a level of complexity and security unimaginable before digital technology. Where the digital industrialist's financial strategy is to extract money through increasingly abstracted derivatives, a more distributist vision would promote the circulation of money through low-friction, peer-driven currencies. Where digital industrialism seeks to use technology to expand markets forever, digital distributism seeks to recycle the same money again and again by investing and spending it in the bounded communities of the real world. Where digital industrialism asks the economy to grow infinitely for its own sake, digital distributism aspires to sustainable prosperity. (2016, 226)

By 'digital distributism' Rushkoff (2016, 231) refers neither to any sort of social democratic wealth distribution through state mechanisms nor a libertarian decentralisation, where alternative power centres spring up on the periphery. Rather it signals a diffusion of power across the network in such a way that value, energy and resources become available to anyone in communal terms. But, as with Rifkin, Rushkoff's optimism is not supported by the facts. Platform capitalism is dominant in the digital plateau and pregnant with the worst nightmares of surveillance capitalism. Most importantly, what Rushkoff is missing in his anarcho-communist crescendo is the significant role the state could assume in the creation of a commons-orientated sociopolitical transition. Central policies are the *sine qua non* for any radical politics to counter neoliberalism.

Rushkoff's analysis sheds ample light on the current digital landscape. It offers an illuminating view of the technological battleground of class struggle while offering substantive weaponry for the commons to subvert the neoliberal hegemony. Digital distributism can significantly support the commons, if integrated into a holistic, post-hegemonic, commons-orientated strategy seeking to decentralise power via horizontally and vertically coordinated mechanisms.

3.9 Envisioning Real Utopias

Erik Olin Wright's work reads as a sociological and political contribution to the commons, freeing up institutional space for strategic action towards a commons-orientated transition. It represents one of the most recent attempts to formulate an emancipatory social science aimed at the socialist transformation of society. The normative principle of this transformation is a radical democratic egalitarian approach to justice, according to which all people should have equal access to the necessary material and social means to live flourishing lives (social justice); and the necessary means to participate in collective decisions affecting their lives as members of a community (political justice) (Wright 2009, 7–8). Freedom is the power to make decisions over one's life, and democracy is the power of integrating freedom in collective decision making. Wright (2009, 73) defines power as the capacity of actors to generate effects in the world. He holds that freedom presupposes equality as the capacity of all people to participate in collective decision making. Wright's egalitarian understanding of freedom is both 'negative' and 'positive', since the liberal ideal of freedom as non-interference combines with the capacity of all people to participate in democratic processes (Wright 2009, 12).

3.9.1 Critique of Marxism

Evidently, Wright's work bears some striking similarities with Castoriadis's project of individual and collective autonomy (Papadimitropoulos 2018c). He, too, has developed a systematic critique of both Marxism and capitalism, arguing that Marx proposed a highly deterministic theory of the demise of capitalism and a relatively voluntaristic theory of the construction of its alternative (Wright 2009, 64). Like Castoriadis, he identifies a number of essential problems with traditional Marxism.

Marx's crisis theory is predicated on the following premises: 1) labour is the source of value and, therefore, profit; 2) competition forces capitalists to replace labour with machinery; and 3) the rate of profit falls. But Marx's law of the falling tendency of the rate of profit seems inadequate, since crises within capitalism do not appear to have an inherent tendency to become ever more intense over time. Capitalism learns to adapt and reform. The labour theory of value, on which Marx's theory of crisis intensification is based, seems no longer sustainable, at least in its full extent. 'While the idea of labour as the source of value may be a useful device for illustrating the idea of the exploitation of labour, there is no persuasive reason for believing that labour and labour alone causally generates value' (Wright 2009, 66). Thus, for the moment there is no good reason to suggest that the internal contradictions of capitalism make it unsustainable in the long run.

Class structures have become more complex over time, rather than progressing into a homogenising proletarianisation (Wright 1985; 2005; 2009, 65–67). We are rather witnessing today the inter-mobility and fragmentation of the working class: the rise of labour aristocracy and freelancers; the opposition between unionised and non-unionised workers; the conflicting interests of different wage categories; the contradictory positions of workers who are exploited by their employer, but may also be running a small business, potentially exploiting other workers. Workers now possess the skills of both capitalists and managers. The collective capacity of the working class to challenge capitalism seems not only to decline within mature capitalist societies, but to replicate the division of directors and executants among the workforce (Wright 2009, 67). Ruptural strategies of social transformation, even if they were capable of overthrowing the capitalist state, do not seem likely to provide a social-political setting for sustaining democratic experimentalism. Like Castoriadis, Wright (2009, 69) holds that the empirical cases of ruptures with capitalism (for example, the Eastern Bloc regimes) have resulted in authoritarian state-bureaucratic regimes rather than true democracies.

3.9.2 A Socialist Transformation Strategy

Wright (2009, 26–34) points out that the relations of domination within capitalist workplaces constitute pervasive restrictions on individual autonomy and self-direction, thus blocking the full realisation and exercise of human potentials. Exploitation, alienation of labour, large economic inequalities, the uncontrolled social externalities of technological change and profit-maximising competition perpetuate eliminable forms of human suffering, thus impeding the universalisation of the conditions for expansive human flourishing.

Wright (2009, 37–43) locates six sources of inefficiency in capitalism: 1) the underproduction of public goods; 2) the underpricing of natural resources; 3) negative externalities; 4) monitoring and enforcing market contracts; 5) pathologies of intellectual property rights; and 6) the costs of inequality. He condemns consumerism on both moral and environmental grounds, arguing that capitalist commodification threatens human values such as child care, product safety, the arts, community, religion and spirituality (2009, 47–57). Lastly, corporate influence limits democracy and fuels militarism and imperialism.

In contrast to both capitalism and traditional Marxism, Wright develops a socialist transformation strategy. He initially distinguishes between three forms of power: economic power exercised over economic resources, state power identified with rule making and rule enforcing over territory, and social power consisting in voluntary collective action. He then attaches these three powers to capitalism, statism and socialism respectively (2009, 73–74). He further makes a distinction between 'power' and 'ownership'. The former is the capacity to direct the means of production, and the latter is the right over property and surplus. Capitalism, statism and socialism differ in terms of the ownership of the means of production and the type of power exercised over economic activities (Wright 2009, 76). But they can combine according to multiple settings of ownership and power.

In contrast to traditional statist versions of socialism, Wright's (2009, 80) socialist transformation strategy is grounded on the distinction between state and social power, state and social ownership, and the possibility of partnerships between the market and socially owned and controlled enterprises. Capitalism, statism and socialism should be then considered as coordinating variables of socialist transformation, geared towards three principal directions: 1) social empowerment over the way the state affects economic activity; 2) social empowerment over the way capitalism shapes economic activity; and 3) social empowerment directly over economic activity (Wright 2009, 82). In short, socialism points to the empowerment of civil society over the state and the market. To this end, Wright (2009, 86–92) illustrates seven pathways:

1. Statist socialism: in contrast to central planning, statist socialism would be orientated towards deepening the democratic quality of the state, aiming to open a genuine pathway to social empowerment.
2. Social democracy: in contrast to state regulation favouring capital, social democracy would regulate capital in ways that enhance social power.
3. Associational democracy: in contrast to associations being heavily manipulated by elites and the state, associational democracy would promote open and deliberative decision-making processes, highly representative of civil society interests. In associational democracy, labour unions, business associations, organisations or civic groups would directly engage in various aspects of political decision making and governance.
4. Social capitalism: in addition to associations of workers or unions exerting power over corporations through co-determination of funds, bargaining over pay and working conditions, and so on, the union movement could create venture capital funds, controlled by labour (as in Canada), to provide equity to start-up firms that satisfy particular social criteria. Consumer-orientated pressure on corporations would be an additional form of civil society empowerment over economic power. Fair trade and equal exchange movements aiming to connect consumers and producers by building alternative global economic networks could also disrupt the economic power of multinational corporations.
5. Social economy: voluntary associations, NGOs, co-ops, community-based organisations, all subsidised through donations, charities, grants and taxes, would directly organise economic activity (for example, Wikipedia, the Quebec economy). An unconditional basic income provided by the state through taxation could furthermore enhance social economy.
6. Cooperative market economy: instead of worker-owned cooperative firms operating in isolation and thus forced to bend to capitalist competitive pressure over time, worker-owned cooperative firms would be incorporated into a cooperative market economy that could provide finance,

training, problem-solving services and all kinds of mutual support (for example, the Mondragon cooperative and the Mozilla Foundation).

7. Participatory socialism: the combination of statist socialism (1) and the social economy (5) with the mission of jointly organising the production of various goods and services. The state becomes more pervasive by getting directly involved in the organisation and production of economic activity. Social power expands from its participation in representative democracy into the productive activity itself.

Wright puts forward a pluralistic and heterogeneous socialist transformation rooted in a centrally coordinated decentralisation of power. But contrary to Castoriadis who was against any type of state- or market-driven reformism, Wright's socialist transformation strategy is premised on the radical democratisation of both the state and economy by civil society. Four of the seven pathways to socialism involve the state. Yet for socialism to be fully realised, Wright holds that state and economic power have to be subordinated to social power on the model of economic democracy (Wright 2009, 92).

3.9.3 Social Empowerment over the State

Social empowerment over the state would include a combination of pathways (1), (2), (3) and (7). In contrast to Castoriadis, Wright (2009, 108–109) claims that a radical egalitarian democracy does not require direct democracy to replace representative democracy, but the deepening of democracy in all three varieties of democratic governance (direct, representative and associational). He introduces participatory forms of direct democracy that could create countervailing power against the privileged groups and elites lobbying for state power. The design principles of this power are the following: bottom-up participation, pragmatic orientation, deliberation, and state-centred decentralisation to local units of action such as neighbourhood councils, local school councils, workplace councils, and so on. Participatory democracy differs from spontaneous activist efforts or projects led by non-governmental organisations or social movement groups, since it aims to change the central procedures of state power rather than occasionally influencing them. Wright cites as an example of participatory democracy the municipal participatory budgeting applied in the case of Porto Alegre in Brazil.

To enhance the democratic quality of representative democracy, Wright introduces proposals for egalitarian public financing of politics, and randomly selected citizen assemblies. He also claims that political institutions can be designed in such a way as to enable secondary associations – labour unions, business associations, organisations or civic groups – to play a positive role in deepening democracy. Centralised administrations are good at imposing uniform rules over homogeneous contexts, but when addressing heterogeneous economic and social conditions, centralised command and control processes are much less effective (Wright 2009, 127). One-size-fits-all regulations are rarely satisfactory, for example, in the context of environment and workplace safety, given that ecologies and workplaces are diverse and complex. Associations could solve this problem and complement public regulatory efforts by gathering local information, monitoring behaviour and promoting cooperation among private actors. Instead of associations providing external pressure by lobbying politicians and agencies for specific rules, they would be included systematically in the central tasks of governance: policy formation, coordination of economic activities, monitoring, administering and enforcing regulations.

The possibilities of an expanded and deepened associative democracy are not limited to the role of encompassing associations in neo-corporatist, peak-level, public policy formation. Associative democracy can also function at the local and regional level to solve problems, and design and implement detailed rules and standards of various sorts. Associations must be relatively encompassing, representing a substantial proportion of the relevant social category; second, the association leadership must be accountable to its membership through meaningful internal democratic processes; and third, the associations must have significant powers to sanction members. Wright (2009, 127–133) cites the example of Quebec in Canada, which is an exemplary showcase of deepening the associational dimension of democracy in the domains of skill formation within regional labour markets, habitat conservation for endangered species, child and elderly care, cooperative housing, education, energy production, and many more.

3.9.4 Social Empowerment over the Economy

Social empowerment over the economy would develop in the direction of market socialism, combining pathways (4), (5), (6) and (7) (Wright 2009, 135–189). Wright employs the term 'social economy' to specify economic activities that spring from civil society. Two prominent examples are Wikipedia and the Quebec social economy. Starting from the Quebec experience, Wright suggests four institutional designs to advance social empowerment: 1) state subsidies targeted at the social economy, 2) the development of social economy investment funds, 3) governance through associational democracy and 4) participatory democratic forms of organisation. By 'social capitalism' he refers to a wide range of institutional mechanisms and social processes that directly impinge on the exercise of capitalist power. Some examples he mentions are labour solidarity funds and share-levy wage earner funds, both pushing capitalism towards a structural hybrid within which social power has greater weight. Finally, a cooperative market economy consists of an association of worker-owned firms such as Mondragon in Spain and the Mozilla Foundation.

A number of scholars have built on the work of Wright to introduce concrete proposals for democratising finance. Hockett (2019, 516–522) calls for the creation of a National Investment Council (NIC) that would provide funding for national development projects in the sectors of clean energy and transport infrastructure. This could be done partly by aggregating funds and partly by issuing and purchasing bonds. The NIC would be coupled with Federal Reserve reforms that would aim to induce public participation in finance by affording every citizen, firm and unit of government a deposit-cum-transaction account.

The first effect would be to end financial exclusion and marginalisation for poor and non-white people. The second would be the more effective control of inflation and deflation. Instead of banks using federal funds to speculate on commodity and other markets, thereby routing funds away from individuals and businesses and inflating commodity prices such as foodstuffs and fuel, a 'QE for the people' would channel money in more socially beneficial directions. A Fed-administered digital dollar backed by Blockchain and accessed via smartphones would further afford greater financial inclusion. Another tool for preserving optimal credit allocation and price stability would be a price stabilisation mechanism that would limit volatility through Fed price modulation (shorting and purchasing activity) with regard to more systematically significant prices than just interest rates, such as labour costs, commodity prices, fuel prices and others.

Block (2019) puts forward a synthesis between socialist theory and radical financial reform. Historically, classical Marxists argued that financial reforms were unlikely to alter the system as long as private property prevailed. They were reluctant to engage in deficit financing or other unorthodox policies. They, therefore, adopted quite orthodox positions on issues of finance such as the return to the gold standard. Radical reformers, on the other hand, imagined the reallocation of credit in the economy through redistribution mechanisms such as 'social credit', time banks or stamped money. Block argues that financial mechanisms can today align these two traditions. Classical Marxists need to acknowledge the relative autonomy of financial superstructure:

> The logic of extracting surplus value at the point of production does not dictate a particular form for a society's financial system. There is great diversity in the structure of financial institutions in different developed market societies, with some heavily relying on public sector financial entities and others demonstrating considerable regulatory effectiveness in keeping destabilising speculative finance in check. In short, state policies have been and continue to be critical in determining what a nation's financial industry looks like. All of this suggests that reform initiatives in this sphere could be successful. (Block 2019, 539)

A major obstacle to socialist reform has been the fear of capital flight and capital strike in the event of the implementation of policies that would threaten the interests of property holders. Capitalist reaction triggers an economic downturn that stirs up public disaffection and anti-leftist populism. Wright has coined the term 'transition trough' to describe periods of extreme public discontent towards democratic socialist reforms. To address this potentiality, Block expands Hockett's franchise model to a set of structural reforms that would weaken the power of capital to resist a broader programme of socialist transition. To begin with, the state could apply the public utility model by granting monopoly rights to firms and banks and further controlling the amount of profit they earn. This would discourage financial speculation, since trading could not exceed the government-set ceiling. A more radical option would be for the government to create in-house franchisees or non-profit institutions equipped with the ability to create money. Regulatory measures would be adopted to prevent unscrupulous trading and predatory lending.

More radical reforms involve creating a national investment bank linked to a set of non-profit, decentralised financial institutions such as credit unions, public banks, community banks and non-profit investment banks to provide credit for underfunded activities such as infrastructure, clean energy, affordable housing and small and medium-size businesses (Block 2019, 535–537). The creation of a non-profit innovation stock market would further open up investment opportunities to the broad public and help high-tech start-ups, cooperatives and B corporations to raise capital for expansion. (Certified B Corporations are businesses that meet the highest standards of verified social and environmental performance, public transparency, and legal accountability to balance profit and purpose.) This way, decentralisation, diversity and competition would weaken large commercial banks and corporations while setting up a more dynamic and sustainable economy:

> This weakening would happen through an incremental shift of consumer savings from for-profit to nonprofit entities. Currently, something close to 90 percent of consumer bank deposits are with large commercial banks, but with the reinvigoration of credit unions and nonprofit banks, we could expect a large-scale shift of these deposits toward more locally institutions as consumers recognize the benefits of reinvesting in their communities. At the same time, savers would have attractive alternatives to putting their retirement funds in mutual funds and common stocks. They would be able to shift to a variety of bonds issued by nonprofit investment banks or the public investment bank, and they could acquire mutual funds invested in the innovation stock market […] With less control over consumer deposits and retirement savings, giant institutions would have to shrink and make do with reduced flows of profits. This, in turn, would reduce the resources to invest in campaign contributions and right-wing think tanks. It would become harder for them to push back against regulators and harder for them to stop the advance of their nonprofit competitors. (Block 2019, 547–548)

Lenore Palladino (2019, 573–591) proposes that the 'parallel credit system' be coupled with a 'parallel equity system'. Palladino attempts to address wealth inequality by claiming not only access to credit but also to equity for all citizens. Since business cycles and macroeconomic risk are likely to trap individuals in a cycle of unaffordable debt repayments, he proposes the creation of a Public Investment Platform that would directly connect individuals to lending or investing opportunities. It would serve as a crowdfunding platform for small companies offering debt or equity securities at little or no cost to the public. It would provide a 'public option' for wealth creation that would compete directly with the private sector and reduce the concentrated power of the 'shadow banking system', which consists of hedge funds and private equity funds involved in risky activities. The Public Investment Platform would be joined by a 'public investment account' that would give a small sum of capital to all citizens in accordance with family net wealth, which would be used as a wealth-building fund.

Michael McCarthy (2019, 611–633) completes the puzzle of reforms by instigating the creation of sovereign wealth funds and inclusive ownership funds. The former would be established by governments through a combination of mechanisms such as levies (taxes and fees on consumption, payroll and capital), leveraged purchases (borrowing at low interest rates to invest at higher rates), ring-fencing existing assets (by transferring existing assets into it) and new money creation. The latter would be adopted by companies with the aim of allocating shares to their workers and increasing their decision-making power in daily management. Workers would also receive dividends, part of which could be channelled to a public fund to pay for welfare benefits and public services.

This whole set of proposals combines Wright's (2009, 191–240) 'symbiotic' and 'interstitial' transitional paths towards socialism. In contrast to a 'ruptural' path of the kind that the former Eastern Bloc experienced, a symbiotic path in the form of a parallel credit system avoids a direct confrontation with capitalist class power, while an interstitial one in the form of a parallel equity system makes relatively small transformations that generate a qualitative shift in class dynamics. While the symbiotic path occupies empty spaces in the dominant financial system, the interstitial path paves the way for a more transversable break with the dominant financial order. The ultimate goal would be the gradual transformation of the private sector into a public one.

This transition would probably not be an easy one. Capital flight and capital strike would lead to the forgoing of new investments, layoffs, the weakening of demand, deflation and economic recession (Block 2019, 547–551). Governments would not be able to offset capital flight by increasing borrowing due to the hostility of international banks and global organisations. Governments would be forced instead to impose capital controls and raise interest rates, aiming to prevent capital outflows. A currency crisis would follow, with the tight monetary policy slowing down economic activity.

However, the proposed reforms might be able to withstand the currency pressure. The central countervailing measure for this would be the expansion of the non-profit sector to offset the capital boycott (Block 2019, 547–551). The combination of capital controls and increased international borrowing by large non-profit banks might be sufficient to avoid a currency crisis and stabilise the economy. Governments would then have gained the political legitimacy necessary to deepen the financial reforms and extend democracy into economic decision making. Wealth and income redistribution, the strengthening of labour rights, the combatting of racial and gender inequality, improved environmental regulations and increased democratic participation in governance could all be supplementary to financial reforms. Finally, education is a critical factor in the provision of adequate economic and technological literacy to the people.

3.9.5 Critique of the Reformist Approach

Overall, the problem with this reformist approach is that it deals with the periphery of the capitalist system, thus leaving untouched the core of capitalist production. To abolish the capitalist system from within, it is essential to alter the mode of capitalist production on the model of commons-based peer production. Credit and equity reforms need to comply with the self-management of the economy and society as a whole. This does not equate to a state-centred leftist approach aiming to nationalise the banks and the means of production. It rather points to a holistic, post-hegemonic strategy that seeks to connect the democratisation of finance with a decentralised, commons-orientated transition.

Wright seems more apprehensive of the radically transformative role of civil society. He conceives of the state, capitalism and civil society as coordinating variables of his socialist transformation, since society as a whole is a hybrid structure comprised of potentially interchangeable overarching powers: economic, state and social. While it is analytically useful to distinguish capitalism, statism and socialism according to the power dominant each time, none of them constitute purely independent powers. The same applies to all units of analysis within each power, be it a firm, a government, a labour union, an association or a cooperative, where complex configurations of capitalist, statist and socialist elements combine. Thus, Wright notes: 'This has critical implications for our understanding of the problem of transformation: emancipatory transformation should not be viewed mainly as a binary shift from one system to another, but rather as a shift in the configuration of the power relations that constitute a hybrid' (2009, 226).

Wright's core argument is that the realisation of a radical egalitarian democracy presupposes the social empowerment of civil society over the state and the economy. He thus brings to the fore the self-instituting power of the people as the main tool of socialist transformation. He incorporates the self-instituting power of the people into a flexible strategic pluralism based on multiple pathways of social empowerment, embodied in a variety of structural transformations.

Wright (2009, 93–95) anticipates a number of potential critiques of his transformation strategy. An initial point of criticism is that models of participatory democracy are non-functional, since people are too apathetic, ignorant or busy to participate. Secondly, a multitude of associations, networks and communities does not guarantee the creation of the social power necessary to effectively control the state and the economy. On the contrary, this could lead to conflicts of interest or, conversely, as conservative critics of socialism have argued, to the tyranny of the majority. Thirdly, according to the critique posed by the revolutionary socialists, a socialist transformation is not feasible in a society dominated by capitalism, as it will sooner or later confront the problem of competition with the capitalist economy, and the dependence of the social economy on capitalism for financial resources.

To address these criticisms, Wright (2009, 93–95) argues that moving along the pathway of social empowerment is not a guarantee of success, but a more favourable terrain of struggle. He conceives the predictions of the revolutionary socialists as pessimistic, since they exaggerate the power of capital and they underestimate the social spaces available for social innovation. Wright (2009, 114) reminds us that when there are opportunities for people to get involved in decision making that directly affects their lives, they do participate in substantial numbers. However, self-institutionalisation could reproduce a reversed bureaucracy if based on rigid procedures that would obstruct or discourage people from participating, resulting in a parody of democracy. People are more likely to support an economic democracy on the models of platform and open cooperativism that can offer them a living along the lines of autonomy, co-ownership and self-realisation. A challenge remains further to calibrate the balance between centralisation and decentralisation in favour of the autonomy of both individuals and the commons. Wright provides one of the most holistic perspectives towards this goal. It is, however, more effective to fit Wright's pluralism into a more coherent post-hegemonic strategy that aims to bring the different facets of the commons under a commons governance.

3.10 The Lack of the Political II

The reformist approach to the commons purports to advance the self-instituting power of the commons from a third institutional axis of civil society coexistent with capitalism and the state into a counter-hegemonic power orientated against neoliberalism. It succeeds in bridging the gap between local and digital commons and transforming the common into a major force of social change. But still there is a significant lack of the political to counter the superpowers of states and corporations.

Bollier recalibrates the liberal state towards the support of the commons rather than the capitalist market. He introduces a green governance model aiming to tackle climate change and protect the natural commons.

Rifkin introduces the collaborative commons as an alternative business model supported by the Internet of Things infrastructure, designed to remain open, decentralised and distributed, thus bringing together local commons and social movements with the digital commons, Internet start-ups and prosumers. Rifkin, however, produces a social democratic version of the commons that cannot but bear the contradictions of capitalism and the state, thereby putting a halt to the self-instituting power of the people.

Scholz attempts to take a more radical stance by elaborating on the model of platform cooperativism, applying algorithmic design to democratic self-management, co-ownership and equitable distribution of value. Yet he seems to oscillate between a radical and a liberal approach.

Bauwens and Kostakis take a more radical stance by connecting cooperatives with the digital commons on the principles of commons-based peer production, instantiated in their sub-model of Design Global–Manufacture Local. Open cooperativism seeks to create a post-capitalist alliance of ethical market entities, a partner state and the commons, with the aim of challenging neoliberal capitalism. This vision falters upon the lack of centrally coordinated macro-policies to apply the principles of the commons at a local, regional, national and international level. This obstacle could be overcome by a partner state embracing the principles of the commons more openly. Arvidsson and Peitersen follow the post-capitalist vision of Bauwens and Kostakis, but they deviate in that they are attuned to a technologically 'updated' Habermasian transformation of the public sphere rather than a more radical approach to the commons that would steer the self-instituting power of the people against neoliberalism.

Rushkoff's model of digital distributism is more in line with the post-capitalist vision of Bauwens and Kostakis in that he envisages a hybrid economy that could force capitalism in the long run to adjust to the commons. The problem with Rushkoff's anarcho-communism is that, by excluding the state, he significantly debilitates a commons-orientated transition.

Wright provides probably the most holistic political alternative for the commons by integrating the self-instituting power of the people into a strategic pluralism based on multiple pathways of social empowerment, embodied in a variety of structural transformations. It can function as an institutional multiformat for the various reformist approaches of the commons exemplified by Rifkin, Scholz, Bauwens and Kostakis, Arvidsson and Peitersen and Rushkoff. Yet it would perhaps be more effective for the commons to fit Wright's strategic pluralism into a more cohesive post-hegemonic perspective that envisions a cross-regional, commons-orientated transition rather than scattered reformats. To this end, a multidisciplinary approach needs to combine politics, finance, law, economics, sustainability science and education under commons governance.

The Anti-capitalist Commons

CHAPTER 4

The Anti-capitalist Commons

4.1 Introduction

The task of Part 3 is to critically review the anti-capitalist literature on the commons, which comprises various interpretations of Marx's work, among others. The first section investigates the relation of the political and the common in a broad spectrum of continental political philosophy, ranging from post-Heideggerianism and postmodernism to strands of autonomous Marxism and post-Marxism. It critically engages with Kioupkiolis's critique of variants of post-Heideggerianism, autonomous Marxism and post-Marxism, as elaborated in the work of Nancy (1993; 1997; 2000), Esposito (2010; 2011; 2012; 2013), Agamben (1993), Hardt and Negri (2000; 2004; 2009) and Laclau and Mouffe (1985). Kioupkiolis (2019) expands the lack of the political in the anti-capitalist commons to point to the crowding out of the self-instituting power of the people in several Marxist and post-Marxist interpretations of the common. He attempts to balance the tension between horizontalism and verticalism by elaborating a post-hegemonic politics of the common predicated on agonistic freedom and radical democracy.

The second section focuses on the work of Dardot and Laval (2014) who, following Castoriadis, among others, have reintroduced the self-instituting power of the people in political discourse as the essential concept of the common.

The third section illustrates a more concrete version of the common, articulated in the post-capitalist framework of Gibson and Graham's work (1996; 2006), which sketches out the philosophical and empirical preconditions of a community economy.

The fourth section deals with the work of Dyer-Witheford (1999; 2006; 2015), De Angelis (2017), and Caffentzis and Federici (2014), who build on the concept of the common as the self-instituting power of the people to introduce variants of autonomous Marxism, ranging from post-capitalism to anti-capitalism.

How to cite this book chapter:

Papadimitropoulos, V. 2020. *The Commons: Economic Alternatives in the Digital Age.* Pp. 139–214. London: University of Westminster Press. DOI: https://doi.org/10.16997 /book46.d. License: CC-BY-NC-ND 4.0

The fifth section examines the conception of the common in the context of classical Marxist views such as those of Žižek (2008; 2010), Dean (2009; 2012), Harvey (2003; 2005; 2010; 2012), Mason (2015) and Fuchs (2008; 2011; 2014).

Overall, the post-hegemonic politics of the commons should engage more critically with the techno-economic dimensions of contemporary class struggle, fragments of which are illustrated by various strands of the common, most notably combined in Bauwens and Kostakis's work. If the commons want to avoid occupying a marginal sub-space and reach a critical mass, it is essential to provide their members with a sustainable livelihood along ecological and democratic lines. To this end, a holistic post-hegemonic strategy needs to bootstrap the spontaneity of the commons, nudged by broader democratic alliances.

4.2 The Post-hegemony of Common Democracy

The disruptive effects of the work of Nietzsche, Heidegger and Freud on traditional and modern philosophy gave rise to various strands of post-foundational philosophy such as post-Heideggerianism, poststructuralism and post-Marxism, which consider the theoretical foundations of modernity such as reason, the subject and God as metaphysical, and reject grand narratives of history and society such as Hegelo-Marxism and Kantianism (Marchart 2007, 2–14). Post-foundationalism should not be confused with anti-foundationalism or 'anything goes' postmodernism, since it does not seek to totally erase concepts such as totality, universality, essence and ground, but to weaken their ontological status. It does not turn into an anti-foundational nihilism or existentialism, nor does it melt down into a postmodern pluralism where all meta-narratives evaporate into thin air. The ontological weakening of foundations does not imply the total absence of ground, but rather the impossibility of a final ground. Freedom and historicity come into play to unfold the undecidability of being and, by extension, the necessity for political decision in the face of radical contingency.

4.2.1 Politics and the Political

A common thread of thought within post-foundationalism builds on the distinction between the political and politics, originating in the work of Carl Schmitt (1996/1932, 26–27), who conceives of the political as the ontological ground that precedes all domains of the social. While politics corresponds to the narrow sense of the political, as constituted, for example, in the state, the political is the essence of society, located in the distinction between friend and enemy. The essential drive of society lies in the conflict and antagonism inherent in the political, which, as such, retains a certain primacy over the social.

For Castoriadis (1991b, 155), politics represents the ontological capacity of the political for self-management, which precedes conflict and antagonism, for it is the *instituting power* of society itself that constitutes meaning. The political is the ontological source of the deliberative power of politics to uphold the 'magma' of the imaginary significations of society. (By 'magma' Castoriadis means the ontological status of society which constantly breeds new forms of meaning not reducible to a determinate set of rules or conditions. Indeterminacy thus is the ontological breeding ground of otherness and difference.) The political consists in the recurring constitution of the *instituted power* by the *instituting power* of the anonymous collective. There is no legitimate or rational source of meaning other than the self-instituting power of the people. Similarly, Claude Lefort (2000, 226) conceives of the political as the moment in which the symbolic form of society is instituted, while Ernesto Laclau (1999, 146) approaches the political as the disruptive moment of the dislocation of the social and the founding moment of society's institutionalisation.

Jean-Luc Nancy, Giorgio Agamben and Roberto Esposito attempt to 'common the political' by substantiating the self-instituting power of the people against the economism of both Marxism and neoliberalism. They contemplate ways of overcoming both the fragmentations and exclusions of gated communities by envisioning collectivities that bring together a plurality of singularities without enclosing them in fixed models – ethnic, cultural, ideological, or any other. They approach politics on the basis of a fundamental sense of coexistence, clearing the ground for social openness, solidarity, plurality and autonomy.

However promising this may seem, a number of critiques have stressed the political limits of this existential thought (Kioupkiolis 2017; Marchart 2012, 173–183; Elliot 2011; Wagner 2006; Dardot and Laval 2014, 14–15). Alexandros Kioupkiolis (2017, 284), in particular, has argued that Nancy, Agamben and Esposito remain stuck on an abstract level of philosophising, detached from any actual politics. He sets out to translate the existential ontologies of the common into more concrete politics by joining them to the political theory of hegemony and antagonism introduced by Laclau and Mouffe.

Nancy's theorisation was intended to refigure the political in light of a new ontological reflection on the common. Nancy (1991; 2000) takes his cues from Heidegger's philosophy and its argument that being-with – *Mitsein* – is essential to existence itself – *Dasein*. Coexistence is an archetypical ontological condition that predates 'society' and 'individuals'. Community is devoid of any essence, since it encapsulates a relation among a plurality of singularities; a reciprocal action based on openness, diversity and change.

In view of his ontology of being-with, the political consists in a social interaction in which singularities undergo consciously the experience of a non-organic community. Nancy's take on the common breaks with both traditional ideas of organic communities rooted in religion and ethnicity and the neoliberal dissolution of the community into an aggregation of individuals. The political implies freedom, equality, infinite justice and struggle, turning against atomisation, totality, homogenisation, sovereignty and the realisation of a fixed identity of soil, blood, community or the self.

Nancy endeavours to 'common the political', that is, to reconstitute politics according to his ontology of being-with. The task of politics would be to establish power on the basis of an incommensurable equal freedom, affirming the incomparable value of any singular being in relation to any other. Equality establishes the actualisation of incommensurable freedom, that is, the shared capacity for the creation of the novel beyond any pre-established framework.

However, Kioupkiolis (2017, 289), among others, has shown that this idea of politics is deeply controversial on account of its ontological framing. It remains on a high level of abstraction, not easily translatable to concrete political praxis. Philosophism can even be politically debilitating in some respects. Nancy fails to grapple with the political in the sense of power relations, divisions and antagonism. Missing is any in-depth engagement with questions of power, hegemony, antagonism and the forging of links among differences in order to construct collective subjects.

Like Nancy, Esposito (2011; 2012; 2013) has set out to conceive of another politics in light of his rethinking of the community. Taking his bearings from Heidegger and Bataille, he approaches the community as an opening to the other and an escape from the self. As in Nancy, community is a relation that joins multiple subjects without tying knots of belonging around language, soil and ethnicity. The common is indeterminate and, therefore, undetermined by any essence, race or sex.

Esposito breaks new conceptual ground by juxtaposing *communitas* with *immunitas*. The word 'community' derives from the Latin *communitas* (*cum* + *munus*). *Munus* means obligation and gift. Community, thus, entails an obligation, which exposes us to others in non-invasive ways. Exposure in its turn stimulates counter-processes of immunisation, that is, the retreat to the self. According to Esposito, immunisation is the present condition we live in, where we are experiencing political fundamentalism, nationalism, racism and fascism. Hence, politics should foster community and freedom to counteract immunisation. Difference should be affirmed as the bond that holds us together, connecting a diversity of singularities rather than exclusionary identities. Esposito admits that it is not an easy task to transform this philosophical formula into actual practice. Most importantly, he does not offer a way out. Philosophical abstraction besets Esposito's theorisation of the political and the community (Kioupkiolis 2017, 291).

In his *Coming Community* (1993), Agamben, too, takes up the themes of the political and the common to outline the politics of a community-to-come, where singularities act in common without holding on to any fixed identity. Pure singularities are indeterminate, variable and open to new possibilities. A community of singularities features a commonality and solidarity devoid of any essence and determinate content. It points to an open space of common appearance, action and co-belonging that cannot be represented by the state. Hence, the coming politics will no longer be a struggle for control of the state, but the opening up of spaces for singularities to freely coexist and interact.

However, like Nancy's and Esposito's, Agamben's politics of a 'community to come' remains vague and elusive. Kioupkiolis sums it up:

> Nancy, Esposito and Agamben remain stuck on the abstract level of a 'fundamental ontology' of being-together. They construe the 'common' as an ontology of co-existence detached from any actual politics. They do not wrestle with topical issues of democratic politics, such as the dominant forms of power and the specific modes of collective action which would uphold democracy in our times. (2017, 284)

4.2.2 Verticalism: Laclau and Mouffe

These valid criticisms notwithstanding, Kioupkiolis (2017, 293) makes the case that post-Heideggerian thought on community can be repoliticised in ways which rescue its value for contemporary politics. To this end, he embarks on politicising the common. A first move in this direction is to politicise ontology by recasting it as partial and value-laden. Ontology cannot lay claim to universal validity, since it is replete with conflict and antagonism. Therefore, the ontology of being-singular-plural is not a fundamental fact of the world, but a value to be pursued. It is not an already existing reality, but a call for democratic politics that need not be totalising but open, collective and deliberative.

Kioupkiolis (2017, 294–296) links the idea of community sketched out by Nancy, Esposito and Agamben with a variety of organisations and social movements, which have surged forth in the last decades, including local and digital commons. The commons exemplify the idea of community put forth by Nancy, Esposito and Agamben: an open relation among a plurality of singularities; a dialogue of plural voices; reciprocal action exposed to diversity and change; a practice of sharing; and politics beyond the sovereignty of capitalism and the state.

Kioupkiolis (2017, 296–302) further connects community politics with the work of Laclau and Mouffe (1985), who combine the plurality of being in common with the politics of hegemony. Laclau and Mouffe integrate often opposing elements from multiple philosophical strands: poststructuralism, psychoanalysis, analytical philosophy, Marxism and liberalism. One could plausibly read their work as a critical dialogue with Schmitt from within a postmodern and post-Marxist perspective. Laclau and Mouffe set out to reconfigure Gramscian hegemony by attuning it with post-Fordism and critiques of essentialism and economism. From their standpoint, hegemony signifies the representation of a totality by a particular discursive articulation of power, which is radically incommensurable with it (Laclau and Mouffe 1985, x). The *hegemon* need not be a revolutionary party or the working class, but any discursive field that takes on community-building action.

By 'discourse' Laclau and Mouffe (1985, 91–101) mean the structured totality resulting from any articulatory practice. Discourse signifies a decentred structure in which meaning is constantly negotiated and constructed (Laclau 1988, 254). The discursive formation cannot be unified in the experience or consciousness of a founding subject (Kant), nor in the progressive unfolding of reason (Hegel), nor in the logical coherence of its elements (structuralism). Subject positions are diverse and dispersed within a discursive formation. The type of coherence Laclau and Mouffe attribute to the discursive formation is close to what Foucault (1969) formulated as *regularity in dispersion*. Whereas Foucault maintained a distinction between discursive and non-discursive practices, Laclau and Mouffe expand discourse to every object of reality. Yet the fact that every object is constituted as an object of discourse dissociates from the realism/idealism opposition. As Laclau and Mouffe put it:

> An earthquake or the falling of a brick is an event that certainly exists, in the sense that it occurs here and now, independently of my will. But whether their specificity as objects is constructed in terms of 'natural phenomena' or 'expressions of the wrath of God', depends upon the structuring of a discursive field. (1985, 94)

At this point, Laclau and Mouffe's analysis meets up with a number of contemporary currents of thought – from Heidegger to Wittgenstein, Althusser and Derrida – that have insisted on the impossibility of fixing ultimate meanings due to the ontological primacy of difference and the subsequent overdetermination of meaning by (all) other meanings. Therefore, only partial fixations of meaning(s) exist. Borrowing from Lacan, they call the privileged discursive points of these partial fixations *nodal points*, that is, privileged signifiers that fix the meaning of a signifying chain.

Hegemony is the precarious articulation of *the particular* and *the universal* through a nodal point or master signifier. The dialectic interplay of particularity and universality introduces chains of equivalence amid conflicting alternatives. A chain of equivalence forms a common axis that connects different demands and projects by configuring the community and assuming the role of its representative. Hegemony, thus, entails the drawing of frontiers, exclusions and processes of concentration of power around common identities and representations. Representatives are considered necessary due to growing fragmentation and social complexity.

From a deconstructive perspective, hegemony is a theory of decision taken in the ontological terrain of antagonism, plurality, contingency and undecidability (Laclau and Mouffe 1985, xi). Antagonism reflects the conflict between 'friend' and 'enemy', whereby the presence of the latter negates the identity of the former and vice versa (Laclau and Mouffe 1985, 101–131). Antagonism is always present, since plurality generates disagreement and undecidability in the field of politics and justice.

Although for both post-Heideggerians and Laclau and Mouffe plurality is constitutive of community and the political, Laclau and Mouffe contradict the notion of plurality found in the work of Nancy, Esposito and Agamben as pure multiplicity. For Laclau and Mouffe, plurality essentially entails antagonism, conflict and division, which call for hegemony and articulation to establish precarious social formations. A randomly dispersed plurality of the common is unlikely to bring about broader social change as it stumbles upon fragmentation, conflict and vested interests. To achieve a minimum of convergence among diverse struggles and reach a critical mass, the commons need to endorse the politics of hegemony, which articulates wider political communities through chains of equivalence sustained by a modicum of collective identity (Kioupkiolis 2017, 297–298).

The hegemonic conception of the plural common converges partly with the thought of Nancy, Esposito and Agamben, since, for Laclau and Mouffe, what holds a radical democratic community together is not a substantive notion of the common good, but the shared values of freedom and equality. Radical democracy is plural, open and inclusive, maximising the autonomy of differences by expanding equality among all spheres of society. Each social struggle should accede to the maximum possible space to freely assert itself, while sharing a common identity promoted by egalitarian principles. Radical democracy comes to address the crisis of representation, which plagues liberal democracies, by escaping the pseudo-dilemma between neoliberalism and communitarianism, that is, between economic individualism and concepts of community based on tradition, language, ethnicity, religion and family. It does so by breaking with the post-political consensus of the 'centre' (Giddens 1994; 1998) and the concomitant topology of extremes by rendering all political positions equally vocal. Put differently, it aims to rearticulate left- and right-wing politics around the reconciliation of equality and freedom. Radical democratic politics manifests in various social struggles: urban, ecological, anti-fascist, feminist, anti-racist, ethnic, regional or that of sexual minorities (Laclau and Mouffe 1985, 143).

From a radical democratic stance, the common promotes the horizontal articulation of a multiplicity of spaces, social relations, movements and democratic practices that retain their partial autonomy with regard to the vertical politics of hegemony. Kioupkiolis (2017, 300), further identifies a tension between the vertical politics of hegemony and horizontal articulations of autonomy such as the commons. Laclau and Mouffe (1985, 133–177) attempt to mitigate this tension by envisaging a left-wing populism that integrates the common into a counter-hegemonic chain of equivalence, articulated against right-wing populism and the post-politics of neoliberalism. In this framework, autonomy is not opposed to hegemony, but is part of the wider hegemonic operation of radical democracy (Laclau and Mouffe 1985, 128, 151).

Kioupkiolis (2017, 300) insists that Laclau and Mouffe have not systematically worked through this tension to reduce the risk of hegemonic politics overshadowing the autonomy of the commons. Laclau and Mouffe neglect the fact that the political plays out in both conflict and consensus, antagonism and solidarity. The ontology of 'being-many-against' is coexistent with the ontology of 'being-many-together'. Most importantly, the identification of the political solely with antagonism and conflict reproduces a reversed essentialism that sneaks into the politics of hegemony in the form of the reification of hierarchy. To further illustrate this tension, Kioupkiolis (2010) contrasts the verticalism of Laclau and Mouffe with the horizontalism of Hardt and Negri.

4.2.3 Horizontalism: Hardt and Negri

Hardt and Negri (2000; 2004; 2009) suggest that capitalism now confronts not so much a working class as a 'multitude' of dispersed subjectivities, collectivities and movements springing up across the globe from post-Fordism onwards. The multitude creates common wealth through 'immaterial labour' that involves the biopolitical communicative and affective dimensions of networked production. With the aid of ICTs, biopolitics covers all aspects of the extended social factory by virtue of the rhizomatic function of immaterial labour which interconnects all social activity, from production to reproduction. Rhizomatic articulation replaces the antithetical binary of identity/difference with the complementary bind of singularity/community, which produces nodes through horizontal interactions of autonomous units. Thus, the Deleuzian 'rhizome' of the multitude features as an alternative to both hierarchy and the postmodern anarchy of dispersed differences.

Hardt and Negri (2009, viii) were the first to dissolve the misconception of the commons as certain properties or natural resources, introducing the notion of the common in the singular. The common represents the spontaneous production of common wealth by a multitude of dispersed collectivities. The common expands from the material world – natural resources – to the social reproduction of knowledge, language, information, affect and so forth. In contrast to Laclau and Mouffe, the common does not arise from the subordination of differences to an overarching particularity, nor is it limited to a horizontal space of autonomy within the broader articulation of hegemony. The common spans a distributed network that encapsulates the dynamic interaction of singularities. Interaction is coordinated by the swarm intelligence of the network via autonomous nodes through which connections unfold horizontally.

The distributed network enacts a new institutional logic, whereby the multitude is established as a constituent self-instituting power driven by the biopolitical reproduction of the community. The Internet and the open source movement are paradigmatic cases of the networked community. Hardt and Negri (2012, 71–72) envisage the digital subversion of capitalism by the self-instituting power of the multitude, which prefigures the advent of an 'absolute democracy' beyond authority, antagonism and exclusion. Absolute democracy would instantiate a collective governance of common wealth through the direct participation of all citizens.

Laclau (2001) and Mouffe (2008) hold that the spontaneism of the multitude slides into a quasi-teleological 'immanentism', that is, a positivism of social change that begs the question. A reversed essentialism slides into the work of Hardt and Negri in the form of the economism of the multitude that constitutes an ontological template of organisation already prefigured and embedded in social dynamics. But the lack of a concrete programme and centralised coordination means that it would do little to unsettle the present balance of power. The nomadism of the multitude cannot translate into an effective political counter-power capable of challenging the hegemony of capitalism.

4.2.4 Beyond Verticalism and Horizontalism: Commoning the Political

Absolute democracy is not feasible on both practical and political grounds. The complexity and the magnitude of contemporary societies, along with the political right to abstain, indicate the necessity of representation. Marina Prentoulis and Lasse Thomassen (2013, 181) have stressed that direct democracy unavoidably involves some inequality and hierarchy. The very realisation of equality presupposes some representational space. Therefore, there is no democracy without representation, no horizontality without verticality, no equality without inequality. Hierarchy and representation are operative in the 'networked systems' of various mobilisations today in the form of 'distributed leadership', stretching from the digital commons to social movements (Nunes 2014, 33–40). Distributed leadership suggests the rotational feature of leadership.

On the flipside, to stipulate that representation is intrinsic to politics, as Laclau and Mouffe presume, is to endorse ontological theses with a strong pretence to universal validity (Kioupkiolis 2010, 145). While various aspects of representation are necessary or appropriate for radical democracy, hegemonic representation is not. The essentialist leanings of the politics of hegemony can be partly attributed to its failure to grasp the innovative potential of creative agency inherent in the multitude. Hardt and Negri locate creative agency in history, inscribe it in social indeterminacy and anticipate its full play in future democracy. A democracy, instead, reformed along Laclau and Mouffe's lines, may be less supportive of freedom and equality. On the other hand, the ontology of a quasi-teleological *vis viva* substantiated in the form of the multitude fails to grapple with macro-structures. It is, thus, debilitating for actual politics.

Kioupkiolis (2019) intends to discharge the various tensions between verticalism and horizontalism. He endeavours to remedy the 'lack of the political' in the anti-capitalist commons by recalibrating Laclau and Mouffe's hegemony to tilt towards the commons and not the other way around. To prevent the absorption of the commons by the bureaucratic institutions of the state or the market, he holds that hegemony and the commons should perform with different strengths at different levels of the political. Hegemony should work outwards: against advocates of oppression, exclusion, homogenisation, injustice and inequality. The commons should work inwards: within the multiple organisations and social movements that abide by the principles of freedom and equality.

Kioupkiolis (2010; 2017, 301–302; 2019) draws on the work of Castoriadis and Foucault, among others, to integrate the two-way political transformation of the common into a post-hegemonic trajectory that transcends the dichotomy between horizontalism and verticalism. Hegemony persists within the horizontal multitudes of *glocal* commons, belying any notion of pure autonomous counter-strategy. Post-hegemony, instead, strives for autonomy, limiting hegemony to the minimum. It advances horizontalism against any residual verticality. Post-hegemony applies the following principles: 1) representation should emanate from the bottom through decentralised decision making based on openness, transparency and diversity; 2) accountability and revocability of representatives would secure democratic control by and for the commons; 3) regular rotation of roles and responsibilities should be exercised with the aim of empowering all the people with relevant skills and knowledge; and 4) self-management would thereby instil an ethical self-transformation through a subjectivation that would induce both individual and collective autonomy.

This new form of collective self-rule in effect prefigures a common democracy that practises political representation, government and self-transformation at its social roots (Kioupkiolis 2019, 203–204). Given that plutocrats and political elites are unlikely to give up their privileges through peaceful dialogue and elections, common democracy should advance deep readjustments in structural asymmetries of power through social struggle. Confrontation or collaboration with the state or maximum distance from it can variably represent the best option in different situations (Kioupkiolis 2019, 207). Common democracy calls for pragmatic hybrid politics, including new citizens' parties, participatory budgeting, civic initiatives and municipal confluences such as the Bologna Regulation for the Commons, Podemos and Barcelona en Comú.

Kioupkiolis aims to politicise the common by commoning the political, that is, by attuning hegemony to a post-hegemonic, non-hierarchical, open and pluralistic logic of the commons. Yet by politicising the common, Kioupkiolis runs the risk of fetishising the political, thus reproducing the essentialism he wishes to abolish. The political assumes primacy vis-à-vis the social, but it does not fully identify with it. The radical imaginary breeds the political and germinates into the social imaginary. The interpenetration of the radical and the social imaginary shakes the bottom-up axis of post-hegemonic recalibration. It instils a free flow of horizontal social interaction. Perhaps what I am suggesting here is a looser sense of the political, without resorting to any sort of radical anarchism or intersubjectivism. Practically, this would translate into the spontaneous mutual coordination of individuals and collectivities; the smooth compatibility between subjectivities and the common rather than a determined political process.

Kioupkiolis has succeeded in filling the gap of the political from within the commons. Post-hegemony can, indeed, be instructive as to how to produce chains of equivalence between alternative formations of community and governance; how to connect local and global commons; how to bring together and coordinate dispersed, small-scale civic initiatives; how to relate to established social systems and power relations in the market and the state, and so on. One could further consider post-hegemony as the political substratum of Bauwens and Kostakis's model of open cooperativism, combined to create a counter-hegemonic power against predatory capitalism and the state. What is still missing on both sides of the common are concrete policies for the commons to reach a critical mass. For the commons to become a sustainable model that can challenge capitalism, they need to provide a steady income to their members and gain broad civil trust, support and involvement. This task points to the creation of a social economy built around the commons. The role of the state and institutions here is pivotal to support the commons in various ways.

4.3 The Self-instituting Power of the Common

The work of Dardot and Laval can be read in conjunction with the attempt of Kioupkiolis to politicise the commons. Dardot and Laval take their cues from Marx, Foucault and Castoriadis, among others, to construe a new political theory of the commons. Like Hardt and Negri, they endorse the singular 'common' (2014, 56, 189–190). The common is not a good but a collective activity that engenders common goods under the constituency of a new collective subject. Like Hardt and Negri, moreover, the common is orientated against the current neoliberal hegemony by bringing to the fore the contradictions of capitalism and the state with regard to the commons. But whereas Hardt and Negri conceive of the common in terms of the multitude, which is supposedly apt to challenge neoliberal capitalism, Dardot and Laval (2014, 57) hold that local and digital commons are fragmented, divided and effectively subsumed under neoliberal capitalism. They, thus, embark on creating a new political conception of the common in a mission to put forward a collective agency for the commons. Their political intent is to juxtapose the counter-power of the common against the superpowers of the state and market capitalism.

Dardot and Laval's concept of the common is based on the interplay of power, law and institution. They understand power in the same vein with Foucault and Castoriadis as a productive force of social relations emanating from below. The commons do not spring up spontaneously from cooperation, as Hardt and Negri claim, but they must be actively striven for, fabricated and instituted. The same accounts for the collective subject of social change, which calls for a drastic transformation of dominant logics and habits among the vast majority

(Dardot and Laval 2014, 397). It pertains to the creation of a novel anthropological type, as Castoriadis would have it.

They thus turn to Castoriadis to demonstrate the common as the self-instituting power of the people. The common identifies with the self-instituting power of the social imaginary of the anonymous collective that creates new significations, norms and laws, forms of living, production and reproduction. The common advances the conscious collective praxis of instituting, which would be ongoing and reflective, thereby constantly challenging instituted norms and laws. This is to be distinguished from Hardt and Negri's constituent power, which accounts for the revolutionary moments in which a polity is founded.

From this vantage point, the current political struggles of the commons are sources of law making, aiming to establish the institutions necessary for the commons to escape the hold of capital and the state (Dardot and Laval 2014, 227). The politics of the common is not reserved to the experts of the state or the party, but extends egalitarian decision making to all domains of society. Thus, the common sets its face against representative democracy by practising participatory models of self-governance in pursuit of common ends (Dardot and Laval 2014, 455). The final gesture of politicising the common by Dardot and Laval (2014, 456–568) is the formulation of a set of propositions that would bring the law of the common into effect:

1. The politics of the common will not emerge from some sort of spontaneous encirclement of capitalism from the outside, nor from mass desertion. It is necessary to construct the politics of the common in all social spheres and on every scale, from the local to the global.
2. There can be no politics of the common without a rethinking of property rights concerning land, capital and intellectual ownership. The common assumes the inappropriability of things and, thus, the common right of use. Traditional ownership rights grant owners absolute use of their property and, therefore, imply no accountability before others. In contrast, the user of what is in common is tied to other users by the co-production of the rules that govern the common use. Rather than seeking to develop a form of property right that broadens ownership to include everyone, there must be a right of use that can be mobilised against property rights. Rights of use, then, rather than rights of property must be the juridical axis for the transformation of society. For there to be common and not simply shared things, there must be co-activity.
3. Labour in the neoliberal enterprise is the product of forced cooperation. The enterprise demands the active mobilisation of the workers while reducing them to simple operatives. The common, instead, is the route to the emancipation of labour via the establishment of workplace democracy.
4. Workplace democracy will be the institutional epicentre of the 'common enterprise', which contrasts both capitalist and state control.

5. The 'common enterprise' must expand into much broader collective associations to avoid being co-opted by market capitalism.
6. Collective associations must establish social democracy not in the form of the social (welfare) state that negates the common as the co-activity of the members of society, but as the return of the institutions of reciprocity and solidarity to the democratic control of society.
7. The state, thus, should transform into institutions of common participatory self-management.
8. The common should entail the institutionalisation of global public goods: (overused) globally indivisible goods (the ozone layer, the climate); (underused) man-made global public goods (scientific knowledge, the Internet); and goods that result from integrated global policy (peace, health, stability).
9. The common should evolve into a non-statist, decentralised federation of self-governing local communities.

Dardot and Laval's proposals sharpen our political understanding of the commons. They serve to draw out the politics of egalitarian, alternative commons and to nudge collective action in positive directions. Yet Kioupkiolis (2019, 95) argues that Dardot and Laval's politics of the common still reads largely as a wish list and a proclamation of principles and end goals of political action. What receives scant response in their work is the obvious and urgent question: How do we get there? How could we put all these propositions into practice, starting from the disabling circumstances that Dardot and Laval astutely lay out? The same criticism, however, can be levelled at Kioupkiolis's post-hegemonic politics. What prevents Dardot and Laval and Kioupkiolis from answering these questions is the absence of the more practical horizon of a post-capitalist transition, engineered by relevant techno-economic tools. Bauwens and Kostakis's counter-hegemonic model of open cooperativism could be a significant fix in articulating a more practical instantiation of the common as the self-instituting power of the people. The latter needs to integrate into a broader post-hegemonic political strategy aimed at putting forward concrete policies that will help the commons reach a critical mass.

4.4 The Community Economy

Gibson and Graham attempt to connect theory with praxis for the purpose of constructing a community economy. They draw on multiple sources to support this venture. Among others, they combine Louis Althusser's concept of overdetermination with Laclau and Mouffe's poststructuralist theory of hegemony to deconstruct capitalism and bring together a diverse alternative economy under a counter-hegemonic, post-capitalist project capable of transforming capitalism into the commons.

4.4.1 Overdetermination and Hegemony

Althusser (1972) appropriated from psychoanalysis the term 'overdetermination' to counter the essentialism inherent in the Marxian philosophy of history and political economy, which is predicated on the axiom that the structure of the economy encapsulates the essence of society, as crystallised in the means and relations of production (Gibson-Graham 1996, 26–29). By contrast, overdetermination asserts that every ontological site or process is constituted at the intersection of all others. Economy is one among many sites of society overdetermining and overdetermined by all others. Overdetermination reveals an ontological emptiness without a core essence. It signifies the openness or incompleteness of every identity; the ultimate unfixity of every meaning; the acentric totality of society that is not structured by the primacy of any social element or location. Society cannot be reduced to the conventional dialectics of A/non-A, supposed to explain the irreconcilable contradictions of capitalism. Instead, overdetermination unfolds on the ontological basis of difference and heterogeneity.

Gibson and Graham approach capitalism not as an essential or fixed entity, but as a differentiated multiplicity that bears a plural identity. If there is no essence or coherent identity of capitalism such as capital accumulation or exploitation, recontextualising capitalism in a discourse of economic plurality destabilises its presumptive hegemony and multiplies the possibilities of alterity (Gibson-Graham 1996, 15).

Gibson and Graham deconstruct the classical Marxist notion of class with the aim of construing an alternative economy based on the proliferation of differences across all fields of the social. In classical Marxism, subjects are social classes, whose unity is constituted around interests determined by their position in the relations of production, which are reduced to two fundamental and contradictory classes or positions: capitalists and workers. The uneven power of capitalists accounts for the exploitation of workers, manifested in the appropriation of surplus labour, that is, labour beyond what is necessary for the worker's reproduction. Capitalism's essence is capital accumulation via exploitation.

Gibson and Graham draw on the work of Stephen Resnick and Richard Wolff (1987) who elaborate a theory of economic difference, which is not reduced to the contradiction between the capitalists and the workers (Gibson-Graham 1996, 17–19). In the discursive space of diverse class positions, individuals may participate in a variety of class processes over time, potentially possessing multiple and shifting class identities. In the words of Mouffe (2005), identity is hybridised and nomadic. The term 'woman' has a different meaning in the context of 'marriage' and 'private life' than in the context of 'feminism' and 'lesbian'. Class processes of exploitation and surplus distribution may also include places outside the factory or the capitalist firm such as households, churches, schools, communities, cooperatives and other sites of (non-)economic activity.

> The different forms of class processes are merely part of an 'economy' that encompasses innumerable other processes – exchange, speculation, waste, production, plunder, consumption, hoarding, innovation, competition, predation – none of which can be said (outside of a particular discursive or political context) to be less important than exploitation. (Gibson-Graham 1996, 20)

Gibson and Graham's core argument is that contemplation of the variety of forms of exploitation and surplus distribution might enable the understanding of capitalism as a field of difference pregnant with post-capitalist possibility. Through the theoretical lenses of overdetermination and hegemony, they see the economy as a diverse space of recognition and negotiation capable of articulating a counter-hegemonic chain of equivalence under a community economy that can bring together the cooperative movement and the solidarity economy with the aim of challenging the current hegemony of neoliberalism.

4.4.2 Class and Second-wave Feminism

One of the driving forces behind this initial deconstruction has been the second-wave feminism inspired by the critique of Marxism and capitalism. By dislocating the economy from its 'base' and relocating it in the class positions dispersed across the totality of the social, the field of reproduction of labour power, which was totally neglected by Marx, now comes to the fore. Women engage in a non-class process of 'reproducing' the capitalist workforce through cleaning, nurturing, clothing and feeding, thus fulfilling the needs of capitalist production (Gibson-Graham 1996, 64). Women have been historically subservient to patriarchy, that is, a system of rules and practices of gender domination.

The struggles against capitalism, patriarchy and gender oppression, combined with the legitimisation of discourses of rights, is due to the rise of identity politics, which takes two opposing directions. On the one hand, it crystallises the critique of capitalism and classical Marxism by poststructuralism and post-Marxism in terms of difference and subject positions stretching across the social. On the other hand, it signals the feminisation of the labour market and the rise of individualism, marking the dominance of neoliberalism following the economic crisis of 1973 and the subsequent decline of social democracy. Feminism, thus, splits basically into a socialist and a neoliberal version, among others.

Gibson and Graham integrate feminism into a post-Marxist and post-capitalist perspective. In contrast to the classical Marxist tradition, which considers the working class as the collective agent of fundamental change and, therefore, the subject of history, Gibson and Graham (1996, 52) follow Resnick and Wolff (1987) in their definition of class as the social process of producing, appropriating (more commonly known as exploiting) and distributing surplus labour along both capitalist and non-capitalist domains. Gibson and Graham (1996, 49–51) invoke the influential work of Wright on the concept of class to illustrate the proliferation of intermediate and occasionally contradictory class locations. A worker, for example, who is exploited by a capitalist enterprise can also own a small business, potentially exploiting other workers. She or he can also be a freelancer, investor and member of a co-op, potentially at the same time.

Gibson and Graham (1996, 55–59) theorise class as an overdetermined social process lying at the intersection of all social dimensions – economic, political, cultural, natural. They understand society as a complex disunity in which class may take multiple and diverse forms. Primitive communist, independent, slave, feudal, capitalist and communal class processes often coexist. The household, for example, features a 'feudal' domestic class process in which one partner produces surplus labour in the form of use values to be appropriated by the other. The state may also be a site of exploitation, as well as educational institutions, self-employment, labour unions and other sites of production not necessarily associated with class. Thus, class struggles do not take place at a particular location in a social structure by fixed identities, but wherever surplus labour is produced, appropriated and distributed. This complex understanding of class suggests a range of non-capitalist class alternatives that could arise out of momentary and partial identifications between subjects constituted at the intersection of very different class and non-class processes and positions.

Traditional Marxism has focused on class relations of exploitation, whereas issues of distribution have often been relegated to the social democratic politics of reform. The privileging of exploitation over distribution stems from the essentialist reduction of economic totality to the core economic relation between capital and labour and the appropriation of surplus value, both of which would be eliminated by the socialisation of the means of production by the socialist state. From this standpoint, social democratic reforms could not touch on the core of the capitalist exploitation and could not, therefore, transform the economy.

Contrary to this essentialist viewpoint, Gibson and Graham (1996, 175–176) introduce a class transformation based on a class politics of distribution by bringing into existence or strengthening non-capitalist processes of surplus appropriation. They envision a diverse economic landscape in which non-capitalist class processes transcend the unsustainable materialistic growth of capitalist class processes by initiating sustainable growth along with non-growth (1996, 177–179). The achievements of second-wave feminism have given Gibson and Graham the confidence to identify with a broader movement that is actively retheorising capitalism and reclaiming the economy through an alternative economic activism aimed at globalising localised politics. Some examples are local movements for stakeholders' rights, aboriginal land rights and sustainable development.

4.4.3 A Weak Theory of a Community Economy

To further this movement, Gibson and Graham (2006, 1–8) introduce a weak theory of social transformation that does not purport to produce an exhaustive knowledge of the 'real', but to enact the 'possible' by opening up spaces for freedom and decision. Weak theory has first and foremost to confront the paranoia, melancholy and moralism of the traditional left – that is, nostalgia for the lost ideals of a failed revolution along with scepticism about any alternative that slightly deviates from those ideals. Weak theory needs to engage affect and emotions into practices of what Nietzsche called self-artistry or self-overcoming, and Foucault called self-cultivation or care of the self. Instead of hanging on to the mastery of 'pure' theories, activism would rather draw on the pleasures of friendliness, trust, conviviality and companionship and indulge in playfulness, experimentation, enchantment and exuberance. Practising weak theory allows us to de-exoticise power and create alternative discourses of subjectivation and collective action.

Gibson and Graham (2006, 53–60) combine Foucault's ethics (1985) with Laclau and Mouffe's poststructuralist theory of hegemony to develop an economic language for a politics of counter-hegemony, aiming to orient economic meaning and activity around non-capitalist points of subjectivation. They intend to dislocate the hegemony of capitalocentric discourse by articulating the language of economic diversity already existing alongside and within capitalism. Their purpose is to reconstruct and further induce collective action around the commons. To do so, they conceptualise economic language in terms of different kinds of transactions, labour and enterprises (2006, 60–72). The criterion Gibson and Graham use to illustrate difference is the production, appropriation and distribution of surplus in a capitalist, an alternative and a non-capitalist format within a diverse economy (Figure 4.1). They thus distinguish between market, alternative and non-market transactions; paid, unpaid and alternatively paid labour; capitalist, alternative and non-capitalist enterprises. What is usually regarded as the 'economy' – wage labour, market exchange of commodities and capitalist enterprise – comprises but a part of produced, exchanged and distributed value.

4.4.4 Transactions, Labour, Surplus

In capitalist market exchange, transactions follow the law of supply and demand in the commensurability of goods and services, voluntarily established by rational, self-interested producers and consumers. But markets are rarely voluntary, free and rational. They are naturally and artificially protected, monopolised, regulated and niched. Transactions are thus governed by context-specific power relations. Alongside capitalist market exchange, there is a huge variety

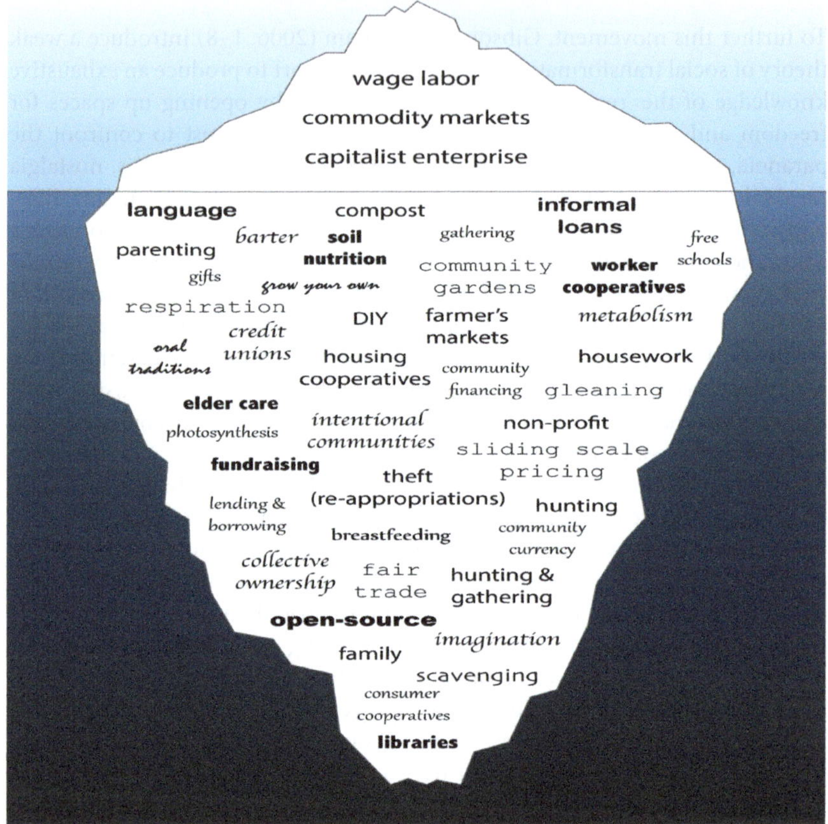

Figure 4.1: Diverse economies iceberg by Community Economies Collective (licensed under a Creative Commons Attribution-ShareAlike 4.0 International Licence).

and volume of non-market transactions such as goods and services shared in the household, provided by nature, given away by people and organisations, allocated by the state or traded within and between communities according to rituals of exchange. Alternative market transactions take place in the informal and underground markets in which goods and services are traded according to local and personalised agreements; in the exchange of commodities between and within worker cooperatives, where prices are set to sustain the cooperative; in the ethical or 'fair' trade of products, where producers and consumers agree on certain price levels; in local trading systems and currencies that foster local interdependency; and in the marketing of public goods and services produced by the state.

Labour also comes in different forms and compensations. Customary wage labour concerns the selling of labour power by workers/employees to employers in return for a monetary wage set at the level of context-specific markets. But there is also alternative paid labour. Worker cooperatives pay a living wage set by the cooperative. Workers in both capitalist and non-capitalist enterprises may receive capital payments according to their stake in the enterprise. Self-employed workers are paying themselves a wage. Others labour in return for payments in kind such as farmers, migrants and residents of a community. There is also the voluntary and unpaid labour performed in the household, the family and the neighbourhood or in the wider community. Yet many would say that this labour is compensated either in the form of money paid by a life partner or in the form of love, emotional support, protection, companionship, the sense of self-worth and reputation.

The main locus for the production, appropriation and distribution of surplus is the capitalist enterprise, where surplus is distributed towards expansion or to shareholders and managers. However, there are many alternative ways in which surplus is distributed both within or alongside the capitalist enterprise. 'Green' capitalist firms distribute part of their surplus to environmental concerns (for example, clean-up, investment in recycling technology and environmental monitoring). 'Socially responsible' capitalist businesses might commit to increasing workers' ownership of the firm or distribute surplus to social and community projects (for example, scholarships for local youth or provision of community infrastructures or services). State capitalist enterprises distribute surplus for the public benefit. Non-profit enterprises are by law not allowed to retain or distribute profits. In worker cooperatives, producers set their own wage and distribute a communal surplus. Self-employed producers set the surplus themselves and decide how to distribute it. In feudal agricultural establishments across the 'developing' world, surplus product is appropriated by the landlord. In many households, domestic work is performed by women and could be seen to be appropriated and distributed by a patriarchal household head.

Gibson and Graham (2006, 71) acknowledge that between the aforementioned economic practices intervene diverse forms of power such as co-optation, seduction, capture, subordination, cooperation, parasitism, symbiosis, conflict and complementarity. To address this alienation, Gibson and Graham (2006, 78) introduce the community economy, which could act as an empty signifier and, thus, concentrate economic power around a new nodal point, constituting a chain of equivalence for different forms of subjectivation and collective action. To do so, they deploy Nancy's concept of community as a form of 'being-with' along with the Foucaultian creation of new forms of subjectivities through embodied practices of ethical self-transformation (2006, 81–88). They attempt to resignify the discourse of the community economy accordingly, placing at the foreground of ethical deliberation and decision four key coordinates: necessity, surplus, consumption and the commons.

4.4.5 Necessity, Surplus, Consumption and the Commons

Necessity involves decisions about how much time to spend in production and in cultural and community practice, how much is a 'living wage', how much of the surplus to set aside for individual and community needs. Necessity varies across income strata, international boundaries, rural and urban contexts, different lifestyles, thereby rendering an ethical discourse indispensable to account for the various forms of interdependencies (trade-offs and flow-ons) that are enacted by relevant decisions on the part of the community. Decisions about necessary labour affect accordingly the production, appropriation and distribution of surplus among the individuals and the community.

Surplus distribution can be exploitative as in the case of appropriation by non-producers (as in the case of capitalist, feudal or slave class processes) or non-exploitative in the case of producer appropriation (in an independent or communal class process). In the diversity economy, surplus distribution takes heterogeneous forms. Save for the impossibility of aggregating incommensurables, Gibson and Graham envisage an (un)quantifiable surplus to be distributed according to the ethical decisions of the community. Relevant questions to be examined are the following: Who is to be included in the decision making over the rate of appropriation of surplus and its distribution? Under what conditions could surplus appropriation not be considered exploitative? How might non-producers have a say in the decision making? What are the social destinations of surplus distribution?

Decisions over necessary labour and surplus distribution have a direct impact on the level of consumption. In contrast to mainstream key economic indicators such as investment/expenditure ratios, debt-saving ratios, ratios of luxury expenditure to necessity expenditure and so forth, decisions of the community economy over how social surplus is to be distributed will aim to counterbalance productive versus non-productive activities, as Marx put it – that is, activities directly involved in production and activities that consume social surplus in replenishing the commons, such as finance, management, and so on.

The commons, thus, refer to commonly used or distributed resources/ infrastructures – whether agricultural land, a gene pool, the atmosphere, a wilderness, a database, a fishery, the Internet, community facilities and support systems or even the whole set of relationships comprising a community economy – that provide direct input into social and physical well-being and reproduction. A crucial decision, therefore, concerns the management of the two-way flow between the commons and the surplus-generating machine of production. In other words, a balance needs to be struck between the commons and the alternative economy.

4.4.6 The Cooperative Enterprise: The Mondragon Case

Gibson and Graham consider the cooperative enterprise to be the best model to strike this balance. However, cooperativism has faced acute criticism. The traditional left has argued that the cooperative movement is insignificant and, therefore, cannot challenge the dominance of capitalism (Gibson-Graham 2006, 109–111). This would require instead a socialist centralised state along with a revolutionary movement. In the view of the revolutionary socialists, cooperative ownership of the means and output of production does not resolve many of the thorny issues associated with the distribution of the proceeds of labour, which include economic rent, that is, payment for land and other non-labour requirements of the production process that influence the price/value of the produced product. In addition, cooperativism has been economically inefficient and prone to group individualism, conflicts of interest and sectorism. Cooperatives are politically conservative and uninterested in solidarity with more political struggles, hence the need for centralised governance of the interdependencies of the various economic sectors.

Gibson and Graham (2006, 111) counter-argue that the essentialism of the traditional left rules out alternative options by offering a limited typology of organisations and practices for overcoming capitalism. They invoke the Mondragon experience as a prominent example of the cooperative movement in Spain (2006, 101–102). Mondragon came into being in the 1950s under the guidance of a Catholic priest, Father Arizmendiarrieta, who inspired a sense of group solidarity in the Basque region, where the first cooperative enterprises in Spain were pioneered. The success of the cooperatives lies, first, in their choice not to heighten local competition and, second, in price protection through high tariffs imposed by the Spanish state on industrial imports. Focus on local markets led to the proliferation of cooperatives and the parallel building of backward and forward linkages among local cooperatives, which then expanded by developing new markets outside the cooperative system. Today, the Mondragon Cooperative Corporation (MCC) involves over one hundred cooperatives, employing more than 30,000 worker-owners in a broad spectrum of sectors, including manufacturing, retail, finance, education, healthcare and insurance.

Admission to membership and governance is open to all democratically, on the principle of 'one member–one vote'. Each cooperative is set up with a number of elected councils that see to day-to-day governance and carry out the decisions made by the annual General Assembly of all councils. The council is made up of general members and a co-op manager appointed for a four-year period. Self-management is based on the free flow of information, access to training, internal promotion, consultation and negotiation about all decisions, including the distribution of surplus, the setting of wage and price levels, investment, consumption, innovation, and so on. Democratic participation, thus, cultivates ethical subjects capable of decision making.

Wages are pegged to a base wage comparable to the base wage outside the Basque region. Wage differentials are minimised to a ratio of 1:6 between the bottom worker and the top manager. The decision to set wage levels at the level of the community and not the individual cooperative prevents the driving of wages down below the community-wide level or the jeopardising of the production of surplus by raising wages above this level. It therefore values community sustainability over personal consumption. 10% of annual profits are allocated to social or charitable institutions, as enforced by Spanish law, and the remaining 90% of the surplus is saved to be reinvested in enterprise development. Members may draw on the interest accumulated in their accounts, but they cannot touch the principal until they retire or resign. This allocation of surplus to 'forced saving' has subordinated personal economic gain to the expansion of the cooperative system. The centrally administered investment fund is a monetary form of commons utilised to create more co-ops and employment.

Innovation is vital for the cooperatives to remain competitive with respect to capitalist enterprises. There is a strong emphasis on efficiency, high productivity, market expansion, new business growth and market development. Job classifications and individual performance goals are important, as they translate into the level of wages and dividends paid to the worker-owners. But automation does not result in unemployment, since workers are employed by other cooperatives or retrained to work in new production processes and paid a maintenance wage. This cost is met by reallocation of surplus at the level of the individual cooperative, supported also by the common funds of the Caja Laboral bank.

The cooperative principles of the MCC have produced a cultural commons fostered periodically through the guiding principle of *equilibrio*, intended to strike a balance between conflicting interests and confront the dangers of exclusivism and group individualism (Gibson-Graham 2006, 105). However, the expansion of the MCC through the appropriation of surplus from non-cooperators has resulted in participating in both exploitative and non-exploitative practices. Thus, the MCC is succumbing to group individualism. Gibson and Graham (2006, 123) admit that this hybridisation is threatening the very identity of the MCC. However, notwithstanding the pitfalls and shortcomings, they hold that the success of the MCC thus far offers important empirical evidence against the degeneration thesis of the traditional left (2006, 124). It can thus function as an example of the 'community economy' that adequately addresses the core concerns of necessity, surplus, consumption and the commons.

Gibson and Graham (2006, 165–196) conceive of the Mondragon experiment as one among many projects, initiated by NGOs and collective finance schemes in concert with local, national and international communities, provincial and municipal governments, that altogether could create a counter-hegemonic community economy against the neoliberal narrative of corporate growth. In contrast to the myth of trickle-down economics, the community economy generates bottom-up, interdependent dynamics of affection, cooperation and solidarity capable of replacing capitalism with the commons.

4.4.7 Critique of the Community Economy

Cooperatives are at a critical crossroads today. There is, indeed, a whole range of emerging areas of development, including local food systems, organic farming and agricultural co-ops, social care, child care, healthcare and community services, affordable housing, environmental stewardship, solar and wind energy, cooperative capital and solidarity services, all showcased in Quebec, Japan, Germany, the US, the UK, Greece, Italy (Emilia Romagna) and Spain (Catalan Integral Cooperative). In addition, the Internet has given rise to platform cooperativism across the globe. The digital commons can further support the transformation of platform cooperativism into open cooperativism between the commons, ethical market entities and a partner state, all sharing common knowledge and practices.

However, Gibson and Graham's theoretical reconstruction of the community economy contains a degree of wishful thinking. Major problems and challenges are yet to be solved. Incompleteness of representation, internal conflicts of interest and bias towards exclusion undermine the democratic role of cooperatives (Simon 2019, 557–571). There is a tendency for established cooperatives to become large organisations, many of them operating transnationally across Europe and internationally, such as Mondragon, some of the large Italian multinational co-ops, international cooperative banks and insurance companies (Restakis 2010). The challenges of growth and the demands of capital most often push towards demutualisation and disconnection from membership and local communities. More and more large co-ops are concerned with maintaining their positions and growing. Consequently, their political role evaporates; they do not envision themselves as organisations with a political and social mission, thus disregarding their cooperative identity. Too many co-ops are unwilling to share their branding and marketing with other co-ops within the movement to convey a collective cooperative idea. Cooperatives are, thus, often absorbed into the capitalist system, turning into private, for-profit, shareholder-owned corporations. This is evident, for example, in the agricultural sector in Canada and Ireland during recent years (Restakis 2010).

Therefore, there is an increasing polarisation and inequality within the cooperative movement, and an increasing divergence of interests and culture between the very large and successful cooperatives and the emergent small and medium-sized cooperatives, with innovative ideas and forward thinking, which remain at the margins. Small and medium-sized co-ops face a whole set of challenges: problems with access to capital and training; lack of entrepreneurial and managerial skills; the absence of institutional support from governments, larger co-ops and NGOs; and the existence of gated communities unwilling to share and cooperate with each other.

4.4.8 Affect, Sexuality, Reproduction

Conclusively, the argument that affect is indispensable for ethical practice and interlayered with thought highlights the crucial role of empathy within a community-orientated economy. In contrast to Arvidsson and Peitersen, who monetise affect, Gibson and Graham demonetise affect and render it the political criterion *par excellence* for managing the economy. Affect should indeed not be subordinate to analytical logic. As Castoriadis (1987, 278) has noted: 'As much as the colour is an equation, to the same extent the dream is the meaning of the dream.' Not everything that counts can be counted, and not everything that can be counted counts. Rather than relying on a cost–benefit analysis to orient policy, the community economy would employ a common stock of affect to address unemployment, poverty, job alienation, solitude and the like. To do away with individualism, nihilism and cynicism, it is necessary to reinvent humanism by rendering affect a central political category.

Yet the identification of affect with labour reproduces the economism it aspires to abolish. It is one thing to resignify a diverse economy in terms of affect, and another thing to identify affect with the economy. Art, culture, enjoyment, entertainment, friendship, sexuality and love intersect with the economy, but that does not qualify them as economic categories. The personal is political to the extent that a free space is recognised within the private and public sphere, untouched by economic categories, even when otherwise named. Economism is renamed to the extent that affection, subjectivation and self-realisation revolve around necessity and not the other way around. Marx himself was acutely cognisant that freedom transcends the field of necessity.

The inclusion of affect and reproduction into the community economy, while enormously important, silences the role of sexuality, by identifying the latter with affection. Sexuality remains by and large a taboo for society in general and for the commons in particular. Sexuality is suppressed by the conjunction of capitalism and neoconservatism, converting either into labour power or into an unspoken pleasure hidden in the private 'chatrooms' of monogamy, prostitution and pornography.

A discourse on the importance of reproduction in the community economy focused solely on affection often tends to identify sexuality with a compulsive sentimentalism producing the reversed sexual suppression of an economically and politically diverse neo-puritanism. Sexual desire and even sexual discourse alone are often synonymous with sexism. Rather than sexuality being the natural coefficient of affection, it has turned into a commodity subject to a cost–benefit analysis, an auction, a transaction, a deal, a negotiation, a neoliberal gender and class struggle. But between neoliberalism, sentimentalism and sexism lies the vitality, spontaneity, pleasure and health of the body and the senses, incorporated into the organic reproduction of society. Feminists, gay movements and various singularities and commonalities have demonstrated in recent decades that the struggle against domination presupposes the affective expansion of freedom into the creation of new values, forms of life and types of relationships. Issues regarding the role of sexuality, affection and gender equality in the reproduction of a commons-orientated economy need to be addressed by a broader, holistic, political perspective that combines concrete policies into a post-hegemonic multi-format strategy.

4.5 Autonomous Marxism and the Common

This section examines the common in the context of autonomous Marxism, which has a deep and wide genealogy, ranging from strands within council communism and anarcho-communism to the activities of the group Socialisme ou Barbarie, founded by Castoriadis and Lefort (Cleaver 1979). Of particular centrality within this orbit of thought is a cluster of theorists associated with the *operaismo* movement of the 1960s and 1970s, including Maria Rosa Dallacosta, Mario Tronti, Paolo Virno, Michael Hardt and Antonio Negri (Dyer-Witheford 1999, 129). What makes the *operaismo* movement a distinct branch of autonomous Marxism is the insight that new modes of knowledge and communication, produced by the post-Fordist deployment of ICTs, operate not only as instruments of capitalist domination, as proclaimed by the Frankfurt School, but also as liberatory resources of anti-capitalist struggle (Dyer-Witheford 1999, 130, 248).

This line of argument integrates postmodern and post-Marxist elements into a neo-Marxist perspective to emphasise not the irreversible, self-contradictory power of capital, as declared by orthodox Marxism, but class struggle as the main driver of social change. This section focuses on the work of Nick Dyer-Witheford, Massimo De Angelis, George Caffentzis and Silvia Federici.

4.5.1 The Circulation of the Common

Following the current of autonomist Marxism, Dyer-Witheford (1999; 2015) builds on the concept of the common, introduced by Hardt and Negri, to advance the circulation of the common against the circulation of capital. Dyer-Witheford (1999, 248) continues on the *operaismo* line of argument to render technology the main terrain of class struggle, reprogrammed to install the circulation of the common against the circulation of capital. He puts forward a particular version of autonomous Marxism, attuned to resonate against a neoliberal or bourgeois interpretation of technology, the latter gathered under various terms such as 'post-industrialism', 'the knowledge society' and the 'information revolution'.

The 'information revolution'

Often former Marxists, a number of theorists such as Peter Drucker (1968), Daniel Bell (1973), Alvin Toffler (1980) and Nico Stehr (1994) pre-empted the end of class struggle, hailing the coming of the information revolution, which is supposed to install a technical fix for the contradictions of capitalism (Dyer-Witheford 1999, 26–64). Post-industrialism marks the transition from industrialism to the information society, where the increasingly systematised relationship between scientific discovery and technological application makes theoretical knowledge the central wealth-producing resource of society. Industry is succeeded by information. Automation progressively liquidates labour, thus either rendering work redundant or creating intellectual and service jobs devoid of toil, drudgery and alienation. Management is now replaced by the technocracy of high-tech and artificial intelligence, introducing new dimensions of autonomy and job satisfaction. Digitisation culminates in the perfection of the market or even its transcendence. Capitalism eventually produces social welfare through better communication and information, yielding a self-regulatory ethical pluralism reflecting consumer society. Democracy gives way to post-democracy (Crouch 2004), where the post-politics of consensus and bargaining (Giddens 1994; 1998) replace democratic politics. Finally, life itself mutates into the synthetic life of cyberspace and artificial intelligence, transforming nature to the benefit of human needs.

Dyer-Witheford juxtaposes the optimistic versions of 'better capitalism' or 'beyond capitalism' with a reinvented Marxism produced by the critical appraisal of various Marxisms. He reminds us that the complexity and ambivalence of Marx's own writings on technology have given rise to different perspectives on the relation of machines to social change (Dyer-Witheford 1999, 114). There is a polarity in Marx's machine writings (Dyer-Witheford 1999, 83–84). At one pole, technology is an instrument of capitalist domination. On the other, it is a means for the liberation of the working class from the strains of capital. Depending on how much emphasis is put on each pole, different future scenarios exist. Dyer-Witheford focuses on three main points of reference: 1) scientific socialism, 2) neo-Luddism and 3) post-Fordism.

Scientific socialism

Scientific socialism, also referred to as classical or orthodox Marxism, extends a line of Marxist thought which conceives of technological development as an autonomous motor of history, heading straight to the dissolution of capitalism and the triumph of socialism (Dyer-Witheford 1999, 78–79). At a certain stage in this trajectory, the technological means of production come into conflict with the relations of production, thus igniting social revolution. Dyer-Witheford (1999, 84) picks up the work of Ernest Mandel as perhaps the most sophisticated recent example of this school of thought, which also represents a magisterial attempt to counter the presumed supersession of Marxism by the 'information revolution'. Mandel argues that there have been three fundamental stages in capitalism: market capitalism, monopoly capitalism and late capitalism. The central feature of late capitalism is the increasing level of automation. Far from representing a post-industrial society, late capitalism consists in the full industrialisation of the economy. The economic centrality of scientific and technological knowledge does not mark an unprecedented historical epoch, but simply represents the specific form of bourgeois ideology in late capitalism.

Capitalist ideology is masked under the veil of the acclaimed omnipotence of technological rationality.

Mandel maintains the Marxian argument that new technologies bring capitalism closer to its inevitable collapse. The centrepiece is the falling rate of profit, consequent on the rising organic composition of capital. Recall that, in the Marxist theory of value, profit is the outcome of the exploitation of living labour through the production of surplus value (S). The rate of profit is the ratio between surplus value and total capital, $S/(C+V)$, where C stands for constant capital (raw materials and means of production) and V for variable capital (labour power). The ratio between constant and variable capital is the organic composition of capital. According to Marx, competition forces capitalists to increase via automation the ratio of constant to variable capital. But the more automation expels workers from production, the more the rate of profit falls, causing faltering investment, class conflict and revolutionary crisis.

Many theorists see this projected inevitability as a special case prevalent only under certain conditions. They invoke the counter-tendencies, some of them identified by Marx himself, against the falling rate of profit: falling costs of the means of production, the absorption of surplus capital in the production of new physical infrastructures, monopolisation and the opening of new areas of exploitation with a low organic composition, accelerating circulation (through advertising, marketing and innovation) and the integration of the world market via telecommunications (Harvey 2010, 94).

David Harvey (2010, 89–101) asserts that Marx's account of the falling rate of profit is unduly simplistic. Castoriadis (1988, 249–253) notes that the rate of profit can fall, increase or remain the same, other factors being variable. For example, automation not only lowers the prices of commodities and labour, but may also lower the price of automating machinery, permitting an increase in the technical composition of capital – more machines relative to workers – while leaving untouched the overall value composition. Dyer-Witheford (1999, 90–91) contends that such possibilities are significant enough to cast doubt on Mandel's teleological certainty. For him, this is not to confirm the post-industrialists' dream of unimpeded market expansion, but to see capitalist crisis as contingent upon social struggles over the scope, scale and velocity of commodification rather than being guaranteed by capital's own contradictory logic. As he puts it: 'the more immediate problem and opportunity is that posed not by the composition of capital and the rate of profit, but by the composition of class, on which depends the rise or fall in what could be termed "the rate of struggle"' (Dyer-Witheford 2015, 28).

Neo-Luddism

Neo-Luddism, the second Marxist interpretation of technology, dates back to the work of the Frankfurt School and authors such as Max Horkheimer, Theodor Adorno and Herbert Marcuse, who introduced the notion of technology as domination, which actually revives the nightmarish aspects of Marx's writings on technology. They stress the manipulative and oppressive character of technological rationality, eventually serving the needs of capital. The analysis of technology-as-domination split during the 1970s and 1980s into two streams: one focused on the labour process, the other on mass media (Dyer-Witheford 1999, 94–98). Contrary to the optimism of post-industrialist theorists, authors such as Harry Braverman and David Noble have claimed that the computerised labour process is simply an extension of Taylorist anti-human authority to the level of cyberspace (Dyer-Witheford 1999, 94–96). On the mass media front, scholars such as Herbert Schiller, Vincent Mosco, Dallas Smythe and Nicholas Garnham have deepened Adorno and Horkheimer's analysis of the 'culture industry' as a means of ideology perpetuation and mind manipulation (Dyer-Witheford 1999, 96). While information society theorists argue that the proliferation of ICTs democratises opinion formation, Schiller counter-argues that the giant media corporations filter the flows of information to intensify the commodification of social relations, excluding anything that is against the interests of owners and advertisers (Dyer-Witheford 1999, 97–98).

The critique of technology-as-domination cuts much deeper than the neutrality thesis adopted by both information theorists and scientific socialists (Dyer-Witheford 1999, 97–102). The neutrality of technology is an illusion, given that the algorithmic setting of machines and computers embodies social choices and political intentions. Therefore, it does not suffice to apply technology in the service of socialist ends instead of capitalist ones, as scientific socialists have it. Neo-Luddites call, instead, for resistance. But they do not go so far as to advocate the redesign of technology in favour of the circulation of the common. They are thus limited to a self-defeating diagnosis by overestimating capital's capacity to command labour with dead labour (Dyer-Witheford 1999, 103). Recall that, for Marx, dead labour is labour embodied in machines. Neo-Luddites recede into a radical pessimism, evoking dystopian visions of indoctrination, surveillance and robotisation. However, in their justified attacks on the automatism of both information theorists and scientific socialists, they have reinvigorated Marx's vision of technology as a contradictory process, yielding countervailing possibilities for contending agencies. This latter strand is extended by theorists as diverse as Bauwens and Kostakis, Rushkoff, Hardt and Negri, Johan Söderberg and Dyer-Witheford himself.

Post-Fordism

Post-Fordism, the third Marxist strand relevant to technology, aggregates a diversity of theoretical positions converging on the technological reconciliation of workers with capital (Dyer-Witheford 1999, 104). From this viewpoint, post-Fordism comes close to the positions of information society theorists. Specifically, the French 'Regulation School' of political economy understands capitalism as a mode of production evolving through different 'modes of regulation' such as Fordism and post-Fordism (Dyer-Witheford 1999, 104–108). Fordism integrated a Taylorist division of labour with intense mechanisation. As such, it marked capitalism's post-Second World War 'golden age', put forward by Keynesian policies. Post-Fordism represents capitalism's response to the multifaceted crisis of the 1970s. It signals a new era of capital accumulation driven by the deployment of ICTs to disaggregate Fordist mass production and cheapen labour by outsourcing it across the globe. From the perspective of the 'Regulation School', this capitalist restructuring was accompanied by flexible specialisation, Japanese management and Swedish humanised workplaces, featuring various models of labour/capital cooperation, which could culminate in the future in a high-tech 'new deal' between capital and workers.

Many Marxists entirely reject the categories of Fordism and post-Fordism as mystifications of capitalism's inhumane development. Yet for Dyer-Witheford (1999, 112), this is not a reason to throw the baby out with the bathwater. Theorists who use the category of post-Fordism have often been more alert to the capital restructuring in the early 1970s than their more orthodox Marxist critics. Yet several versions of post-Fordism underplay conflict and class struggle within this capital restructuring. Ultimately, they go along with a post-Marxist politics that claims to go 'beyond' capital and class. Dyer-Witheford (1999, 13) criticises, in particular, the post-Marxism of Laclau and Mouffe on the grounds that it dissolves the distinction between capital and class into the populist pluralism of social movements. However, he is mistaken to assume that Laclau and Mouffe's project is not radical enough to challenge capitalism, since their goal is, precisely, to form a counter-hegemonic political alliance against neoliberalism. Interestingly, I argue later on that this alliance might fill the gap of the political in Dyer-Witheford's own circulation of the common.

Cycles of struggle: The socialised worker

After having brought to light the deficiencies of all three Marxist approaches to addressing the challenges put forward by information theorists, Dyer-Witheford (1999, 127–514) elaborates a critical version of autonomous Marxism that builds upon class struggle supported by ICTs. To analyse class struggle, autonomists use the concept of class composition, which consists in the decomposition and recomposition of the cycles of struggle between labour and capital.

The autonomists identify three major cycles of struggle in the twentieth century, revolving around the professional worker, the mass worker and the socialised worker (Dyer-Witheford 1999, 143–169). Taylorism eroded the craft skills of the professional worker of early capitalism, transforming him into the mass worker of the Fordist assembly line, thus furthering what Marx called the formal subsumption of the worker to the needs of capital. The mass worker reacted through the strengthening of unions, the negotiation of a social wage, including welfare, unemployment benefit, pensions, health insurance, and so on, and the eruption of social movements, including women, students, and black and immigrant communities in the 1970s. Capital responded with the post-Fordist restructuring of the factory base through automation and the globalisation of manufacturing, backed by the neoliberal policies of Reagan and Thatcher. Capital succeeded, thus, in splitting up the production cycle and dispersing the workers once organised under working teams. What followed was the dismantling of the unions and the welfare state, with repercussions that resonate up to the present.

Capital's informational restructuring gave rise to the subject of a new cycle of revolutionary struggles: the socialised worker. Negri (1988, 90) uses the term to refer to the expansion of the working class to society through the commodification of reproduction, communication and consumption, which intensifies the circulation of capital via the technologically advanced circuits of advertising, marketing and finance. The feminist wing of autonomous Marxism, represented by the work of Mariarosa Dalla Costa and Selma James, has argued that the reproduction of labour power within the social factory occupied a crucial but neglected role (Dyer-Witheford 1999, 135). Marx downplayed the role of gender, as represented by the unpaid labour of women. The socialisation of labour blurs waged and non-waged labour. The activities of women, students, consumers, shoppers and viewers are now directly integrated into the production process, actualising what Marx called the real subsumption of society into capital. The concept of the socialised worker is in fact a synthesis of 'old working-class theory' with the rise of 'new social movements' through the spectrum of a neo-Marxist perspective that combines the postmodern element of difference with the Marxist element of class struggle.

Autonomous Marxism analyses capitalism as a collision of two opposing vectors: capital's exploitation of labour and workers' resistance (Dyer-Witheford 1999, 138). The role of technology is twofold: it can be utilised as an instrument of capitalist domination, shattering scientific socialism's myth of automatic scientific progress, while functioning as a site of class struggle. Unlike the Frankfurt School theorists, autonomist theorists do not find the scope of the social factory grounds for despair, since now the expanded network of social relations refracts into a multiplicity of points of conflict with capitalist domination. If capital interweaves technology and power, this weaving can be redone to the benefit of class struggle. Technoscience, Negri (1989, 85–86) suggests, becomes the main site for the reappropriation of power.

The global cyber-proletariat

Dyer-Witheford (1999, 248–262; 2015) uses the autonomist concept of 'cycles of struggle' to update class composition in the digitised era. He focuses on cyberspace, where ICTs appear not just as instruments for the circulation of commodities, but simultaneously as channels for the circulation of struggle. In this newly socialised space of capital encompassing all sites of the social factory, the cybernetic spiralling of the capitalist vortex multiplies the sites of its disruption, destabilisation and destruction. As Dyer-Witheford puts it:

> Our travels along capital's data highways have discovered rebellions at every point: people fighting for freedom from dependence on the wage, creating a 'communication commons', experimenting with new forms of self-organisation, and new relations to the natural world. Such movements are incipient and embattled, yet undeniable. Indeed, without in any way diminishing the magnitude of the defeats and disarrays suffered by counter-movements over the last twenty years, I suggest that there are now visible across the siliconised, bioengineered, post-Fordist landscape the signs of a strange new class recomposition. (1999, 261)

Dyer-Witheford (2015, 32) distances himself from Hardt and Negri's concept of the multitude, and focuses on proletarianisation, understanding the latter as a contradictory process both of and against capital. He draws on several authors who have built on Marx's (2008/1848, 33) definition of the proletariat as the class of modern wage-labourers who, having no means of production of their own, are reduced to selling their labour power for subsistence. Karl Heinz Roth (2010) uses the term 'global proletariat' to refer to the displacement of agrarian populations from the land by biotech corporations; the consequent engagement of vast surplus populations in the electronic supply chain and in the diffuse 'service sector'; the mobilisation of women both for waged and unpaid domestic labour; and the escalation of unemployment, underemployment, insecure labour and unpaid work. Ursula Huws (2003; 2014) coined the term 'cybertariat' to emphasise the precarious nature of digital labour such as neo-Taylorised clerical, data entry and office work, crossing with unpaid labour at home. Huge numbers of jobs in the digital economy fall under this term inasmuch as they are routine, subordinate and poorly paid.

Dyer-Witheford (2015, 133–138) introduces the term 'global cyber-proletariat' to cover all these diverse aspects of proletarianisation, ranging from the physical exploitation of workers in coltan mines and electronics factories in Africa and China to women's unpaid domestic labour and the digital labour of prosumers on the Internet. Proletarianisation goes hand in hand with de-proletarianisation, that is, the expansion of professional and intermediate strata, and of capital's managerial sector, staffed by the boom of university and college 'edu-factories' (Dyer-Witheford 2015, 126). Yet the rise of the middle class is haunted by re-proletarianisation in times of crisis, generating both right- and left-wing populism (Dyer-Witheford 2015, 141). Most importantly, the expansion of both proletarian segments and intermediate strata with their contradictory locations is subordinated to capital's info-tech oligarchy of the '1 per cent' (Dyer-Witheford 2015, 141–143). To provide some indicative figures: by 2013, the richest 1% of the world controlled $110 trillion, or 65 times the total wealth of the poorest 3.5 billion people; of 3 billion workers globally, only 1.6 billion receive a wage or salary; the other 1.5 billion are engaged in subsistence activities, living on less than 2 dollars per day (Dyer-Witheford 2015, 134, 142).

Proletarianisation and de-proletarianisation are traversed by new imperialist world conflicts, new economic crises and migrant flows, 'upward and downward' moving proletarians and realignments of capital. In this constant flux of the capitalist vortex, class composition is both fractal and fractioned; fractioned insofar as it varies sharply from region to region, fractal in that it is fractured into multiple points of class struggle across the globe, with each one often bearing different but overlapping regional and national features (Dyer-Witheford 2015, 129). Capitalism does not progress into better capitalism by virtue of an ever-expanding middle class, as the information theorists would have it, but evolves into digital capitalism, which applies automation in all domains of the social factory to transform the labour process into a new type of fixed capital that sustains the cycle of production, circulation and finance (Dyer-Witheford 2015, 33). Digital capitalism propels its moving contradiction – the simultaneous induction and expulsion of labour – into a new circulation of struggle.

The circulation of the common

Marx deemed the cellular form of capitalism to be the commodity. He famously modelled the circulation of capital in the formula: $M\text{-}C\ (LP/MP)...P...C'\text{-}M'$. Money (M) buys the commodity (C), that is, labour power (LP) and the means of production (MP), to produce (P) new commodities (C') that are sold for more money (M') divided into costs, profit and reinvestment.[11] Dyer-Witheford (2006) reverses Marx's formula to generate from the circulation of struggle the circulation of the common. The commodity is a good produced for exchange between private owners. The common is a good produced to be shared among collectivities. Dyer-Witheford calls these collectivities associations, whether tribal assemblies, socialist cooperatives or open source networks. If C stands for the common and A for association, the circulation of the common consists in the following formula: $A\text{-}C...P...C'\text{-}P'$ repeated ad infinitum. Associations organise shared resources to produce more shared resources, which in turn provide the common wealth for the formation of new associations.

Dyer-Witheford (2006) distinguishes three sub-circuits within the circulation of the common: the terrestrial commons (that is, the customary sharing of natural resources in traditional societies), planner commons (that is, command socialism and the liberal democratic welfare state) and networked commons (that is, the free associations of open source software, peer-to-peer networks, grid computing and the numerous other socialisations of technoscience). He envisions a twenty-first-century communism as a complex unity of terrestrial, planner and networked commons. The terrestrial commons correspond today to the need to preserve the biosphere from a predatory capitalism responsible for climate change. The great message of the green movement is the imperative of new habits and norms in production and consumption. Interestingly, Dyer-Witheford is one of the few authors to explicitly address the issue of sexuality in relation to the creation of a new subjectivity. He calls for a shared corporeality, stretching from safe sex to recycling, emissions and cloning.

As such, the terrestrial commons develop alongside the planner commons. Dyer-Witheford (2006) contrasts this with the libertarian utopia of spontaneous, decentralised, individualised coordination. He deems it impossible to address global poverty and climate change without an ethic of public ownership and planned resource allocation at all levels, municipal, national and global. The planner commons encapsulate a radical democratic regime based on a de-statification that devolves administrative power to a multiplicity of associations. As he puts it: 'The role of government is redefined as supporting collective initiatives rather than substituting for them, diffusing rather than concentrating control, nurturing social transformation from the bottom up rather than engineering it from the top down.' (Dyer-Witheford 1999, 209) The terrestrial and the planner commons are info-mediated by the networked commons of ICTs. The digital commons produce a post-scarcity software economy in which collaborative creation and shared use generate more robust and abundant goods. Peer-to-peer networks of micro-fabricators, designers, activists, prosumers and all sorts of citizens constitute the networked socialisation of co-production and co-governance. Networked horizontalism shares the means of production and governance along the currents of the terrestrial and planner commons.

With regard to ICTs, communication commons could provide extensive opportunities for citizen involvement in technological research, development, design and strategy. Publicly funded organisations and programmes could assist communities to conduct research and develop technologies shaped to their needs, while monitoring, testing, evaluating and debating the consequences of specific lines of R&D both at universities and corporations. *Contra* the corporatisation of technoscience, the networked commons can contribute to the commonification of scientific research and knowledge along democratic and ecological lines. Thus, the circulation of the common could sustain the circulation of struggles towards a new cooperativism, which links worker cooperatives with the commons (Dyer-Witheford and de Peuter 2010).

Critique of the circulation of the common

Dyer-Witheford's circulation of the common is much in line with Bauwens and Kostakis's model of open cooperativism, with the exception that he remains mute as to the relation of the common to the market. He alludes to the complex interdependencies and possible contradictions of the three circuits of the commons. He lacks, however, a political appraisal of the critical interconnections both within and outside the commons. He posits the circulation of the common against the circulation of capital. But he does not touch on the grave dependence of the commons on capital and the state. How can the commons compete with the superpowers of corporations? Once again, the absence of concrete policies to mobilise a critical mass to join the commons is telling. For this reason, post-hegemonic holism helps articulate a chain of equivalence between sociopolitical power and the advance of the common against the current neoliberal assault. The coalescence of relevant economic and sociopolitical powers is indispensable to creating the institutional, monetary and legal tools for the empowerment of the people against the subordination of the common to predatory capitalism and the state.

Dyer-Witheford offers one of the most detailed and nuanced analyses of class composition in the digital age, of which just a brief outline has been presented here. He contributes to the renewal of neo-Marxist thought by promoting the circulation of the common against the circulation of capital. But let us play devil's advocate here and consider for a moment a plausible counter-argument. Let us assume that there is a considerable part of the middle class, either salaried professionals or freelancers, particularly in the USA, Northern Europe, Canada and Australia, with an average annual salary in the range of $35,000 to $65,000,[12] who are more or less satisfied with their job and their current standard of living. Let us take here the example of a coalminer in Australia, who earns $65,000 a year and might also own a block of rental units and a portfolio of shares in leading companies or have a share in another small business. Potentially his wife also has a part-time job or contributes to the family business, and they live happily together with their children. It is highly unlikely that they would condescend to a potential diminution of their salary if that was the cost of exiting the capitalist economy and entering the commons. How are these groups of professionals going to be convinced or incentivised to join the circulation of the common? What if capitalism progresses into a regulated, ethical, green cyber-capitalism, alleviating its periodic crises? What would then be the purpose of the commons apart from constituting a marginal socio-economic system subordinate to capitalist operation?

The discussion should not focus on whether capitalism is suicidal or not, but on the comparative institutional advantages of the commons with regard to the core structural contradiction of capitalism, that is, the division between directors and executants. One of the main challenges lying ahead for the commons is how to transform the cynical, individualistic, self-interested maximiser of our current capitalist societies into a *homo cooperans*. This involves the task of nudging a novel anthropological type that combines the liberal ideals of freedom and pluralism with the right to equality and economic democracy. Post-hegemonic holism expresses precisely the need to radically transform the core structure of society by cross-fertilising top-down and bottom-up commons strategies into cross-regional policies that span the entire psyche and body of the social. The ultimate goal is to transform capitalism into the post-capitalism of the commons.

4.5.2 *Omnia sunt communia*

De Angelis (2017) offers another formulation of the circulation of the common against the circulation of capital. Drawing on systems theory, cybernetics and autonomous Marxist-feminist political economy, he approaches the commons as social systems in which resources are pooled by a community of subjects engaging in commoning, that is, the self-governing and reproduction of the community and its resources (2017, 119). The commons are tripartite systems consisting of the following elements: 1) the common-pool resources or common wealth, 2) the community and 3) commoning. Silke Helfrich (Bollier and Helfrich 2012) has emphasised the praxis of commoning as a social process: the commons is neither the resource nor the community that determines protocols for its stewardship, but the dynamic interaction between all these elements. De Angelis, too, highlights the relational/contextual character of the commons. It is the social relations of commoning and governing the commons that give to a good the meaning of a common good. As he puts it:

> The limit to what can be considered a common good is entirely contextual and political, depending on the political boundaries, imaginative capability and involvement in doing in commons that a community can give itself […] Starting from the position that we should not confuse the commons with resources held in common, I approach commons as social systems in which resources are pooled by a community of subjects who also govern these resources to guarantee the sustainability of the resources (if they are natural resources) and the reproduction of the community, and who engage in commoning, that is, doing in commons that has a direct relation to the needs, desires and aspirations of the community. (2017, 63, 90)

De Angelis's approach to the commons differs from Ostrom's in that the analytical distinction of the latter between limited common-pool resources and open access commons may not entail a categorical exclusion but an unavoidable interrelation. De Angelis (2017, 146) portrays a post-capitalist vision of commons-based peer production in which the commons is the main socio-economic and political system, and open access is a necessary subsystem within the commons, allowing for the reverse co-optation of capitalism and the state. Open access is a loophole of state and market operation into the circulation of the common and vice versa. This point is crucial in theorising the relation of the commons to capitalism and the state and can be further analysed through De Angelis's critique of Marx.

From the circuit of capital to the circuit of the common

In chapter 4 of *Capital*, Marx identifies two formulas for the circulation of commodities: C–M–C and M–C–M′, where C stands for commodities, M stands for money and M′ for more money than originally invested, including profit. C–M–C represents the simplest form of circulation of commodities, as manifested by merchants and petty traders, and M–C–M′ is the general formula of capitalism, wherein money is invested into the production of commodities to generate profit. Capital accumulation fuels the cycle of capitalist growth ad infinitum.

De Angelis criticises Marx for largely focusing on capital, thereby neglecting the role the commons play in social reproduction, since capital has fed off the commons since its inception. De Angelis's goal, instead, is to subsume the circuit of capital to the circuit of the commons (Figure 4.2). To do so, he draws on the work of radical feminists such as Silvia Federici (2012) to represent the work of reproduction as a sub-circuit of the capital circuit (De Angelis 2017, 188, 189). In the capital circuit at the bottom of Figure 4.2, money (M) buys labour power (LP) and the means of production (MP) come together in production (P) as commodities (C) to produce new commodities (C′) and money (M′). In the reproduction circuit at the top, the money obtained in exchange for labour power (LP) is used to buy commodities (C) that are processed in the household through labour (P*), which reproduces physical and psychological labour power (LP*) to be sold again to capital. Thus, the unpaid labour in the household and numerous other sites of social interaction reproduces the labour power of capital. To the extent that patriarchal relations are dominant, the great bulk of reproduction labour is performed by women. Both paid and unpaid labour are part of capitalist production, expanding capital's work period to 24/7 long before post-Fordism.

De Angelis (2017, 192–194) zooms out of the specific reproduction of labour power and regards the top circuit in Figure 4.2 as applicable to any commodity according to the formula C–M–C. He integrates the formula C–M–C into the commons circuit, thus aiming to subsume capitalism into the commons. The formula C–M–C describes not only the general metabolism of the reproduction of labour power, but also the circuit of production of commodities involving the self-employed, petty producers, craft people, small organic farmers, associations, and so on. For De Angelis, the circuit C–M–C is but a moment of social reproduction. Thus, it is integrated into the *commons circuit* (Figure 4.3), where Cs stands for the commons, CW for common wealth and A for an association or the community. Common wealth is divided into the non-commodity form (NC) pooled together within the sphere of the commons and the commodity form (C) acquired from within the market economy. The commons enter the market economy either as a buyer – on the left-hand side of the formula – or as a seller – on the right-hand side of the formula – or receive money as a transfer from an outside source (the state or another organisation).

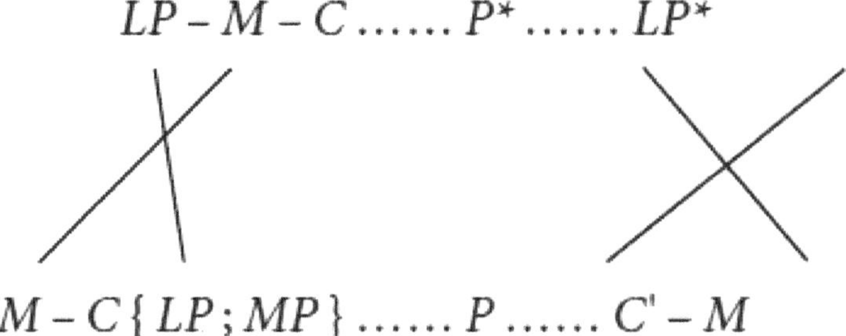

$$LP - M - C \ldots\ldots P^* \ldots\ldots LP^*$$

$$M - C\{LP\,;MP\}\ldots\ldots P \ldots\ldots C' - M$$

Figure 4.2: Coupling between production and reproduction circuits (from De Angelis 2017, 189).

$$\left.{}^{NC}_{\,C}\right\}CW\Big\}\,Cs\ldots cm\ldots Cs\,\Big\{{}^{A}_{CW}\Big\{{}^{NC}_{\,C}$$

Figure 4.3: The circuit of the commons (from De Angelis 2017, 193).

Whereas money in capitalism is an end in itself, in the commons it is a means for the social reproduction of the commons.

De Angelis's (2017, 312) core argument is that the commons need to develop a relational stance towards capitalism and the state with the aim of structurally coupling them from a position of power and changing them in favour of the commons. To this end, he introduces the mechanisms of 'boundary commoning' and 'structural coupling' (2017, 265–355). Whereas the former describes the internal cooperation between different commons, the latter entails the making of external deals with capital and the state, allowing the commons to expand within capitalism and reach a critical mass through a 'middle class explosion'. De Angelis hopes, thereby, to subvert capitalism towards a post-capitalist commons.

Critique of the circuit of the common

By expanding Marx's commodity formula into social reproduction as such, the latter incorporated into a 24/7 market economy, De Angelis, like Gibson and Graham, cannot avoid but fall into the trap of a reversed economism. By generalising the activity of labour to sociality by and large, there is no space left for free time. De Angelis fails to distinguish sufficiently between the economy and different societal activities.

De Angelis (2017, 64–74) has successfully conceptualised the interdependence between material and immaterial commons, highlighting the reproduction basis of the digital commons: food, care, energy, housing, education, social relations. Software and hardware need energy and minerals for their industrial production, while software developers themselves need to eat, rest and reproduce. Once again, one cannot but notice the complete absence of sexuality in De Angelis's discourse on reproduction, unless abstractly identified with social relations. Moreover, De Angelis does not offer a solution as to how the immaterial production of the digital commons can connect to material commons and reproduce common wealth in the long run. He develops a tautological version of the commons which is supposed to gradually outflank the state and capital by reducing the power of the latter to regulate the complexity and variety of the former. De Angelis begs the question, as he expects the commons to grow by creating the common wealth that will allow it to interlace, multiply and outpace the state and capital. The issue is, precisely, how to create the common wealth necessary for the multiplication of the commons given the grave dependence of the latter on the state and capital. From this standpoint, reformist strategies such as Bauwens and Kostakis's model of open cooperativism could significantly complement De Angelis's post-capitalist vision of the commons.

Like Dyer-Witheford, De Angelis (2017, 180, 359–387) advocates a synergy with social movements. He, too, distances himself from the multitude of Hardt and Negri, considering it a fuzzy concept and, by extension, not consistent with issues of social justice, redistribution of wealth or the ecological transformation of social production. But De Angelis's own approach is somewhat vague. He acknowledges the deep relation of the commons movement to law, politics and the media. Yet he does not provide any concrete proposal as to how this relation could develop in the interests of the commons. A post-hegemonic politics of the common could address this deficit by articulating a chain of equivalence between various social movements and the commons, hypostatised into relevant orthogonal policies and practices.

4.5.3 The Reproduction of the Common

The work of George Caffentzis (2013) and Silvia Federici (2004; 2012) can be read in conjunction with De Angelis's work. Caffentzis and Federici (2014) represent a more radical version of the commons, as they reject the 'capitalist commons' introduced by Bauwens and Kostakis for fear of the commons being co-opted by market mechanisms. Like De Angelis, they hold that the digital or immaterial commons cannot have an autonomous substance in their own right, as they depend for their reproduction on both capitalism and the material commons. The digital or immaterial commons should connect, instead, to the material commons and form an alliance of anti-capitalist commons, orientated against capitalism and the state. Caffentzis and Federici (2014, 101) regard the commons as 'associations of free individuals' established by way of commoning, that is, constitutive social practices of self-governance rooted in autonomy, equality, reciprocity, collective decision making and power from the ground up.

They do not, however, suggest any concrete solution as to how the commons can reproduce themselves under conditions of grave dependence on the state and capital. They advocate a continuous class struggle of the commons. Yet they do not indicate any specific form this struggle could take with respect to the state and capital. Interestingly, they point to the inherent contradictions of the commons, such as disorganisation, disempowerment, claustrophobia, patriarchy, xenophobia and gated communities. But they do not offer any resolution of these contradictions. Most importantly, they do not see the potential inherent in technology to bridge the gap between material and immaterial production and help the commons reproduce themselves within, against and beyond capitalism and the state.

Reproduction, unpaid labour, sexuality

The work of Federici (2012) is of particular importance, since it represents a feminist approach to the commons that brings to the fore the gender biases inherent in the social reproduction of capitalism. She develops a feminist critique of Marx:

> At the center of this critique is the argument that Marx's analysis of capitalism has been hampered by his inability to conceive of value-producing work other than in the form of commodity production and his consequent blindness to the significance of women's unpaid reproductive work in the process of capitalist accumulation. Ignoring this work has limited Marx's understanding of the true extent of capitalist exploitation of labour and the function of the wage in the creation of divisions within the working class, starting with the relation between women and men. (2012, 92)

Marx famously illustrated that the wage hides the unpaid labour that goes into profit. But the identification of labour with the wage also hides the extent to which family and social relations have become relations of production in the social factory of capitalism (Federici 2012, 35). Federici (2012, 33) holds that the family is essentially the institutionalisation of unwaged labour, of women's wageless dependence on men and, consequently, the institutionalisation of an unequal division of power that has disciplined both men and women. Sexuality is a form of labour, serving the needs of capital. Sex is work for women, a duty that has been subordinated to the reproduction of labour power (Federici 2012, 25). The economic dependence of women on men is the ultimate control over sexuality as work, rendering it one of the main occupations for women, with prostitution underlining every sexual encounter. For this reason, she holds that a wage paid to women would secure the economic independence of women with respect to men's income.

Federici considers the reproduction of human beings the foundation of every economic and political system and places the struggle against sexual discrimination in an anti-capitalist framework. She goes along with De Angelis and Caffentzis in arguing that the digital commons do not question the material basis of the digital technology of the Internet (2012, 142–146). She makes the case that digitisation and automation cannot robotise 'care' except at a terrible cost for the people involved. However, she does not elaborate on what an anti-capitalist framework would be like. She calls for the communalisation/collectivisation of housework, rendering the 'commoning' of the material means of production the primary mechanism by which a collective interest and mutual bonds are created. Yet she does not explain how to reverse the co-optation of the commons by capital. Federici does not see the link that the digital commons can provide between material and immaterial production in transcending both the state and capitalist production.

Paradoxically, Federici (2012, 147) believes that it is women, historically the house-workers and house-prisoners, who must take the initiative to reclaim the house as a centre of collective life on which the economy is built. But by assigning the task of commoning/collectivising reproduction primarily to women, she concedes to a naturalistic conception of 'feminity', thereby reproducing the gender biases she wishes to abolish. Federici eventually produces a generalised argument, resulting in a limited view on a rather nuanced problem. Patriarchy reigns supreme partially due to women themselves often condescending to a sexist distribution of labour, which attributes to both women and men 'naturally' predetermined gendered roles of femininity and masculinity. This often produces a reverse exploitation that assigns to men the role of the 'hunter', the 'provider', the 'protector', the 'macho', and so on. Patriarchy often switches roles with matriarchy, either via direct oppression or indirect sentimental compulsion, sexual strikes, passive aggression and other forms of gender struggle. Federici poses the problem as a gender struggle of women against men when it would be better addressed as a struggle of both men and women against bi-gender oppression and capitalist exploitation. To quote Simone de Beauvoir: 'The point is not for women simply to take power out of men's hands, since that wouldn't change anything about the world. It's a question precisely of destroying that notion of power' (Card 2003, 202).

The Foucaultian concept of power

Foucault's analysis of power could be illuminating here, as he points to the multidimensional power dynamics that flow across the various social strata. Power is a form of governmentality that introduces a mode of action upon other actions. 'To govern, in this sense, is to structure the possible field of action of others' (Foucault 1982, 790). Power is not the domination of one individual over another, of one group over another, of one class over another; it is not an attribute in the possession of some, with others being subject to it (Foucault 2003).

Power 'comes from below'. It is intentional and productive, but impersonal and non-subjective inasmuch as it expresses a variety of anonymous aims and objectives (Foucault 1978, 94–96). Power is relational, decentralised, multidirectional and mobile. But power is also transitionary. Power comes always with resistance. Power produces resistance as anti-power, resulting in a relentless struggle of anonymous bodies, desires, thoughts, forces, energies, and so on.

Yet what Foucault misses in his governmental analysis of power is the sadomasochism often lying in the initial contradiction of capitalism that forms the core structure of society: the division between directors and executants (Papadimitropoulos 2018d). The psychodynamics of slave and master variously reverberate across feudalism, colonialism, racism, fascism and capitalism. A contemporary analysis of power ought to take into account the capitalist division between directors and executants, which penetrates the social factory, exerting an asymmetric economic power of capital over class (Balibar and Wallerstein 1991). Feminism often takes a neoliberal turn that perpetuates the vicious cycle of sadomasochism, with women reproducing men's corporate power. Corporate fascism becomes bi-gendered, spreading across the social factory and often aligning with the extremes of political power: Nazism and Stalinism.

Escaping the pitfalls of economism

Capitalism floods society and Federici unwittingly goes with the flow. It is one thing to consider the circuit of capitalist production expanding in the social factory by subsuming social reproduction as such, and another to identify labour with life as a whole. The latter entails the hidden assumption that time is money, that is, concealed labour, as Marx would have it. But still, can we imagine a free living space beyond money? The commons movement endeavours to address this question when it deviates from economism and envisages the abundance of the commons gradually overcoming the scarcity of market capitalism on the model of post-capitalism. Indeed, can we imagine a non-militaristic version of a *Star Trek* society where scarcity will have become obsolete and human beings free to enjoy the abundance of the commons? The point I want to raise here is that we should allow ourselves to envision a space uncolonised by the economy; a space of playfulness, affection, sexuality, creativity, spontaneity and self-realisation; a space of unconditional freedom equivalent to the cultural expression of difference and plurality. The task of post-hegemonic holism would, then, be to further the emergence of commons-orientated subjects capable of supporting a post-capitalist economy based on the commons.

4.6 Communism and the Common

The argument so far has been that there is a significant lack of the political in all three camps of the common: the liberal, the reformist and the anti-capitalist.

They lack a critical political reflection that would translate into a set of concrete policies that could incite a critical mass to join the commons. The last stage in reconfiguring this argument is to oppose the post-hegemonic politics of the common to the communist horizon, which represent two radically different concepts of the common: the common as the self-instituting power of the people and the common as the idea of communism. The first is horizontally articulated, whereas the latter comprises a variation of classical Marxist themes of the common, some of them espousing the party as the main agent of communism, and others adopting more hybrid formats.

In the wake of the 2008 financial crisis and the expansion of neoliberalism thereafter, several radical voices have cast doubt on non-statist horizontalist politics such as the Occupy movement and the Spanish and Greek Indignados, since they are considered to lack organisation, leadership and strategy, thus fading into a narrow, ephemeral and impotent reaction. Given the concentration of power in the capitalist elites, collective action that does not come to grips with state institutions is destined to failure (Juris and Khasnabish 2013, 379, 385–386). Several such critics have, thus, revived the forceful politics of communism, reasserting the classic role of the state and the party for a potent revolutionary politics (Badiou 2009; 2010; Dean 2009; 2012; 2016; Žižek 2008; 2010; 2013).

The idea of communism encapsulates several values that throb at the heart of the commons such as common ownership, egalitarianism and collective self-government. Yet at the core of the same tradition figure policies and practices that are at odds with the pluralism, openness and horizontalism of the commons such as the centrality of the state and the party, top-down direction, totalitarian control, authoritarianism, violence, terror and the idolatry of leaders (Kioupkiolis 2019, 96–97). Therefore, the signifier is not up for resignification, since it clashes head-on with the self-instituting power of the people, which has been elaborated here as the quintessential concept of the common. I go along with Kioupkiolis (2019, 97) who holds that communism makes no sense in a bid for a post-hegemonic politics that could win over large swathes of people. My twist is that central mechanisms are essential to any serious social change. To further illustrate this argument, I take up here three prominent proponents of the communist idea, Slavoj Žižek, Jodi Dean and David Harvey. The chapter concludes with the more hybrid approaches of Paul Mason and Christian Fuchs.

4.6.1 The Idea of Communism

Žižek's (2010, 217) political ontology takes its cues from Hegel, Marx and Lacan to reclaim a communist past of state and authoritarian politics, incarnated in the dictatorial power of the party. Žižek rejects any postmodern, post-industrial and post-Marxist dynamics. His professed position is that what the left needs today is a Jacobin-Leninist party to impose the classic communist principles of strict egalitarian justice, disciplinary terror, political voluntarism and trust in the people (Žižek 2010, 217, 219).

Four antagonisms and the privatisation of the general intellect

Žižek (2010, 211) takes on Marx's notion of communism not as an ideal, but as a movement which reacts to the actual social antagonisms of capitalism. He identifies four such antagonisms today (2010, 212–213): the looming threat of ecological calamity, the inappropriateness of the notion of property for so-called intellectual property, the socio-ethical implications of new technoscientific developments (especially in biogenetics), and new forms of apartheid, new walls and slums.

The first three antagonisms revolve around what Hardt and Negri call the 'commons': the commons of external nature plagued by pollution and over-use, the commons of culture (language, communication, education, infrastructures) facing privatisation, and the commons of internal nature (the biogenetic inheritance of humanity) threatened by new biogenetic technology. The fourth antagonism – the gap that separates the excluded from the included – differs qualitatively from the others in that it reveals the proletarianisation setting the ground for the reaction against the enclosure of the commons, the latter marking out a new phase of separation of the people from the objective conditions of their lives (Žižek 2010, 214).

The central problem today, for Žižek (2010, 221), is how the late capitalist hegemonic role of 'intellectual labour', foreseen by Marx as the evolution of the 'general intellect', affects Marx's basic scheme of the separation of labour from its objective conditions, and of revolution as the subjective reappropriation of those conditions. Žižek (2010, 221) argues that Marx's classic notion of commodity fetishism in which 'relations of people' assume the form of 'relations of things' has to be radically revised, since, in immaterial labour, the relations of people are themselves the very material of exploitation. As he puts it:

> Far from being invisible, social relationality in its very fluidity is directly the object of marketing and exchange: in 'cultural capitalism', one no longer sells (and buys) objects which 'bring' cultural or emotional experiences, one directly sells (and buys) such experiences. (2010, 221)

Žižek (2010, 224) argues that the contemporary production of multitude, rather than sowing the seeds of revolution, creates excess capital that initiates a new privatisation process by means of new enclosures. He admits that the expansion of the relations of production outside the factory setting requires a revision of Marx's conceptual scheme (Žižek 2010, 224). He sides with Negri in claiming that exploitation is no longer possible in the classical Marxist sense. Marx did not envisage the possibility of the privatisation of the general intellect itself. Exploitation today increasingly takes the form of rent. The result is not the self-dissolution of capitalism, but the gradual transformation of the profit generated by the exploitation of surplus labour into rent appropriated by the privatisation of the general intellect (Žižek 2010, 224–225).

Whereas today's intellectual workers are, superficially, not separated by the objective conditions of their labour (their PCs), they remain cut off from the social field of their work, from the general intellect, because the latter is privatised by capital in terms of intellectual property (Žižek 2010, 225). Capitalist competition is not strictly defined in terms of lower costs and higher levels of exploitation, but in terms of the monopolisation of the general intellect (Žižek 2010, 225). The same holds true for natural resources (for example, oil, gas, etc.), the exploitation rate of which is set according to the rent paid to the owners of the resource relative to its scarcity. This is *par excellence* the case with the United States, which remains the dominant financial power due to its reliance on the extraction of rents, either on the basis of its advantages in technological and financial innovation or from intellectual property rights.

Three fractions of the working class and the need for representation

For Žižek (2010, 225–226), the general intellect today splits into three fractions of the working class: the enlightened postmodern hedonism and liberal multiculturalism of the intellectual class, the populist fundamentalism of the working class, and the more extreme forms of the outcast fraction. Capitalism has sought to control these fractions by putting workers in competition with each other along the lines of race, sex, ethnicity, religion, and so on. Examples of this social disparity are the wage gap between men and women, wage distinctions between blacks and whites as well as Hispanics and Asiatics in the United States, and so on (Harvey 2010, 62). Capitalism advances various forms of social darwinism, that is, the scientific propaganda of the survival of the fittest, imposed by elites on society over millennia so as to 'divide and rule'.

Žižek (2010, 226) calls for the unity of the proletarians under a revolutionary party that will take over the state and impose the 'dictatorship of the proletariat'. The goal is to centrally transform the state to operate in a 'non-statal way' that feeds on the direct involvement of grassroots movements, the circumvention of the state apparatus and reliance on the collective will of the people (Žižek 2008, 155). Communism is based on the tetrad of people–movement–party–leader (Žižek 2013, 188). People and movements are coordinated by the party and the leader.

Žižek (2008, 337–80) is highly critical of the anti-statist left – from Simon Critchley to Hardt and Negri and Alain Badiou – who take a stand in favour of grassroots self-organisation. For Žižek, social activism, revolts and grassroots movements do not suffice to change the system, since they lack organisation, strategy and efficiency. Mass mobilisations of thousands of people organising themselves horizontally remain a minority movement in today's societies; hence, the need for representation. People do not know what they want, and they, therefore, demand a master to guide them; hence, the centrality of the party and the leader (Žižek 2013, 189).

Critique of 'statist' Marxism

Žižek is right to insist on the crucial role of proper leadership and the state in a communist revolution. However, the exercise of power from outside or above is at odds with egalitarian self-government and autonomy. Kioupkiolis (2019, 110) is right to counter-argue that parties, leaders and representatives should act as 'vanishing mediators' who empower society, enlarge the scope for collective self-activity, but make themselves gradually redundant. This is exactly the meaning of the commonification and 'destatification' of the state found in the work of Bauwens and Kostakis and Dyer-Witheford respectively. This is also the meaning of the post-hegemonic politics of the common put forward by Kioupkiolis. The common thread binding these approaches is the self-instituting power of the people articulated by Castoriadis and Dardot and Laval.

Kioupkiolis (2019, 108) correctly holds that Žižek champions a communist conservatism insofar as he dreams of the worst nightmares of authoritarian communism – the state, the Party, the Leader/Master, disciplinary terror and political voluntarism. The resurrection of the gulag for outcasts and dissidents would not be appealing at all to the contemporary 'liberal' cognitariat, the highly educated, networked and impoverished middle-class youth and hipsters, even to the 'populist' working class who easily fall prey to authoritarian and racist versions of capitalism that promulgate the exclusion of immigrants.

Žižek is right to argue that the identity politics of postmodern difference reproduces the mainstream values of individualism, profit, hedonism and competition, recycling cynicism, nihilism and conformism in the vortex of cultural capitalism. Whence, I argue, comes the need to integrate postmodern difference into the pluralism of the commons. I go along with Žižek in advocating a holistic, transnational, centralised, leftist, counter-hegemonic alternative to capitalism. Yet this does not entail the abolition of democracy and the establishment of the dictatorship of the proletatiat by the hegemony of the party/leader. Post-hegemonic holism rather stresses the need for a radical deepening of democracy on all levels of the social. A constructive elaboration on contemporary techno-social innovation built on the commons, as in the cases of platform and open cooperativism, bears the potential to open up a more democratic horizon rather than a revival of top-down Leninist-Stalinist communism. In any case, the tension between verticalism and horizontalism in either a Marxist or post-Marxist perspective would rather advance grassroots self-governance.

4.6.2 The Crowd and the Party

Jodi Dean offers a deeper understanding of the contemporary technological landscape than Žižek. She endorses Žižek's Lacanian Marxism to construe a communist political theory with the aim of politicising the left to subvert communicative capitalism.

Communicative capitalism

Dean draws on the work of Saskia Sassen (1996) and David Harvey (2005) to demonstrate the current convergence of networked telecommunications and globalised neoliberalism into a communicative capitalism that traps contemporary subjects into an intense circulation of information for the purposes of commodification and profit maximisation. Instead of technology rendering the market the site *par excellence* of democratic aspirations, communicative capitalism repurposes democratic ideals in ways that strengthen globalised neoliberalism. The high-tech fantasy of abundance, participation and wholeness dissolves into the circulation of content for the sake of circulation, generating the very negation of communication, that is, a communication without communicability (Dean 2009, 26). The instability of meaning in communicative capitalism corresponds to what Žižek terms the 'decline of symbolic efficiency'. It designates the decline of meaning itself.

The semblance of access, inclusion and participation propagated by communicative capitalism hides the underlying inequalities of the networks, producing a deadlock democracy incapable of bringing about a progressive political and economic change. Impressive popular spikes, eruptions and spectacles in the media do not provide alternative practices of collective engagement, challenge corporate ownership of the telecommunications infrastructure or redirect financial flows towards the most disadvantaged. Instead, communicative capitalism seizes, privatises and monetises the social substance. As Dean puts it:

> Instead of leading to more equitable distributions of wealth and influence, instead of enabling the emergence of a richer variety in modes of living and practices of freedom, the deluge of screens and spectacles coincides with extreme corporatisation, financialisation and privatisation across the globe. Rhetorics of access, participation and democracy work ideologically to secure the technological infrastructure of neoliberalism, an invidious and predatory politico-economic project that concentrates assets and power in the hands of the very, very rich, devastating the planet and destroying the lives of billions of people. (2009, 23)

The common and the commons

Dean uses Cesare Casarino's distinction between the common and the commons to illustrate both the potentials and impasses of the commons. Glossing

Hardt and Negri, Casarino and Negri (2008) distinguish between the common as the capacity of the general intellect and the commons as the concrete instantiation of the common as in the cases of land, resources, language, technology, etc. Whereas the commons are finite and characterised by scarcity – the digital commons excluded – the common is infinite, as it comprises the surplus nature of creativity, language, affect, thought and communication.

In line with Žižek, who pointed out the contemporary commodification and privatisation of the general intellect, Dean (2012, 136) pinpoints six fields of the expropriation of the common by networked communications: data, metadata, networks, attention, capacity and spectacle. Central to these fields is the 'power-law distribution' introduced by Albert-Lázló Barabási (2003), that is, the 80/20 rule that accounts for the winner-takes-all format of the new economy and the 'long tail'. Networks do not exhibit a rhizomatic organisation as Hardt and Negri would have it, but display an asymmetric growth based on preferential attachment that gives rise to hubs and hierarchies. What Barabási, however, omits is that hierarchy does not come naturally, but stems from pre-existing power asymmetries constitutive of network infrastructures that channel the flow of attention accordingly; hence, media concentration and the subsequent mind manipulation by corporate elites.

Interestingly, Dean (2012, 146–148) detects a contradiction between the abundance of the digital commons and the scarcity of human capacity to process all the information available to convert either into commons or commodities. Sharing in the commons does not always result in common wealth, and production either in the commons or in communicative capitalism comes up against limits inherent to communication as such. The crux of Dean's argument is that the common, finally, is co-opted by communicative capitalism (2012, 20). Hardt and Negri's dream of the multitude overthrowing capitalism is simply untenable, since it fails to build a concentrated political force capable of confronting the capitalist mode of production and replacing it with a communist one. Instead of perpetuating the division between the common and capitalism by transposing social change to the future subversion of capitalism, people ought to seize the division right here and now and turn it against capitalism. To promote this, Dean brings into the discussion the role of the communist party in the political struggle.

Dead-end democracy and the psychodynamics of the party

Dean takes issue with Brown (2015) who argues that de-democratisation is the central force in the convergence of neoliberalism and neoconservatism. Brown makes the case that neoliberalism is undoing basic elements of democracy, thus inaugurating a new era of post-democracy, marking the substitution of politics by technocracy and economism. Dean, on the other hand, holds that the problem is not democratisation, but the failure of the left to juxtapose another politics against globalised neoliberal capitalism. Like Žižek, she asserts that the appeal to democracy is a dead end for left politics (Dean 2009, 94). The left should not rely on the procedural form of democracy, but on the collective power of the people, the latter resonating with the party. Dean (2012, 20) observes that the goal of the party is the creation of a mode of production and distribution where the free development of each is compatible with the free development of all. She understands communism in the Marxian sense of a self-conscious collective action driven by voluntary cooperation that is not forced or out of control (2012, 157).

Dean offers a psychodynamic approach to the party inspired by the crowd. She attributes to the crowd four unconscious features: the desire to grow, a state of absolute equality, the love of density and the need for direction (2012, 75–101). Like Žižek, Dean holds that the crowd lacks organisation, endurance and scale. Therefore, it needs a party and a leader. She conceives of the party as the polymorphous and porous body of communism stretching across the entire field of society, focusing the inarticulate cries of the crowd into the collective will of communist politics (2012, 135). The crowd does not have a politics, but it is the opportunity for politics (Dean 2012, 11–12). She brings up the case of Syriza to demonstrate the dynamic relation between the crowd and the party (2012, 21–22). Syriza's initial victories came from a broad alliance with social movements and local solidarity networks. Dean claims that despite Syriza's betrayal of its supporters, it nevertheless signalled a political innovation that shifted the terrain of the possible.

Critique of the left

Perhaps what one can infer from Syriza's defeat is not its capitulation as such, but the moral derailment of the populist left along with its failure to offer a viable alternative. If Syriza purports to be a radical left party, then it should aim at overthrowing capitalism rather than assuming another mild, centre-left, social democratic position. To do so, Syriza and the left in general should more generously endorse the commons and create the conditions necessary for a social economy based on the commons. This presupposes the design of concrete policies intended to clash head-on with capitalism, rather than employing gentle tactics and manoeuvres.

As with Žižek, Dean's argument is overly generalised, turning into a vague call for political struggle. Dean points to the creation of a collective mode of production and distribution, but she does not acknowledge the existence of commons-based peer production, which is alive and kicking. Dean lacks a firm understanding of peer production, thus leaning on a communist conservatism, notwithstanding the violent coefficients of Žižek's state of terror. Rather than dismissing altogether horizontal forms of self-organising, it would be politically more beneficial to examine more closely the potential of technology to support a post-hegemonic politics of the common and drive both capitalism and the state towards a post-capitalist, commons-orientated transition. The diversity of the crowd could then be absorbed into the pluralism of the commons, perhaps bringing Marx's ideal closer to reality.

4.6.3 Historical Geographical Materialism

David Harvey carries on the Marxist legacy to offer one of the most compelling neo-Marxist analyses of contemporary capitalism. Harvey (2010, 40) seeks to answer the questions of how does capitalism survive, and why is it so crisis-prone. The basic motor of capitalism is competition, which keeps the system running through a process of creative destruction that comes to rationalise an inherently irrational economic system, leading to reconfigurations, new models of development, new spheres of investment and new forms of class power (Harvey 2010, 11, 43). The system is destined to constantly push its limits and renovate to accumulate capital and survive. Harvey (2010, 47) identifies five potential barriers to capital accumulation: 1) insufficient initial capital; 2) scarcity of labour and means of production, including natural limits; 3) inappropriate technologies and organisational forms; 4) resistance by labour; and 5) lack of efficient demand. Crises break out in various historical and geographical settings due to the fluid character of capitalist development and the perpetual repositioning of one barrier at the expense of another (Harvey 2010, 117). Credit and liquidity crises, stagflation, secular stagnation, over-accumulation, under-consumption, class struggle and profit squeeze are some of the forms of the capitalist crisis.

Over-accumulation crises and spatio-temporal fixes

Central to the evolution of capitalism is technological innovation, which is a double-edged sword: it can destabilise and, at the same time, open up new paths of development for surplus capital absorption (Harvey 2010, 101). Harvey goes along with Marx's insight that technological change plays a key role in producing crises of one sort or another. As already noted, Marx argues that technology inevitably produces a tendency for the rate of profit to fall. Harvey (2010, 101) considers Marx's argument an oversimplification. The most frequent form of the presumed tendency for the rate of profit to fall is the capital surplus absorption problem or capital over-accumulation, defined as a mismatch between surplus capital and surplus labour or a lack of opportunities for profitable investment. In this case, over-accumulated capital is devalued or destroyed. Devalued capital can take many forms: abandoned factories, empty offices, unsold commodities, idle money, declining assets in stocks, shares, land, properties, etc. (Harvey 2010, 45–46).

Capitalism resolves its over-accumulation crises through spatio-temporal fixes, engineered by the state–finance nexus (Harvey 2003, 89). Capital can accumulate in two ways: it can exploit labour in production to create the surplus value that sustains the basis of profit, or it can search for new opportunities across the globe for profitable reinvestment. In the second case, capitalism progresses into an imperialism that arises out of a dialectical relation between two distinct but tightly intertwined sorts of power: state and capitalist power (Harvey 2003, 27–30). Capitalist imperialism consists in an often contradictory fusion of state-empire politics and the molecular processes of capital accumulation in space and time.

State power mobilises human and natural resources towards political, economic and territorial/military ends, whereas capitalist power flows across and through states via the production process, trade, commerce, money, technology transfers, currency and asset speculation. Whereas the statesman seeks a collective advantage that sustains or augments the power of their own state vis-à-vis other states, the capitalist seeks an individual advantage commensurate with the accumulation of capital. Whereas the statesman is responsible to a citizenry or, more often, to an elite group, the capitalist is responsible only to shareholders. State power fuses with capitalist power inasmuch as the elite group that influences state policies identifies or aligns with capital, albeit in a contradictory manner. The endless accumulation of capital, for example, produces periodic crises within the territory of the state. Different state regulation, on the other hand, creates the basis for different versions of capitalism, uneven geographical development and geopolitical struggles. Therefore, to understand capitalist imperialism, one needs first to grapple with the theory of the capitalist state in all its diversity.

Different states create different imperialisms, as in the case of the French, Dutch, British and Belgian imperialisms from 1870 to 1945. Imperialist practices, viewed from the perspective of capitalist logic, exploit the uneven geographical conditions under which capital accumulation occurs, such as the uneven patterning of natural resources and geostrategic advantages as well as the asymmetric exchange relations that facilitate the concentration of wealth and power in certain places rather than others (Harvey 2003, 31–32). This is precisely the case with modern European colonialism.

Three stages of capitalist imperialism

The first major crisis of capitalist over-accumulation occurred in Europe in 1846–50, forcing the bourgeois revolutionary movements to join capital under the banner of the modern nation-state, and altogether expand geographically across the globe (Harvey 2003, 42–49). Marx and Engels (2008/1848, 33) define the bourgeoisie as the class of modern capitalists, owners of the means of production and employers of wage labour. The ruling class (landlords, the aristocracy, the king and the clergy) rejected the idea that the problem of over-accumulation could be solved by internal reforms and redistribution among the bourgeoisie and wage labour. To avoid the civil war that would emerge out of class struggle, it sought solutions through external trade and colonial/imperial practices (Harvey 2003, 125).

Social darwinism in the form of tribal nationalism and outright racism legitimised the plundering of colonies and the extraction of tributes from 'barbarians, savages and inferiors' who had failed to mix their labour with the land and progress accordingly (Harvey 2003, 42–45). Colonialism produced one of the most oppressive and violently exploitative forms of imperialism ever invented. Hannah Arendt (1968) correctly sees the fascism of Nazism as the apogee of the nationalistic monstrosity, marking the historical-geographical trajectory of European colonialism from 1870 until 1945.

Imperialism is not a modern historical phenomenon. The geographical accumulation of wealth and state power have gone hand in hand since the invention of money, private property and slavery (Karatani 2014). What is unique in the case of capitalist imperialism is the rise of the bourgeoisie, that is, the emergence of the middle class of merchants who gradually asserted their money power to reconfigure state forms and assume a commanding influence over military institutions, administrative and legal systems (Harvey 2010, 48). Ultimately, the rising bourgeoisie joined forces with feudal lords and monarchs to embark on colonising the globe.

The second stage of capitalist imperialism took place in the post-war period from 1945 to 1970, when the political rule of the bourgeoisie operated under global US dominance and hegemony (Harvey 2010, 49–62). Against the backdrop of the Cold War and economic stagnation following the Second World War, the United States decided to circulate its surpluses through Canada, Australia, Western Europe and Japan, aiming to restabilise the global market and stimulate effective demand for its products. A new financial order was established by the Bretton Woods system that set up a fixed exchange rate by pegging all currencies against the US dollar, which, in turn, was pegged to the price of gold, fixed at $35 an ounce. At the time, US gold reserves made up two-thirds of global gold reserves.

Decolonisation followed suit to allow open trade to flourish and capital accumulation to accelerate. The whole enterprise was accompanied by a battery of institutions such as the World Bank, the International Monetary Fund and the Organisation for Economic Cooperation and Development, designed to coordinate economic growth between the advanced capitalist powers and to bring capitalist-style development to the rest of the non-communist world. That was a period of remarkably strong economic growth in the advanced capitalist countries, with the problem of over-accumulation contained until the late 1960s by a mix of internal adjustments and spatio-temporal fixes within and beyond the United States (Harvey 2003, 58). In short, nationalist bourgeois imperialism, after 1945, took the form of Fordist capitalism, characterised by a Taylorist system of mass production and consumption, nationally regulated economies, regulation of world trade and exchange relationships between currencies, and the emergence of welfare states.

This second stage in the global rule of the bourgeoisie ended with the economic crisis of the 1970s, which was due to the fiscal crisis in the US caused by the rising costs of the military conflict in Vietnam. The US responded by printing more money, resulting in a world-wide stagflation of high unemployment and inflation, signalling another disconnect between idle capital and labour capacity. The new crisis of over-accumulation gave rise to neoliberalism (Harvey 2003, 62–86). Gold was abandoned as the material basis of the monetary system, and the flow of money was totally liberated from state controls.

Threatened in the realm of production by Europe and Japan, the US reasserted its hegemony through finance. Financialisation now came to stimulate both demand and supply through credit, which is vital to productive investment and the reallocation of capital. 'In the same way that capital can operate on both sides of the demand and supply of labour (via technologically induced unemployment), so it can operate through the credit system on both sides of the production-realisation relation' (Harvey 2010, 115). Rather than relying on the state to stimulate demand, capital uses credit to boost production and control the money flow. For example, the supply of credit to both property developers and homeowners fuelled a massive boom in housing and urban development in the US, followed by the mortgage crisis of 2008 (Harvey 2010, 115).

The US banks in concert with the financial centres of London, Frankfurt and Tokyo were now given the exclusive right to recycle the vast quantities of petrodollars being accumulated in the Gulf region in the form of credit and all sorts of financial products such as stocks, bonds, options, derivatives, currency values, commodity futures, securitisation and the like. Speculation, thus, became the by-product of credit, and of what Marx calls fictitious capital, that is, capital detached from value produced in the real economy.

Digitisation spread credit and speculation across the globe. Computers installed the post-Fordist model, which enabled capitalist restructuring in the field of production, thereby allowing capital to reduce costs (including the devaluation of labour) through outsourcing and offshoring (Harvey 2003, 62–86). Computer networks allowed corporations to organise on a transnational level by breaking down the production process into small units managed by subcontracted firms of corporations around the globe, distributed according to the location of the most attractive conditions for economic investment (low wages, low corporate taxes, weak unions, political stability, and so on). Fuchs describes post-Fordism as follows:

> The post-Fordist economy is a flexible regime of accumulation that is enabled by ICTs and is based on the outsourcing, decentralisation, and 'flexibilisation' of production: lean management, just-in-time production, the flattening of internal hierarchies in corporations, small

organisational units in corporations, delegation of decision making from upper hierarchical levels to lower ones, decentralisation of organisational structures, teamwork, strategic alliances, innovation networks, semi-autonomous working groups, network organisations, tertiarisation and informatisation of the economy, triadisation of international trade and of capital export, participatory management, a new phase of economic globalisation, diversified quality production, automation and rationalisation mediated by computerised ICTs. (2008, 110)

Globalisation is the post-Fordist nomadism of capitalism in space and time (Fuchs 2008, 111–112).

The global rise of multinational corporations was further supported by the neoliberal policies of Reagan and Thatcher, which resulted in the dismantling of the welfare state and the privatisation of public assets. Neoliberalism, finally, came to refer to the privatisation of everything and the socialisation of risk; so-called socialism for the bankers (Harvey 2010, 10). This became amply evident in the mortgage crisis of 2008 when the state stepped in to bail out the bankrupt banks with taxpayers' money to the tune of $700 billion. Neoliberalism, thus, produces a systemic 'moral hazard' in which banks do not have to suffer the consequences of high-risk behaviour (Harvey 2010, 11).

To sum up, Harvey identifies three stages of capitalist imperialism: the bourgeois imperialisms of 1870–1945, the post-war US hegemony of 1945–1970, and the neoliberal hegemony from 1970 onwards. Capitalist imperialism evolves through spatio-temporal fixes to crises of over-accumulation, engineered by the state–finance nexus. Rather than being the enemy of capital, as many libertarians would have it, the state has functioned historically as the helping hand of capitalism, providing the institutional framework and manipulating the molecular forces of capital accumulation. As Harvey puts it:

Capital accumulation through price-fixing market exchange flourishes best in the midst of certain institutional structures of law, private property, contract, and security of the money form. A strong state armed with police powers and a monopoly over the means of violence can guarantee an institutional framework and back it up with definite constitutional arrangements. State formation, coupled with the emergence of bourgeois constitutionality, have therefore been crucial features within the long historical geography of capitalism. (2003, 89–90)

Accumulation by dispossession

The central mechanism of capitalist imperialism has been what Harvey calls 'accumulation by dispossession'. Harvey draws on Marx's concept of primitive accumulation, further expanded by Rosa Luxemburg in space and time, to refer to the strategy of capital of releasing, co-opting and leveraging a set of assets (including labour power), often through fraud, robbery, plunder and raw violence, at very low (and in some instances zero) cost.

The first instance of accumulation by dispossession was the primitive accumulation described by Marx in terms of the commodification and privatisation of land, beginning in Britain; the forceful expulsion of peasant populations; the conversion of common property rights into private property rights; the commodification of labour power; colonialism; the monetisation of exchange and taxation, particularly of land; slavery; the national debt bondage; and, finally, the credit system (Harvey 2003, 145). Primitive accumulation, in short, entails the appropriation of cultural, natural and social capital as well as confrontation and supersession (Harvey 2003, 146). Marx considered primitive accumulation as a one-off event that sparked capitalist development. Rosa Luxemburg (2003/1913) showed instead that capital accumulation is an ongoing process that is essential to the reproduction of capitalism.

Harvey (2003, 147–149) advanced the concept of 'accumulation by dispossession' from the shadowy position it held prior to 1970 to a central feature of capitalist logic, manifested today in the sectors of finance, biogenetics, agriculture, real estate, culture and public assets. He demonstrates the new wave of enclosures of the commons through land dispossession and debt peonage, the commodification of the world's stockpile of genetic resources, the depletion of the global environmental commons (land, air, water), the co-optation of cultural forms, histories and intellectual creativity, the privatisation of hitherto public property, and the reversion of common property rights to the private domain.

Alongside accumulation by dispossession, the collapse of the Soviet Union and then the opening up of China released hitherto unavailable assets for over-accumulated capital to seize upon (Harvey 2010, 16). Capitalism evolves by opening new markets, while deploying more sophisticated methods of arbitrage (buying cheap and selling dear) to produce more money from money. Capitalism survives not only through spatio-temporal fixes that absorb capital surpluses into productive activity, but also through destruction spurred by speculation (Harvey 2003, 135). Ponzi schemes, structured asset destruction through inflation, asset stripping through mergers and acquisitions, debt incumbency that reduces whole countries to debt peonage, the raiding of pension funds and their decimation by stock and corporate collapses, credit and liquidity crises are all the (un)intended consequences of creative destruction (Harvey 2003, 147; 2010, 11).

Creative destruction is the outcome of a zero-sum game, a trial-and-error process that promotes the survival of the fittest in the jungle of the market. Inequalities, power asymmetries, even unfairness and ruthlessness are all indicators of a 'meritocracy' depicted as the natural law of the strongest; social darwinism at its best. This interpretation is miles away from the liberal ideal of self-regulating free markets, which operate as sites of voluntary exchange based on private property rights and free trade, designed to foster technological progress and rising labour productivity to satisfy the wants and needs of all. This utopian vision of a world of individual freedom and liberty for all is undermined, among other things, by capitalism's basic condition of survival: credit-fuelled capital accumulation at a compound rate of 3%. Harvey (2010, 112) argues that a 3% rate of capitalist growth is simply untenable, given that it requires 3% of reinvestment to keep up with future demand.

To sum up, credit, privatisation, crisis manipulation, leveraging, speculation and devaluation of assets (including labour and land) are the neoliberal solutions to the problem of capital over-accumulation, combined with the classic predatory practices of monopoly capitalism such as cartels, fixed pricing, tax evasion, bribery and the like. The whole system is supposed to be kept in check by state intervention through anti-trust policies, regulation and quantitative easing. But endemic corruption perpetuates economic crises, the repercussions of which resurrect the racism and nationalism that had once bound nation-state and empire together (Harvey 2003, 188). Populism surges today under the banner of neoconservative neoliberalism. Populist politics is the natural outcome of capitalist crises, managed by elites to blame the inherent contradictions of capitalism on immigrants. Capitalism retreats in times of crisis into racism and fascism to mitigate the rage of people and reboot the circulation of capital accumulation under nationalist terms.

The contradictions of the commons

Resistance, however, escapes populist co-optation in the case of progressive social movements and various struggles over dispossession, outlined by Harvey as follows:

> The struggles of the Ogoni people against the degradation of their lands by Shell Oil; the long-drawn-out struggles against World Bank-backed dam construction projects in India and Latin America; peasant movements against biopiracy; struggles against genetically modified foods and the authenticity of local production systems; fights to preserve access for indigenous populations to forest reserves while curbing the activities of the timber companies; political struggles against privatisation; movements to procure labour rights or women's rights in developing countries; campaigns to protect biodiversity and to prevent habitat destruction; peasant movements to gain access to land; protests against highway and airport construction; literally hundreds of protests against IMF-imposed austerity programmes – these were all part of a volatile mix of protest movements that swept the world and increasingly grabbed the headlines during and after the 1980s. (2003, 166–167)

The effect of all these movements was to shift the terrain of political activity away from centralised state mechanisms into a less focused political dynamic of social action, spanning civil society. Yet Harvey (2003, 168, 177–179) detects some internal contradictions within the anti-capitalist social movements that cut to the heart of the commons. Localism, gated communities, vested interests, atavism, traditionalism and conservatism are some of the regressive elements of social movements that reverberate within the commons. The danger is to see all these social movements as by definition 'progressive' or, even worse, to place them under the homogenising and nebulous concept of Hardt and Negri's 'multitude' that will magically rise up to power and extinguish capitalism (Harvey 2003, 169).

The problem with socialism

Harvey (2010, 120) goes along with Marx who recognised some positive elements within capitalist production. On the negative side, capitalism has produced abhorrent class violence and has caused world wars, increasing inequalities, severe environmental degradation, the loss of biodiverse habitats, spiralling poverty among burgeoning populations, neocolonialism, serious crises in public health, alienation, insecurity and anxieties. On the positive side, capitalism obliterated feudal relations and replaced a world of superstition and ignorance with a world of scientific enlightenment capable of liberating people from material want and need. Material living and well-being have significantly increased on average, travel and communications have been revolutionised and knowledge proliferates.

> From this standpoint it could be said that primitive accumulation was a necessary though ugly stage through which the social order had to go in order to arrive at a stage where both capitalism and some alternative socialism might be possible [...] It was, within the Marxist/communist revolutionary tradition, often deemed necessary to organise the equivalent of primitive accumulation in order to implement programmes of modernisation in those countries that had not gone through the initiation into capitalist development. This sometimes meant similar levels of appalling violence, as with the forced collectivisation of agriculture in the Soviet Union (the elimination of the kulaks) and in China and Eastern Europe. (Harvey 2003, 163, 165)

The problem with socialism, however, for Harvey, was precisely that it attempted to co-opt insurgent movements into the centralised mechanisms of the party that revolved around the aristocracy of labour. Socialism, thus, came at the cost of innumerable exclusions. Social movements such as feminism and environmentalism remained outside the agenda of the traditional left (Harvey 2003,

170–171). What the left should do today, instead, is to directly attack class relations by incorporating social movements and civil society into a much broader politics of social change. Somehow the left must find a way to move beyond the amorphous concept of the 'multitude' without falling back into localism (Harvey 2003, 179). This presupposes the incorporation of the commons into the macro-politics of the left, without the former losing their autonomy vis-à-vis the state (Harvey 2011).

Harvey abstains, however, from introducing any concrete policies through which the left could rise to challenge capitalism. Most importantly, he recycles a narrow, economistic, neo-Marxist analysis. The survival of capitalism does not merely depend on its capacity to achieve 3% compound growth. Capitalism can manoeuvre through crises and business cycles by hoarding or recycling profits into the spiral of creative destruction ad infinitum. Capitalism is not going to disappear simply by losing a big chunk of money. Harvey at times rests on the allegedly indissoluble contradictions of capitalism and loses sight of the central contradiction of capitalism, which is the division between directors and executants. Capitalism's power does not reside in capital itself, but in its mode of production. To change the system from within, it is necessary to alter the mode of capitalist production into post-capitalist self-management. Harvey supports activism, community and labour movements and clearly sees the advanced role of technology in both renovating and undermining capitalism. He welcomes automation and artificial intelligence, but he does not open up a clear path towards a socialist engineering of technological innovation (Harvey 2019). This path presupposes a holistic, post-hegemonic strategy that redeploys centralised mechanisms to diffuse power to the crowd via concrete policies.

4.6.4 Post-capitalism

Paul Mason (2015, xiv–xix) reiterates the narrative put forward by a number of authors so far that information technology has a revolutionary potential to pave the way for the transition from a capitalist economy of scarcity to a post-capitalist economy of abundance. As shown thus far, post-capitalism is modelled after a number of reformist and anti-capitalist variants of the commons. Mason probably represents the most statist version of post-capitalism. He advocates a leftist social democracy or networked socialism with a strong emphasis on the role of the state in a commons-orientated transition.

The information argument

Mason (2015, xiii, 112) argues that capitalism is a complex and adaptive system that is losing its ability to adapt due to the essential features of information. He draws on a number of authors as diverse as Marx, Benkler and Rifkin (Mason

2015, 109–145) to claim that information technology has four specific effects that mainstream economics struggles to cope with: 1) the zero marginal cost effect; 2) the creation of massive positive externalities through network effects; 3) the amplified asymmetry of information; and 4) the separation of work from wages.

Paul Romer showed in 1990 that the non-rivalrous nature of information drives the marginal cost of digital goods over time towards zero, thus eroding profits (Mason 2015, 117–126). After the costs of production have been incurred in the product, the cost of reproduction is almost nil. The Deloitte consultancy group calculated that the falling price of information bandwidth, storage and processing power is exponential (Mason 2015, 165). Competitive advantages and monopoly pricing are undermined by information's free circulation. Napster, Gnutella, Bittorent, PirateBay, Kindle, iPad, Wikipedia, Wordpress and hundreds of software applications – some of them open source – have cost creative industry and the media (books, music, films, software, news, visual arts) billions of dollars. On the flipside, filesharing and downloading is beneficial not only to the millions of 'pirates', but to artists themselves, who earned very low royalties anyway. Now they can advertise their work for free and gain more money from concerts, presentations, exhibitions, and so on. Finally, high information content is added also to physical goods, sucking them into the same zero-price vortex as digital goods. For example, computer-simulating stress tests on aircraft engineering significantly reduces the costs of production, thus pushing prices down, all other factors being equal.

Corporations respond by imposing ownership on information and extending copyright. They capture the positive externalities – or, in Marxian terms, the use value – of shareable information and enclose them with strict intellectual property rights (Mason 2015, 131–133). Externalities such as pollution and shareable information are respectively negative and positive spillovers of production that are not embedded in the true costs and benefits of the product or service. Info-monopolies such as Facebook, Google and Amazon base their business model on the positive externalities of network effects generated by Internet users, coupled with intellectual property rights. Kenneth Arrow showed that strong intellectual property rights result in the under-utilisation of information as in the case of info-monopolies. An economy that aims at the full utilisation of information cannot have a closed market or absolute intellectual property rights.

The networked economy and the end of capitalism

Mainstream economics assumes that free markets operating under conditions of perfect competition and perfect information reach a state of equilibrium where the maximum possible social good is achieved (Mason 2015, 118). Market failures and imperfections such as monopolies, patents, trade unions and price-fixing cartels are only temporary. Critics of mainstream economics such as Joseph Stiglitz have claimed that the general assumptions of perfect information and efficient markets are wrong due to the asymmetry of information between economic agents, and subsequent power imbalances (Mason 2015, 120). Adverse selection, moral hazard and monopolies of knowledge are examples of asymmetric information.[13]

Benkler has demonstrated that info-tech makes possible a non-market economy based on a demographic that pursues its self-interest through non-market actions (Mason 2015, 127–131). Info-tech supports the rise of a networked economy based on the spontaneous interaction of people using information pathways and forms of organisation that no longer respond to the dictates of the market and managerial hierarchies. Digital platforms and mobile applications allow for an increased sociality where non-monetary motivations come to occupy a larger space of non-market activity, thus shrinking the capitalist market. Mason (2015, 109–145) stresses that this is not a simple rebalancing between public goods and private goods, but a precursor of a transition towards a post-capitalist world of zero-priced goods, shared economic space, non-market organisations and non-ownable products.

The networked economy creates an abundance of free and shared goods, where the law of supply and demand is inapplicable. Whereas in capitalism supply creates its own demand, with market-clearing prices matching supply and demand, production in post-capitalism is based on real-time and transparent computation of demand (Mason 2015, 160–164). Automation speeds up the post-capitalist transition by reducing necessary labour, blurring furthermore the distinction between work and leisure. It erodes the link between value and labour altogether (Mason 2015, 179). Capitalism responds by creating new needs and skills and commercialising every aspect of social life on the Internet and beyond (Mason 2015, 164). But, still, class struggle resists.

Marx had already anticipated in the 'Fragment on Machines' a knowledge-based route out of capitalism, in which the main contradiction is between technology and the market mechanism. Mason (2015, 144) traces two ways out of this contradiction: either a new form of cognitive capitalism emerges and consolidates firms, markets and networked collaboration, or a conflict takes place between the network and the market system that results in the abolition of the market system and its replacement by post-capitalism. Capitalism collapses because it cannot exist alongside the shared knowledge produced by the general intellect.

Information technology, far from creating a new and stable form of capitalism, is disintegrating it (Mason 2015, 112). Information does not produce an informational capitalism via another creative destruction that 'updates' capitalism, but breeds a peer-to-peer mode of production that tends to dissolve capitalism's core structural contradiction between directors and executants. Mason (2015, xix) reproduces the autonomous Marxist argument that information gradually pushes that contradiction to its limits by contrasting the abundance of the network against the scarcity of the hierarchy.

Updating class struggle

Mason uses Marxist crisis theory to accentuate the role of the class struggle in the transition from capitalism to post-capitalism. For Marx, competition drives capitalists to replace labour with machinery, the result being the tendency of the profit rate to fall. Capitalism offsets this tendency by various counteracting tendencies. However, Marx believed that the counteracting tendencies eventually break down, leading to a cyclical crisis, the 'snowballing effect' of which brings capitalism to a halt.

Mason (2015, 31–77) calls upon a variant of Nikolai Kondratieff's theory of 'long waves' of capitalist growth to correct both Kondratieff and Marx. Contrary to Marx, who claimed that capitalism is doomed to failure, Kondratieff argued that capitalism generally adapts and mutates. He assumed that capitalist development has the form of fifty-year cycles consisting of twenty-five years of economic upswing followed by twenty-five years of downswing (Mason 2015, 33). The cause of the long cycles, according to Kondratieff, lies in the economy, not in technology or global politics. Take-off is caused by capital accumulating faster than it can be invested, the effect being either the search for an expanded supply of money or the increased availability of new, cheaper technologies (Mason 2015, 37–38).

The first long cycle began with the factory system in Britain in the 1780s and was terminated around 1849. The second long cycle involved the global deployment of railways, steam ships and the telegraph, ending sometime in the 1890s. The third cycle took off with the harnessing of electricity, the telephone, scientific management and mass production and experienced its downswing during the Second World War. The fourth cycle was powered by transistors and factory automation, producing the longest economic boom in history. The peak was the oil shock of 1973, after which a long period of instability took hold. The fifth cycle supposedly began in the late 1990s, driven by the Internet and mobile communications. But it has stalled. The reason for this, according to Mason (2015, 47–48), is neoliberalism and the nature of information, which erodes capitalism from within.

Schumpeter took Kondratieff's wave theory to develop a techno-determinist account of boom and bust (Mason 2015, 45). For him, capitalist cycles are not driven by the rhythm of investment, but by technological innovation that prompts the 'creative destruction' of old and inefficient models. Carlota Perez, a modern follower of Schumpeter, emphasises the response of governments at crisis points to invert Kondratieff's cause and effect: governments drive technology, and technology drives the economics (Mason 2015, 47). Mason gives a Marxian twist to all three. The problem with the Schumpeterian version of wave theory is that it is obsessed with innovators and technologies, and does not see classes (Mason 2015, 73). The same goes for Kondratieff and Perez: they do not see that class struggle drives capitalism into post-capitalism.

> Long cycles are not produced by just technology and economics, the
> third critical driver is class struggle. And it is in this context that Marx's
> original theory of crisis provides a better understanding than Kondra-
> tieff's 'exhausted investment' theory […] Kondratieff's account – which
> said that the fifty-year cycles were driven by the need to renew major
> infrastructure – was far too simplistic. Better to say each wave generates
> a specific and concrete solution to falling profit rates during the upswing
> – a set of business models, skills and technologies – and that the down-
> swing starts when the solution becomes exhausted or disrupted […] The
> tendency of the rate of profit to fall, interacting constantly with
> the counter-tendencies, is a much better explanation of what drives the
> fifty-year cycle than the one Kondratieff gave. (Mason 2015, 77)

Mason employs Marx's crisis theory only to deviate from it by upgrading the
role of class struggle in the transition from capitalism to post-capitalism. Marx
noticed that the fundamental flaw of capitalism, that is, the tendency of the
profit rate to fall, is due to the main contradiction between the forces of production (workers, machinery) and relations of production (owners of machinery vs non-owners). The solution, however, does not rest on the passage from
private to communal property via the state, but on the transformation of the
capitalist mode of production into a post-capitalist one. The main contradiction of capitalism is not an issue of (state) ownership but of self-management.
The solution is the abolition of the division between directors and executants
and the establishment of self-management across all spheres of the social.
Mason (2015, 177–181) contends that the agent of social change is no longer
the working class, but the networked individual who occupies the social factory
and whose lifestyle is not solidarity but impermanence.

Classical Marxists, including Marx himself, underestimated the constitutive
nature of political agency in the course of capitalism's history, ranging from
the spatio-temporal fixes of the capitalist state to class struggle itself (Mason
2015, 75–76). Rudolf Hilferding dispensed with the thesis of the 'snowballing
crisis' and conceived of capitalism as a state-directed, heavily monopolised and
national system (Mason 2015, 59). But he mistakenly assumed that monopoly
capitalism would lead to a long and stagnant crisis period that would give way to
socialism. Rosa Luxemburg moved crisis theory to the post-colonial collapse of
capitalism, caused by the lack of new markets. But she could not see at the time
that capitalism could create new markets within existing markets (Mason 2015,
61–63). The mistake of both was to consider monopolised state capitalism as the
only pathway to post-capitalism (Mason 2015, 71). The dialectical progression
from free market to monopoly and from colonisation to global war and revolution was simply a fallacy exposed in 1989, with the collapse of the Soviet Bloc.

The role of class struggle came to prominence through the autonomous
Marxists after the 1970s. Information technology has triggered since then the

fourth and prolonged stage of state capitalism in the model of neoliberalism, supposed to produce a new wave of capitalist growth driven by ICTs. Information capitalism, however, has not yet emerged or, at least, has stalled due to the stagnation of the last two decades (Mason 2015, 91–106). The current period presents an anomaly in Kondratieff's cycles or waves of global capitalist growth. This anomaly cannot be explained in terms of the classical Marxist theory that traces crises to one abstract cause. Mason (2015, 71–72) argues, instead, that the economic explanation must be concrete and take into account the real structures of capitalism: states, corporations, welfare systems, financial markets. Put simply, capitalism is a complex system consisting of multiple moving parts, the explanation of which requires a focused analysis on the parts in question each time. It therefore requires a poststructural analysis contingent on the evolution of capitalism and class struggle.

Envisaging post-capitalism

Neoliberalism offsets the tendency of the profit rate to fall by suppressing labour costs and massively expanding financial profits (Mason 2015, 71). The conundrum of rising profits alongside falling investment is explained by the fact that firms use profits to build up cash reserves as buffers against a credit crunch. They also pay down debt while distributing profit to shareholders through buy-back schemes. They are minimising their exposure to risk while speculating in the financial markets. The state, on the other hand, uses a mixture of quantitative easing and austerity policies to boost growth. The result is secular stagnation. Neoliberalism is on life support. It is just 15 trillion dollars worth of balance sheet expansion, backed by zero interest rates.

Information technology comes into play to install a post-capitalist model of production based on the networked economy that disrupts top-down centralised capitalism. Class struggle now occupies centre stage. Yet Mason (2015, 273–274) argues that the post-capitalist transition will need the state to create the necessary framework, since the networked economy operating via peer-to-peer projects, collaborative business models and non-profit activities is typically small-scale. Class struggle is fragile. The top-level goals of a post-capitalist project should be the following (Mason 2015, 269–270):

1. The reduction of carbon emissions so that the world has warmed by only two degrees Celsius by 2050.
2. The socialisation of the finance system to prevent other boom–bust cycles that could destroy the world economy. This could combine controlled debt write-offs with a 10–15 year global policy of 'financial repression'. It would include the restructuring of the banking system to favour non-profit local and regional banks, credit unions and peer lending and a well-regulated

space for complex financial activities that rewards innovation and discourages rent-seeking behaviour.
3. The prioritising of information-rich technologies to address issues of social welfare (health, sexual exploitation, digital illiteracy).
4. The gearing of technology towards the automation of the economy with the aim of freeing up basic commodities and public services, rendering work voluntary and turning economic management primarily into an issue of energy and resources, not capital and labour.

The first step towards achieving these goals would be the creation of a global institute or network for simulating the long-term transition beyond capitalism based on current economic data. Ideally this would be an open source project supported by the state that would draw on real-time data. Based on those data, the state should switch off the neoliberal machine and reshape markets to favour sustainable, collaborative and socially just outcomes (Mason 2015, 271–272). However unrealistic this prospect, it marks out a holistic and centralised planning. The state should act as an enabler of new technologies and collaborative business models; it should suppress or socialise monopolies; pay everyone a basic income; allow patents and intellectual property to taper away quickly; coordinate and plan infrastructure; and 'own' the agenda for responses to the challenges of climate change, demographic ageing, energy security and migration (Mason 2015, 273–289). With energy and banking socialised, the short-term goal would be to progress the economy towards high automation, low work and abundant cheap or free goods and services (Mason 2015, 283). Money and credit would have a much smaller role in the economy and returns on investment would come in a mixture of monetary and non-monetary forms. The long-term goal would be the creation of an abundant gift economy, which prioritises use value over exchange value. The post-capitalist transition involves, thus, a mix of planning, state provision, markets and peer production.

Critics from different and contrasting sides have argued that Mason's argument is naïve, optimistic, utopian, one-dimensional and techno-determinist (Fuchs 2016; Milanovic 2018; Mullin 2015; Pitts 2015). Some have claimed that information capitalism is already alive and kicking, as evidenced by the enormous profits of info-monopolies (Fuchs 2016; Milanovic 2018). While this is true, it cannot exclude the possibility of the disruptive effects that info-tech might have in the long run. Some crucial questions to be addressed are the following: Can the positional power of info-monopolies be outcompeted by networked individuals? Can networked individuals self-organise towards this goal? Might the state support the self-organisation of networked individuals against neoliberal capitalism? The answer to these questions depends, among other things, on grassroots action, political volition and democratic deliberation. Notwithstanding the pitfalls of an info-determinist approach with respect to the political, Mason's post-capitalist vision actually represents one potential version of future class struggle, the outcome of which will be determined by the interplay of a number of factors coming together at the crossroads of politics, technology and economics.

4.6.5 The Critical Theory of the Commons

Christian Fuchs elaborates on the technological aspect of class struggle. He lays the groundwork for a contemporary critical theory of media and information studies, which reflects the emergence of commons-based peer production. His work could, therefore, read as a technological update of the critical theory of Frankfurt School.

The Frankfurt School

Critical theory originated in the work of Friedrich Hegel and Karl Marx. In the twentieth century it came to refer specifically to the Frankfurt School, and more particularly the work of George Lukács, Theodor W. Adorno, Max Horkheimer, Jürgen Habermas and Herbert Marcuse (Fuchs 2011, 11–26; 2016, 5–22). The Frankfurt School drew on the philosophical predicates of Hegel and Marx to engage with ideology critique, among other things. In the Marxian analytical framework, ideology is a partial, simplified and distorted representation of reality, reflecting the interests of capitalists, boiling down to capital accumulation. It is reinforced by the neoliberal presumption that the essence of human nature is competition over the forces and relations of production. Marx (1975, 175) unveils, among other things, the religious facet of ideology by considering religion as the opium of the people. Yet he focuses on the economic dimension of ideology, as manifested in the exploitative capitalist relations of production. Exploitation is the result of capitalist domination over the forces and relations of production.

In *Capital*, ideology critique takes the form of commodity fetishism and alienation, where the social relations of production are perceived as economic relations among commodities and money. Money becomes a fetish, an end in itself rather than a force of production. George Lukács (1972/1923, 83) built on Marx's concept of alienation to introduce the concept of reification, which reduces humans to the status of things. Max Horkheimer (1974/1947, 15) reformulated Lukács's concept of reification into the notion of instrumental reason, which transforms humans into automatic machines serving capital accumulation. Capitalist ideology departs from the basis of economy to dominate the superstructure of society in terms of instrumental reason, which pervades science, politics, culture and the media. Herbert Marcuse (1964, 138) coined the term 'technological rationality' to describe instrumental reason. Capitalist ideology uses technology to create a one-dimensional human who employs a calculative logic according to the rules of capitalist domination. Technoscience, thus, becomes a tool for capital accumulation.

Fuchs (2011, 58–72) adopts Marcuse's dialectics to articulate his critical theory of media and information economy. Dialectics dates back to Heraclitus, Plato and Aristotle to reflect the contrasts inherent in the cosmos, thought and rational argumentation. In modern political philosophy, it is redeployed by Hegel and Marx to reveal the inner contradictions of capitalism. Marx (1867, 744) observes that contradictions are the source of all dialectics. A contradiction consists of two opposing poles that require and exclude each other at the same time. The tension between opposing poles can be resolved in a process that Hegel and Marx called 'Aufhebung' (sublation) and 'negation of negation': a new third quality that emerges from the contradiction between two poles. For Marx, the major contradiction of capitalism is between the forces and relations of production, that is, between capital and workers, or owners and non-owners of the means of production. This contradiction is partly sublated in times of crisis by a creative destruction that reboots the capitalist system to restart a new round of capital accumulation. Its true sublation, however, can only be achieved by overthrowing capitalism and establishing socialism.

Stalin's attempt to establish socialism was based on a deterministic interpretation of Marx's dialectics according to which proletarian revolution and socialism are inevitable developments, following the dialectical and historical progress of capitalism into communism (Fuchs 2011, 54–55). Stalin's dialectics was functionalist and structuralist, underestimating the role of human subjects in dialectical processes. Dialectics was mixed with a Protestant ethic to eventually produce a terrorist ideology. This distorted the humanistic element of Marx by resorting to a labour fetishism that reproduced the bourgeois morality of family, performance and hard work (Fuchs 2008, 347). The Marxian principle 'From each according to his ability, to each according to his needs' was transformed into 'From each according to his ability, to each according to his labour' (Fuchs 2016, 15).

Marcuse sought to avoid deterministic dialectics by shifting the structural-functionalist dialectic towards a human-centred dialectic (Fuchs 2011, 59). He reintroduced the Hegelian-Marxist dialectics of subject–object, where the subject transforms the object and vice versa. Society is shaped by the dialectic of freedom and necessity. Whereas necessity consists in the laws of nature, freedom is the capacity of humans to transform nature. In contrast to the objectivism of positivism and the subjectivism of postmodernism, Marcuse takes up the Hegelian dialectic between essence and existence to inscribe a normative dimension on critical theory (Fuchs 2011, 39). Unlike positivism, which ascribes a neutral or value-free character to knowledge, and postmodernism, which dissolves into a culturalism of signs, symbols and representations, critical theory introduces a political perspective on knowledge (Fuchs 2011, 28–34; 2016, 13–14). It understands theory and knowledge as a terrain of antagonism and conflict without resorting to a post-Marxist classless analysis of the political. Following young Marx, Marcuse conceives of cooperation as the essence of society, which contradicts the actual existence of competition (Fuchs 2011, 31, 40–41). Contrary to the relativism of postmodernism, he posits that there are universal human characteristics such as sociality, cooperation and the desire for wealth, happiness and freedom. He interprets Marx's work as an ethics of cooperation that needs to be liberated from capitalist ideology. Cooperation results in a categorical imperative that, in contrast to Kant, stresses the need for integrative democracy.

The dialectics of agency and structure

Fuchs (2008, 59) proceeds via Marcuse into a rereading of Marx, focusing on human practice and its application to contemporary society and technology. The dialectic of subject and object takes on the form of a dialectic of crisis and social struggle, the goal of which is the critique of capitalist domination and exploitation and its sublation by a classless society. To this end, he translates the Marcusean dialectics of subject and object into the contemporary dialectics of agency and structure (Fuchs 2008, 59–71). Human actors are conditioned by societal structures and vice versa. Fuchs builds on the social theory of Anthony Giddens and Pierre Bourdieu to conceive society as a dynamic and dialectical system consisting of three core subsystems:

> the economic system, in which values and property that satisfy human needs are produced; the political system, in which power is distributed in a certain way and collective decisions are taken; and the cultural system, in which skills, meaning and competency are acquired, produced and enacted in ways of life. (2008, 215)

Fuchs (2011, 46) adheres to Marx's distinction between the base and the superstructure of society. He considers the economic system the foundation of society that forms the necessary but not sufficient condition for the political and cultural system. The dialectics of agency and structure permits the reformulation of the economy by the human actors involved in the political and cultural system. Fuchs focuses on information and the media:

> Media operate at the structural level of society, whereas information is a property of the actor level of society. Media are structural properties of society that enable and constrain human cognition, communication and cooperation (information processes). Human information processes are form-giving processes in society: in the threefold process of cognition, communication and cooperation, humans transform, create and recreate social structures. Human knowledge is externalised by humans with

the help of media that store representations of this knowledge (sounds, images, writings, moving images, multimedia, etc.). Media are complex objectifications of human knowledge […] Information and the media are based on a subject–object dialectic that takes place within society: there is no subjective information (cognition, communication, cooperation) without media structures, and there are no media structures (that objectify, i.e. represent, subjective knowledge) without human cognition, communication and cooperation. (2011, 90–91)

Fuchs interprets the Internet as a technological catalyst of social struggle (Fuchs 2008, viiii). He considers the media and information economy in contemporary society as fields for the display of power and domination (2011, 5). He sees power in the Spinozan sense of 'transformative capacity', the capability to intervene and alter or affect the outcome of politics in the broader sense (2011, 4).

Power is a political structure; it can be defined as the disposition over means required to influence collective processes and decisions in one's own interest. Domination is a specific form of power; it refers to the disposition over the means of coercion required to influence others, collective processes and decisions. (Fuchs 2008, 67)

Domination establishes asymmetric power relations by force and violence (Fuchs 2008, 213). In the media and information economy, domination takes the form of a concentration of economic capital in a handful of corporations that manipulate public opinion, policies and consumer decisions to their own interests (Fuchs 2011, 5). 'The centralisation of ownership and wealth results in a situation in which a few actors dominate national and international public opinion and have a huge influence on public institutions such as the media, education, politics, culture and welfare' (Fuchs 2011, 110). Thus, the media transform into power structures and spaces of power struggle (Fuchs 2011, 6).

Fuchs (2014, 151) blends the autonomist Marxist argument regarding the circulation of struggle with the dialectics of critical theory to argue that the development of informational productive forces is itself contradictory and comes into conflict with the capitalist relations of production, as evidenced in the case of FOSS, the digital commons, cooperatives and social movements. Contrary to scholars such as Bell, Toffler, Drucker, Stehr and Castells, who speak of the emergence of a post-industrial society/knowledge society/information society/ network society, boosted by the development of ICTs, Fuchs (2014, 144) argues that what the last decades have experienced is not a new type of information society, but the transformation of industrial capitalism into digital capitalism driven by information and knowledge production. Contemporary society is an information society in terms of its forces of production. In terms of its relations of production, it remains a capitalist one (Fuchs 2014, 150). Fuchs (2014, 144) sides with scholars such as Nicholas Garnham (2000; 2004/1998), Peter

Golding (2000) and Frank Webster (2002; 2006) who object to the information society hypothesis, stressing instead the continued exploitative character of capitalist class relations.

Transnational informational capitalism

Fuchs (2008, 104) speaks of transnational informational capitalism to underscore the role of information and knowledge in globalised capitalist production. He approaches knowledge as a dialectical social process of cognition, communication and cooperation (2008, 117). Knowledge is neither subjective nor objective, postmodern nor positivist, but encapsulates a subject–object dialectic:

> The notion of informational capitalism grasps this subject–object dialectic, it conceptualises contemporary capitalism based on the rise of cognitive, communicative and cooperative labour that is interconnected with the rise of technologies of goods that objectify human cognition, communication, and cooperation. Informational capitalism is based on the dialectical interconnection of subjective knowledge and knowledge objectified in information technologies. (Fuchs 2008, 104)

Following the autonomist Marxist tradition, Fuchs expands the Marxian notion of exploitation from industrial labour to knowledge and digital labour, enabled by computers and mobile phones. Digital labour refers to the blurring of labour and play. In the social factory, work resembles play, and entertainment becomes labour-like (Fuchs 2014, 267).

Fuchs (2008, 202) builds on Hardt and Negri's notion of the multitude to include traditional industrial workers, knowledge workers, houseworkers, the unemployed, migrants, retirees and students. He redefines the multitude as an expanded notion of the proletariat who produce material or knowledge goods and services directly or indirectly for capital, and are deprived or expropriated of resources by capital (2011, 280). Fuchs (2011, 279–280) replaces Negri's term 'social worker' with the term 'knowledge worker' to refer to workers who directly produce knowledge goods and services (for example, hardware, software, data, statistics, advertisements, media content, films, music, etc.), and 'workers' who indirectly produce and reproduce the conditions of capital and wage labour such as natural resources, education, sociality, affect, communication, sex, housework, care, and so on.

Fuchs replaces the term 'immaterial labour' with the term 'informational labour' to distance himself from the subjectivism of autonomous Marxism (2008, 103). Informational labour is not detached from nature and matter, but is material itself. It denotes the brain's materiality involved in cognition, communication and cooperation. *Pace* Hardt and Negri, Fuchs (2014, 275–279) claims that it is a mistake to assume that 'immaterial labour' brings about the end of the labour theory of value. Parents, citizens, consumers, Internet prosumers, radio listeners and television viewers are all part of the multitude that employs informational or digital labour to produce the commons of capital's own social and natural reproduction (Fuchs 2008, 202). The amount of this labour time can be measured by counting the hours of unpaid work on the Internet, which can be characterised as indirect common surplus value (Fuchs 2008, 209). Corporations consume the common surplus value produced across the whole range of the social factory, including nature, knowledge, communication, entertainment, culture and public infrastructures (Fuchs 2011, 286). Capitalism, thus, exploits the multitude and society as a whole.

The antagonism between e-cooperation and e-competition: economy, politics and culture

The commons, however, also use capital to reproduce themselves. The multitude makes use of fixed capital (for example, computers and software) for its own benefit as in the case of FOSS developers, the digital commons, Internet prosumers (for example, file sharing) and citizens themselves who use media and Internet services at near-zero marginal cost. Capitalism and the commons constantly feed off each other. The Internet has now shifted the antagonism of capital and the commons into the digital realm. 'Transnational network capitalism has an antagonistic character, knowledge and new technologies do not have one-sided effects, but should be analysed dialectically: they are embedded into a fundamental antagonism of capitalism, the one between cooperation and competition, that has specific manifestations in the various subsystems of society' (Fuchs 2011, 130). The antagonism between cooperation and competition plays out in the antagonism between information as a common/public good and as a commodity. The anti-rivalrous nature of information resists commodification. This resistance stems from the fundamental antagonism between use value and exchange value, with the latter dominating the former; the main aspect of a thing being not its usefulness but its commodification (Fuchs 2008, 164–165). The anti-rivalrous nature of information renders the Internet an antagonistic and contested space where class struggle takes the form of the contradiction between cooperation and competition, pervading the three subsystems of society: economy, politics and culture.

In the Internet economy, the contradiction between cooperation and competition unfolds in the antagonism between the information gift economy and the informational commodity economy (Fuchs 2008, 148–209). The logic of cooperation uses information as a gift that circulates in the global peer production of the multitude, as manifested in the case of platform cooperativism, FOSS development, the digital commons, the makers movement, social movements, and so on. The logic of competition, on the other hand, uses information as a commodity on the model of platform capitalism that exploits user-generated content for the purposes of capital accumulation.

The contradiction between cooperation and competition expands in online politics via the antagonism between e-participation and e-domination (Fuchs 2008, 213–294). The logic of cooperation spreads into e-participation which aims at digital inclusion via forums of grassroots digital democracy, cyberprotest, rational free online speech, critical online public spheres and counter-publics. Fuchs (2008, 163) parts ways here with Lessig's and Stallman's liberal concept of freedom on the net, where digital knowledge can be both commodified and non-commodified. He holds that digital knowledge should not be exchanged for money as a commodity, but provided for free. The logic of domination is based on commodification, resulting in a digital divide marked by information warfare, electronic surveillance and the repression of online plurality and tolerance.

In cyberculture, the contradiction between cooperation and competition takes the final form of antagonism between socialisation and alienation (Fuchs 2008, 299–333). The logic of cooperation takes place in the virtual socialisation of cooperative online participatory communities who represent a unity in diversity of identities and shared meanings through forums of cyber-friendship and cyber-love, high-quality cyberscience, critical online journalism and participatory e-learning. The logic of competition, on the other hand, occurs in the virtual alienation of commodified virtual communities that produce identity marketing, symbolic capital, one-dimensional online journalism, cyber-hate, high-speed cyberscience, inauthentic art and individualised e-learning.

Envisaging communism

Fuchs's (2011, 290–291) core argument is that the Internet is a dialectical space that contains both positive and negative potentials: the advancement of civil society, public discourse, active prosumptive usage by the masses, more open, discursive and democratic forms of education plus the new model of commons-based peer production, all contrast with the corporate appropriation of Web 2.0, digital exclusion and digital divides, the exploitation of Internet prosumers, the fragmentation of the public sphere and the creation of an e-literate online elite. The net result is a class-structured online space that is dominated by corporations that use the Internet as a medium of capital accumulation and advertising (Fuchs 2011, 310).

> Digital media are technologies of domination and liberation at the same time. These potentials are, however, not equally distributed. In a class-based society, we can always take the dominative use of technologies for certain, whereas alternative uses aiming at liberation are much more fragile and precarious. Only political praxis can bring about humanity's emancipation from repression. (Fuchs 2016, 219)

Fuchs (2011, 110) situates the media and information economy within the societal totality and sees them as being embedded within political struggles. He advocates for a human-centred Internet in a human-centred society based on an association of free produsers, critical, self-managed, surveillance-free, beneficial for all, freely accessible for all, classless and universal (2011, 317). The commons-based Internet opposes the corporate-dominated Internet that tends to be exploitative, one-dimensional, undemocratic, surveillant, unequal, access-restricted, fostering economic concentration, individualistic, class-divided and fragmented. The commons-based Internet has to be integrated into political movements that clash with the capitalisation of society, corporate domination, commodification and the imperialistic colonisation of the Internet by capitalist logic (Fuchs 2011, 318).

Fuchs (2011, 311) envisions a post-capitalist world where there is no money, no exchange and profit, where work is voluntary and goods are available for free. He defines communism in the Marxian sense of the association of free prosumers (2011, 330–331). Communism points to the sublation of class in a classless society. It is based on self-management which fosters cooperative production and enriches individuality. Societies contain both elements of private property and common ownership over the means of production (Fuchs 2011, 343). Communism does not put an end to individual consumption, but to the exploitation of the labour of individuals by a small group of capitalists. In communism, the forces of production have increased to such an extent that the springs of common wealth flow abundantly, allowing the economy to flourish on the principle: 'From each according to their abilities, to each according to their needs' (Fuchs 2011, 331–332).

A first step towards communism is the creation of an associationist movement that brings together students, intellectuals, knowledge workers and traditional workers in struggles against capitalism. An alternative Internet would contribute to the commons transition through the peer production of open access projects, open content projects, free software, open source projects, alternative online news media, collective digital art projects, cyberprotest, public online media, public access projects, the struggle for net neutrality, the creation of free wireless networks, non-commercial and non-profit virtual communities, and so on (Fuchs 2011, 345).

> The task is to construct political projects that aim at the connection of the multiplicity of subject positions that are immanent in the multitude and have the potential to advance struggles that transcend capitalism and anticipate a participatory alternative to capitalism, that is, grassroots socialism […] The political task is to create a political unity in plurality of the multitude so that the internal antagonisms are externalised and can be synergistically combining the strength of the now fragmented powers be directed against the capitalist class. (Fuchs 2011, 347–348)

Marxist dialectics vs post-hegemonic discourse

Fuchs's terminology echoes here Laclau and Mouffe's politics of hegemony: 'grassroots socialism', 'subject positions', 'unity in plurality', 'antagonisms'. Yet Fuchs is being critical of post-Marxism without, however, engaging in a detailed critique of Laclau and Mouffe's work. He goes along with the broadening of the notion of class to include non-workers without, however, acceding to a classless analysis (2011, 329). Fuchs (2011, 31) concurs, instead, with Žižek's statement that postmodernism and post-Marxism have, by assuming an 'irreducible plurality of struggles', accepted 'capitalism as the only game in town' and have renounced 'any real attempt to overcome the existing capitalist liberal regime'. This argument, however, is overly generalised and mistaken, especially in relation to Laclau and Mouffe, whose work is radically democratic and profoundly anti-capitalist.

The major problem rests on Fuchs's dialectical methodology which clashes head-on with the post-Marxist methodology of discourse theory. Dialectics is a formalistic simplification of ontological heterogeneity. It is occasionally and partially useful as a methodological tool, not as a transcendental principle of immanence, as Fuchs would have it. The dialectical methodology is valid when used to diagnose, among other things, the main contradiction of capitalism between directors and executants. But it is invalid when advanced to an ontological principle. Following Castoriadis, the heterogeneity of ontological difference crystallises a creation *ex nihilo* that cannot break down into a binary logic. And when it does so, it risks turning into a reversed ideology, a reversed rational mastery (Papadimitropoulos 2016), a reversed instrumental rationality that eliminates or absorbs ontological difference into two hegemonic poles of causal explanation. It reproduces the reversed neopositivism of a two-valued logic embedded into the totalitarian hegemony of socialism that seeks to become science.

The advantage of discourse theory over dialectics is to conceive the real as overdetermined, as being one and many at the same time: a guitar is a musical instrument, a design, a commodity, an embodiment of human labour, a natural combination of wood, sound and strings and an emotional attachment, all at once. Dialectics distorts the polysemia and similitude of things. To identify and contradict presupposes the logic-ontology of difference, which is 'pure' multiplicity infused with the meaning of the political which overdetermines the social. This is not to deny the central contradiction of capitalism between directors and executants, but to situate it in a broader class struggle that takes into account identity politics along with the broadening of the notion of class to include often contradictory class and subject positions.

This has direct consequences for Fuchs's understanding of the political, the primacy of which over the economy discounts the fact that in order to eat and survive, humans need to possess the ontological capacity to search for food in a self-organised manner. Thus, the capacity of humans to self-organise and not the economy per se is the precondition of survival. The economy is the necessary but not the sufficient condition for survival. Coextensive to any emergent social structure is the self-instituting power of agency stemming from the radical imaginary of the anonymous collective, as Castoriadis would have it. What is missing, further, from Fuchs's analysis is the psychoanalytic dimension of affection, which is not reducible to the rationalistic and formalistic schema of dialectics. Dialectics is a useful tool of human agency for simplifying complexity and understanding social change, but not as an ontological nor an epistemological principle per se. By identifying the political with the Marxist dialectics of critical theory, Fuchs undermines the political itself. He underestimates the political inherent in the self-instituting power of the people which transcends a dialectical understanding of the real. Fuchs abstains from the statism of the Communist Party, but still lacks a coherent post-hegemonic grasp on the political.

Notwithstanding the defects of Marxist dialectics, Fuchs's work contributes enormously to building a holistic alternative to neoliberalism, which could be further integrated into a post-hegemonic politics of the common that could create political unity in plurality; connect grassroots socialism with current institutions; produce chains of equivalence between alternative formations of community and governance; and combine horizontalism with verticalism in favour of agonistic political commons that share political values or goods, subject to recurrent question, conflict and revision (Tully 2008, 311–312). Lastly, the virtue of Fuchs's work consists, among other things, in providing a set of concrete policy proposals that could be immensely valuable for a post-hegemonic, commons-orientated transition:

1. Economic redistribution from high-profit corporations and the rich towards low-income classes by increasing taxation of capital and high incomes
2. The full cancellation of the debts of developing countries
3. The introduction of a basic income guarantee for all (financed by, for example, a Tobin tax)
4. Subsidies for self-managed cooperatives, local hardware production and commons-based Internet projects based on free software technologies
5. The introduction of rigidly regulated employment contracts
6. The reduction of working hours without loss of income for employees
7. The establishing of unions
8. Provision of free universal basic services in health and education
9. Universal availability of ICT infrastructure and network connectivity for free or at very low prices for all
10. Support for digital literacy and digital involvement for all
11. Large-scale implementation of open social software tools that support participatory democracy in education, the media and civil society
12. The introduction of global privacy and data-protection laws

4.7 The Lack of the Political III

Kioupkiolis has succeeded in politicising the common by commoning the political, that is, by attuning Laclau and Mouffe's hegemonic politics to the non-hierarchical, open and pluralistic logic of the commons. The post-hegemonic politics of agonistic freedom and radical democracy can be instructive as to how to connect local and global commons; how to unite and coordinate dispersed, small-scale civic initiatives; and how to relate to established social systems and power relations in the market and the state. Post-hegemony is coextensive with the work of Dardot and Laval who build upon the concept of the common as the self-instituting power of the people to further conceptualise the common as an institutionalised right.

Missing, however, in both approaches is a thorough elaboration of the technological and economic implications of the commons. The lack of concrete policies for the commons to reach a critical mass is still telling. This gap can be filled by envisioning a multidisciplinary account of the common that could bring together local and digital commons on the model of open cooperativism. For the commons to become a sustainable model that can challenge capitalism, they need to provide a steady income to their members along with conditions of autonomy, sharing, openness and self-realisation. The ultimate goal is to harmonise the basic ideals of freedom and equality under a holistic regime of pluralist and radical democracy capable of gaining broad civil trust, support and involvement. This post-hegemonic task implies the creation of a post-capitalist economy built around the commons. The role of the state and international institutions is pivotal to introducing the policies necessary to this end.

Dyer-Witheford and De Angelis were among the first to illustrate a post-capitalist model by formalising the circulation of the common alongside the circulation of capital. As with Bauwens and Kostakis, the abundance of the commons coexists with the artificial scarcity of market capitalism until the latter is forced to adjust to the former in the long run. However, they also lack the policy proposals necessary to flesh out this post-capitalist transition. Caffentzis and Federici take a more radical stance by advocating the autonomous development of the commons against capitalism and the state. They do not, however, explain how the commons can survive, reproduce and solve their own contradictions under conditions of grave dependence on capitalism and the state.

Gibson and Graham sketch out a more concrete version of a community economy that could circulate alongside capitalism and transform the latter into post-capitalism. As in the case of the autonomous Marxists, the problem with their approach is that they downplay the significant role that the state could assume in that transformation. The problem with the communist approach of Žižek, Dean and Harvey, on the other hand, is that they overemphasise the role of the state at the expense of the self-instituting power of the people. Mason and Fuchs strike a balance between the state and the commons by introducing a number of concrete policies aimed at advancing the self-instituting power of the people against capitalism and the state. This set of policies could be further integrated into a holistic, post-hegemonic strategy for a post-capitalist, commons-orientated transition.

CHAPTER 5

Conclusion: Reformatting the Commons

A key strand of the core argument put forward in this book is the significant lack of the political in the commons literature. The political is understood within the theoretical framework of Castoriadis's concept of the common as the self-instituting power of the people, promoting individual and collective autonomy. The political embraces direct democracy as the core moral value of society, advancing agonistic freedom, plurality and antagonism.

Whereas all approaches to the commons put forward the self-instituting power of the people as the quintessential concept of the common, they do not fully address the political in terms of radical democracy and power structures. Theorists often rest on a limited or ideological standpoint that runs counter to a holistic approach, which would translate into a set of concrete policies supportive of the commons' sustainability. For this reason, the political has been analysed here through the spectrum of a post-hegemonic perspective, aimed at rendering the commons the dominant socio-economic paradigm vis-à-vis capitalism and the state. Post-hegemony seeks to integrate the economic, technological, sociopolitical and environmental facets of the commons into a holistic, multidisciplinary account of the common.

5.1 Liberal, Reformist and Anti-capitalist Arguments

5.1.1 The Liberal Argument

Ostrom shifted the discourse on incentives from the methodological individualism of neoclassical economics to the institutional structure of collective agency. She reinvigorated the historical concept of the common as the self-instituting power of the people, highlighting the democratic elements of participation and inclusion in the collective management of common-pool resources. Her design principles for the commons – the demarcation of clear boundaries, the matching of rules with local needs and conditions, the modification of rules by

---

How to cite this book chapter:
Papadimitropoulos, V. 2020. *The Commons: Economic Alternatives in the Digital Age.* Pp. 215–226. London: University of Westminster Press. DOI: https://doi.org/10.16997 /book46.e. License: CC-BY-NC-ND 4.0

users themselves, the monitoring of resources and the imposition of sanctions on free-riders – have been broadly accepted and utilised in multiple settings on rural, urban and digital commons.

Yet the self-management of common-pool resources by local communities is overshadowed by the superpowers of states and corporations, thus limiting the self-instituting power of the people. Ostrom's non-mainstream use of institutional economics and game theory conceals the exploitation and power asymmetries inherent in capitalism and the state. She does not take into account the contradictory logics that bring the commons into conflict with the state and capitalist markets. Local commons are in tension with institutional macro-structures and open access commons such as public infrastructures and the digital commons. They are politically debilitating at higher levels. In short, Ostrom downplays the political as antagonism, struggle and power structures. Today, a number of efforts attempt to expand Ostrom's design principles to the digital commons and link the latter with rural and urban commons. Absent, however, is a holistic account that encompasses a multidisciplinary framework for the commons.

Lessig and Benkler expand the common as the self-instituting power of the people from local to digital commons. Contrary to local eco-commons, the digital commons are open, plural, voluntary and international. Modularity and granularity allow for mass participation, flexibility and distributed leadership. Hierarchies tend to be flat and reversible, with the type of affiliation that binds the commons being loose and fluid. The ground of the common is not any ethnic or local identity, but a shared sense of purpose and an ongoing interaction and collaboration along symmetrical rules and ethical lines.

Lessig and Benkler consider commons-based peer production as a third institutional model that offers substantial degrees of freedom and power in addition to state and market operation. It produces significant information and allocation gains compared to managerial hierarchies and markets by introducing a more refined, flexible and cost-efficient information processing, better attuned to the variability of human creativity than managerial hierarchies (firms, states) and markets. Its success, therefore, requires that we modify our conceptions about incentives, the role of property and contract in the domains of information-dependent production, and the theory of the firm and organisational management, including the state and adjoining institutions.

Whereas Lessig takes a liberal stance on the commons, Benkler oscillates between liberalism and anarchism. His ambivalence revolves around the scope and role of commons-based peer production in relation to state and market operation. Lessig and Benkler stress the current battle between corporations and the digital commons. To prevent the corporatisation of cyberspace, they propose the expansion of commons-supporting licences and copyrights enforced by adequate lobbying, litigation and legal reforms, embedded in the generalised production of open source knowledge and peer-to-peer networks. Rather than clashing head-on with capitalism, commons-based peer production is anticipated to render predatory capitalism obsolete through superior working anti-models, running code and a healthy commons that will trump polemics.

Yet monetary motivations still prevail either by necessity or by choice. Commons-based peer production runs mostly on a voluntary and activist mode. It occupies a marginal space in the socio-economic landscape, unable to offer its members a living. Given its grave dependence on the state and capitalism, it cannot reproduce itself into a sustainable mode of production that can challenge neoliberalism. Neither local nor digital commons alone can provide a viable alternative. The digital commons are not yet replicable in other sectors of the economy. The current impotence of the commons vis-à-vis capital and the state resides in the absence of a link between local and global (digital) commons. This void is indicative of the broader lack of the political which accounts for the strategic non-choice of the liberal commons to band together dispersed initiatives into a coherent political strategy capable of opposing the neoliberal status quo. Dardot and Laval and Kioupkiolis correctly note that the liberal approach to the commons cannot address the repercussions of the contradictions of capitalism and the state.

5.1.2 The Reformist Argument

The reformist approach to the commons purports to advance the self-instituting power of the people from a third institutional axis of civil society into a counter-hegemonic power directed against neoliberalism. Bollier recalibrates the liberal state to support the commons rather than the capitalist market, introducing a green governance model with the aim of tackling climate change and protecting the natural commons. He documents a number of initiatives that attempt to bridge the gap between local and global commons and progress the commons into a counter-hegemonic project beyond capitalism and the state.

Rifkin advocates a social democratic commons-orientated transition, in which the developed nations in concert with the big corporations would be the leaders of the Third Industrial Revolution, intended to gradually coalesce around the collaborative commons and transform capitalism into post-capitalism. As with the liberal approach to the commons, Rifkin's wishful thinking bypasses the contradictions of capitalism and the state, thus reproducing the lack of the political. He has succeeded in linking local with global commons via the Internet of Things infrastructure, best served by self-management. Yet the transition to the commons is not merely a technical issue of algorithms programming win–win partnerships between the state, capitalism and the commons. It requires a shift to another model of society based on real democracy; hence, the need for the creation of a novel anthropological type anchored in the abolition of the division between directors and executants and the establishment of individual and collective autonomy.

Scholz adds a cooperative twist to the collaborative commons by juxtaposing platform cooperativism against platform capitalism (the so-called sharing and gig economy). Platform cooperativism consists of online business models based on democratic self-governance, platform co-ownership and equitable distribution of value. The idea is to use the algorithmic design of apps such as Uber in the service of a cooperative business model and bring together the roughly 170 years of the cooperative movement with commons-based peer production. But Scholz, too, oscillates between a moderate and a radical thesis. He contends that it is unrealistic to anticipate that platform co-ops will dominate capitalist markets. Rather, he envisions a more diversified economy. Therefore, there is a tension here between the alleged radicalism of platform cooperativism and his projecting a mixed economy.

A more radical line of argument holds that platform cooperativism would rather integrate into commons-based peer production. Bauwens and Kostakis attempt to bridge Ostrom's local commons with Benkler's digital commons by incorporating the ecological model Design Global–Manufacture Local (DG–ML) into the commons, supported by the Internet and free software/hardware. They give a challenging spin to platform cooperativism by introducing the model of open cooperativism between the commons and ethical market entities, operating in terms of open protocols, open supply chains, commons-based licensing and open book accounting. Open cooperativism aims at the creation of a commons-orientated economy based on shared resources from which actors can draw and to which they can contribute according to their needs and capacities. The commons are ideally backed by a partner state through taxation, funding, regulation, education and so forth.

Bauwens and Kostakis's core argument is that firms that cooperate with the digital commons, and therefore have access to a vast pool of knowledge, obtain a competitive advantage over proprietary firms that rely solely on their private R&D. The hybrid of post-capitalist commons can beat capitalism on its own ground: that is, competition. The cooperation of ethical market entities with *glocal* commons, supported by a partner state, can create an abundance of value that will force capitalism to adjust to the commons in the long run.

Bauwens and Kostakis's strategy comprises both state and market mechanisms along democratic, ethical and ecological lines. It aims to gradually transform capitalism and the state into the commons. Yet the commons cannot currently compete with the capitalist behemoths on various grounds: capital, know-how, skills, political power, etc. Bauwens and Kostakis's model requires a holistic political strategy to translate into centrally coordinated micro/macro-policies stretching across the entire body of the social. This could be achieved by a partner state applying the principles of the commons at a local, regional, national and international level.

Arvidsson and Peitersen follow in the footsteps of Bauwens and Kostakis, deviating only by tracing out a technologically 'updated' Habermasian transformation of the public sphere. Rather than attuning to a more radical approach to the commons that would steer the self-instituting power of the people against neoliberalism, they conform to a mainstream approach. They envisage the romantic reconciliation of affect with the commitment of the Enlightenment to rationality and measurement through the financial monetisation of productive publics, supported by the Internet and open source software/hardware. But this vision bears little resemblance to the current status of the commons, which are largely co-opted by finance capitalism.

Arvidsson and Peitersen acknowledge that Internet neutrality is currently under threat from political and commercial forces, which are planning to impose biased standards favouring their own commercial interests. The last decades have already witnessed a state of 'information feudalism', where firms and corporations make billions out of monetising users' personal data and online activity. To reverse this, they go along with Lessig, Benkler and Bollier to advocate for traditional political lobbying and activism to safeguard network neutrality and regulate social media companies. The ultimate political goal would be a global New Deal around sustainability and social responsibility. But this is simply to ignore the contradictions of capitalism and the state, which undermine the concept of the common as the self-instituting power of the people. The common should not limit itself to a social democratic paradigm, but should aim at deepening democracy and empowering citizens themselves. Arvidsson and Peitersen do not fully address the political in terms of individual and collective autonomy.

Rushkoff's model of digital distributism is more in line with Bauwens and Kostakis's post-capitalist vision in that he envisions a hybrid economy that could force capitalism in the long run to adjust to the commons. However, the exclusion of the state from Rushkoff's account is significantly debilitating for a commons-orientated transition.

Wright provides probably the most holistic political alternative for the commons by integrating the self-instituting power of the people into a strategic pluralism opening up multiple pathways of social empowerment, embodied in a variety of structural transformations. As such, it can function as an institutional multi-format for the various approaches to the commons. Wright's seven pathways to socialism provide a rough map of the direction of social empowerment. It is, however, perhaps more efficient to fit Wright's pluralism into a more cohesive post-hegemonic strategy aimed at unifying the different commons under a common democracy.

5.1.3 The Anti-capitalist Argument

Kioupkiolis detects a tension between Laclau and Mouffe's verticalism and Hardt and Negri's horizontalism. Whereas Laclau and Mouffe consider top-down procedures to be a *sine qua non* for radical democratic politics, Hardt and Negri favour a bottom-up approach. Kioupkiolis attempts to reconcile Laclau and Mouffe's hegemonic politics with the non-hierarchical, open and pluralistic logic of the commons. His post-hegemonic politics of agonistic freedom and radical democracy can, indeed, be instructive as to how to politicise the common and connect local and global commons; how to unite and coordinate dispersed, small-scale civic initiatives; and how to relate to established social systems and power relations in the market and the state. In short, post-hegemony could render the self-instituting power of the people the central axis of the political in the commons.

Post-hegemony goes along with the work of Dardot and Laval to the degree that they build upon the concept of the common as the self-instituting power of the people introduced by Marx, Proudhon and Castoriadis. What is absent in both Kioupkiolis's and Dardot and Laval's account is a more thorough elaboration of the technological and economic conditions of the commons. This gap can be filled by a holistic, multidisciplinary account of the commons that can bring together local and global commons under post-capitalism. For the commons to evolve into a sustainable mode of production capable of challenging neoliberalism, they need to provide a steady income to their members along with the political conditions for democracy and self-realisation. This task points to the creation of a social economy built around the commons. Unlike Castoriadis, this book makes the case that the role of the state and international institutions is pivotal to introducing the policies necessary to this end. The commons should not abstain from market and state operation, but rather strive to gear both to the interests of commoners.

Dyer-Witheford and De Angelis were among the first to envisage a post-capitalist transition by formalising the circulation of the common against the circulation of capital. As with Bauwens and Kostakis, the abundance of the commons necessarily transacts with the scarcity of market capitalism until the latter is forced to adjust to the former. But they also lack a set of concrete policies to activate this transition.

Caffentzis and Federici oppose both state and market operation. They advocate, instead, the autonomous development of the commons against capitalism and the state. They do not, however, develop an account of how the commons can survive and solve their own contradictions under conditions of grave dependence on capitalism and the state.

Gibson and Graham offer a more concrete demonstration of a post-capitalist community economy. But, as in the case of the autonomous Marxists, they downplay the role that the state could assume in this project. The problem with the communist approach of Žižek, Dean and Harvey, on the other hand, is that they overemphasise the role of the state at the expense of the self-instituting power of the people. Mason and Fuchs seek to strike the right balance between the state and the commons by introducing a number of concrete policies, employing both commons and state mechanisms to promote and safeguard the self-instituting power of the people.

5.1.4 Towards Post-hegemonic Holism

The final step here is to integrate all three approaches to the commons into a holistic, multidisciplinary account that encompasses finance, economics, technology, politics, education and law under commons governance. To this end, this chapter summarises key proposals from all three approaches to the commons, which are by no means exhaustive. These proposals could play out in multiple patterns of cross-fertilising strategies that could variously advance the self-instituting power of the people beyond capitalism and the state. Rather than approaching the commons in terms of scattered and often contrasting theories, it would be far more beneficial for both theory and praxis to consider them in tandem with a flexible, multi-format set of policies from which political agents can draw accordingly. This is not to resort to a politics *à la carte* nor to diminish conflict as the essential element of the political. On the contrary, post-hegemonic holism sets pluralism and antagonism as the main stage of progressive politics. Since there can be no single theory capable of carving out a unique pathway to a post-capitalist, commons-orientated transition, implications for policy depend on which set of proposals would be more relevant under the ever-changing global conditions of class struggle:

5.2 Liberal, Reformist and Radical Formats

The liberal format

1. The expansion of Ostrom's design principles – the demarcation of clear boundaries, the matching of rules with local needs and conditions, the modification of rules by users themselves, the monitoring of resources and the imposition of sanctions on free-riders – from local to digital commons (free software and Blockchain technologies). Ostrom's design principles could apply also on a reformist and radical format.
2. The design of patents and intellectual property to taper away quickly.
3. Municipal funding of neutral broadband networks, state funding of basic research, and possible strategic regulatory interventions to negate monopoly control over essential resources in the digital environment.
4. Commons-based licensing (GNU, Creative Commons, Copyfair).
5. A number of post-Keynesian policies have been introduced by several authors to address the shortcomings of neoliberalism: Mariana Mazzucato calls for the 'socialisation of investment' by an 'entrepreneurial state' investing in innovation to address major societal problems such as climate change and elderly healthcare (Jacobs and Mazzucato 2016, 14); Stiglitz (2016) suggests changes to executive compensation schemes,

macroeconomic policies to reduce unemployment, greater investment in education and infrastructure and the reform of capital taxation; Yanis Varoufakis (2011) advocates a Green New Deal funded by Eurobonds as a first step before reimagining the corporation. A further step would be to shift the terrain from post-Keynesianism to post-capitalism through the creation of commons-centric partner states willing to invest heavily in the commons. Rather than reimagining the corporation, post-Keynesianism should reimagine the commons by transforming the state accordingly.

6. Interestingly, DIEM25, the party founded by Yanis Varoufakis, included in its agenda (DIEM25 2019) a number of policies in favour of the commons that could push for a more radical transformative politics by:
   - enhancing regulations on data protection (GDPR) and e-privacy
   - strengthening anti-trust laws
   - enforcing cross-platform interoperability and e-portability of data
   - introducing the concept of data unions
   - decommodifying data through the establishment of a public data commons, thereby establishing a Digital Commonwealth
   - supporting alternative business models such as platform cooperatives
   - fighting tax evasion by platform companies and imposing a digital tax/ dividend on the collecting/processing and sale of personal data
   - establishing a digital rights framework for e-citizens (the right to encryption, the right to computation, the right to an algorithmic opt-out and opt-in)
   - transforming intellectual property by limiting its scope and broadening the 'fair use' concept

The reformist format

1. The adoption of a different language of the commons that would reflect their multiple patterns.
2. The creation and use of distributed ledger platforms such as Blockchain and Holochain that can advance cooperation on digital networks and boost a parallel commons ecosystem running both online and offline.
3. The state could install open platforms inviting citizens to assist city councils in urban planning, government websites encouraging citizen feedback about public services, participatory budgeting programmes allowing citizens to co-determine spending decisions, government support for co-housing, volunteer networks for the elderly, and so on. Free and open source software could become the default infrastructure in public administration and education. Instead of schools turning into the quasi-captive extensions of large software corporations' marketing departments, they could educate students in the use of open source software, which would then have spin-off effects for higher education, municipal governments and the general public. State-endorsed open design protocols for information services, housing, ride-hailing services and energy

grids could foster open source innovation and benefit local communities, preventing proprietary lock-ins by larger companies.

4. Regulation of platform co-ops.

5. Open cooperativism between productive communities, ethical market entities and for-benefit associations. Open design, open protocols, open supply chains, open value accounting that promote abundance vs scarcity and collaboration by mutual coordination, which can in turn sustain a circular economy. Cosmolocalism could bring together digital, rural and urban commons, energy cooperatives, eco-villages, the degrowth movement and Transition Towns.

6. A commons-centric partner state that implements direct democratic procedures and introduces commons-friendly policies in taxation, law, education and research. The partner state could support new forms of common–public partnerships similar to the cases of Barcelona en Comú, Bologna, Naples and Ghent (Bauwens and Niaros 2017). A common–public partnership is a joint enterprise between a commons association, a state or local authority and a trade union or experts, which applies co-ownership and distributed democratic control of surplus value (Milburn and Russell 2019). The democratic structure and surplus distribution is contingent on the nature of the joint enterprise, be it the establishment of energy company infrastructure, the collective purchasing of a market building, initial subsidisation of a platform taxi cooperative, the purchasing of land for a community land trust, and so on. A common–public partnership constitutes a self-expanding circuit of radical democratic self-governance and centrifugal financialisation that could transfer wealth from one initiative to another, thus transforming surplus value into common use value. Centrifugal financialisation would allow a circulation of common use value against the centripetal circulation of capital.

7. A partner state could establish public forums of democratic participation such as a Commons CityLab, where an Assembly of the Commons (representing citizens) and a Chamber of the Commons (representing members of generative enterprises) could work in concert with government representatives and knowledge institutions to generate public–private–common partnerships on the model of Ostrom's polycentric governance. Additional measures would include the provision of adequate regulation, financing and legal support for commons initiatives (Bauwens and Niaros 2017, 62–79).

8. The DECODE project has built alternative digital platforms in Barcelona and Amsterdam to bring the data economy back under democratic control and give citizens control over their data. It documents a number of business and revenue models that could help secure the sustainability of the commons. By building a set of technical, economic, social and legal tools, they contribute to a multidisciplinary approach to the commons, further promoting commons-based peer production on the models of platform and open cooperativism.

9. The deepening of democracy in all three varieties of democratic governance (direct democracy, representative and associational). Participatory forms of direct democracy could create countervailing power against the ordinarily powerful groups and elites influencing state governance. The design principles of this power are the following: bottom-up participation, pragmatic orientation, deliberation, state-centred decentralisation to local units of action such as neighbourhood councils, local school councils, workplace councils, and so on.

10. The commons-orientated structural adjustment of capitalism towards more sustainable and socially responsible business models such as open sharing and collaboration models, 'inclusive capitalism', the 'benefit corporation', 'flexible purpose corporation', 'low-profit limited liability company' and 'not-for-profit', which prioritise value creation and money circulation by distributing currency to more people and enterprises.

11. In addition to associations of workers or unions exerting power over corporations through the co-determination of funds, and bargaining over pay and working conditions, the union movement could create venture capital funds, controlled by labour (as in Canada), to provide equity to start-up firms that satisfy particular social criteria. Consumer-orientated pressure on corporations would be an additional form of civil society empowerment over economic power. Fair trade and equal exchange movements aiming to connect consumers and producers by building alternative global economic networks could also disrupt the economic power of multinational corporations.

12. The creation of a social economy: voluntary associations, NGOs, co-ops, community-based organisations, all subsidised through donations, charities, grants and taxes (for example, Wikipedia, the Quebec economy). Social economy could merge with platform and open co-ops on the principles of cosmolocalism and commons-based peer production.

13. Egalitarian public financing of politics, and randomly selected citizen assemblies. Political institutions could be designed in such a way as to enable secondary associations – labour unions, business associations, organisations or civic groups – to play a positive role in deepening democracy.

14. The creation of a National Investment Council (NIC) coupled with Federal Reserve reforms that would create a 'QE for the people' channelled to commons initiatives; a Fed-administered digital dollar backed by Blockchain and accessed via smartphones would further guarantee greater financial inclusion.

15. The creation of a national investment bank linked to a set of non-profit, decentralised financial institutions such as credit unions, public banks, community banks and non-profit investment banks to provide credit for the commons.

16. The creation of a non-profit innovation stock market would further open up investment opportunities to the broad public and help the commons raise capital for expansion.

17. The creation of a commons-orientated Public Investment Platform joined by a Public Investment Account.

18. The creation of sovereign wealth funds and inclusive ownership funds.

19. An unconditional basic income could further enhance the social economy and the commons.

The radical format

1. The socialisation of the banking system to promote the democratic finance of the commons: social and ethical lending by credit unions and public banks, non-profit local and regional banks, crowdfunding (for example, Goteo), complementary currencies, time banks. This would include the restructuring of the finance system to reward techno-social innovation and discourage rent-seeking behaviour. It would, thus, advance commons-friendly finance structures based on bounded investing such as union pension funds, affordable housing investment funds, communities, interest groups and a mutually supportive range of businesses, where money ends up circulating rather than being sucked up by a company foreign to the ecosystem.

2. Post-hegemonic horizontalism against any residual verticality: 1) representation should emanate from the bottom through decentralised decision making based on openness, transparency and diversity; 2) accountability and revocability of representatives would secure democratic control by and for the commons; 3) regular rotation in roles and responsibilities should be exercised with the aim of empowering all the people with relevant skills and knowledge; 4) self-management would thereby instil an ethical self-transformation through a subjectivation that would induce both individual and collective autonomy.

3. Economic redistribution from high-profit corporations and the rich towards low-income classes by increasing taxation of capital and high incomes (for example, Tobin tax or high taxes on rent seeking).

4. The commonification of social media.

5. An alternative Internet would contribute to the commons transition through the peer production of open access projects, open content projects, free software, open source projects, alternative online news media, collective digital art projects, cyberprotest, public online media, public access projects, the struggle for net neutrality, the creation of free wireless networks, non-commercial and non-profit virtual communities, and so on.

6. The full cancellation of the debts of developing countries.

7. The introduction of rigidly regulated employment contracts.

8. The reduction of working hours without loss of income for employees.
9. The establishing of unions.
10. Provision of free universal basic services in health and education.
11. Universal availability of ICT infrastructure and network connectivity for free or at very low prices for all.
12. Support for digital literacy and digital involvement for all.
13. Large-scale implementation of open social software tools that support participatory democracy in education, the media and civil society.
14. The introduction of global privacy and data-protection laws.

References

Agamben, Giorgio. 1993. *The Coming Community*. Minneapolis, MN: University of Minnesota Press.

Aigrain, Philippe. 2012. *Sharing: Culture and the Economy in the Internet Age*. Amsterdam: Amsterdam University Press.

Althusser, Louis. 1972. *Politics and History*. London: New Left Books.

Andersson, Krister P. and Ostrom, Elinor. 2008. Analysing Decentralised Resource Regimes From a Polycentric Perspective. *Policy Sciences*, 41(1), 71–93.

Anzilotti, Eillie. 2018. Worker-owned Co-ops Are Coming for the Digital Gig Economy. *Fast Company*. Last accessed 21 January 2019. https://www.fastcompany.com/40575728/worker-owned-co-ops-are-coming-for-the-digital-gig-economy.

Arendt, Hannah. 1958. *The Human Condition*. Chicago, IL: University of Chicago Press.

Arendt, Hannah. 1968. *Imperialism*. New York: Harcourt Brace Jovanovich.

Aristotle. 1932. *Politics*. Cambridge, MA: Harvard University Press.

Arrow, Kenneth. 1950. A Difficulty in the Concept of Social Welfare. *Journal of Political Economy*, 58, 328–346.

Arrow, Kenneth. 1962. Economic Welfare and the Allocation of Resources for Invention. In Robert Nelson (Ed.), *The Rate and Direction of Inventive Activity: Economic and Social Factors*, pp. 609–626. Princeton, NJ: Princeton University Press.

Arterton, Christopher. 1987. *Teledemocracy: Can Technology Protect Democracy?* Newbury Park, CA: Sage.

Arvidsson, Adam. 2009. The Ethical Economy: Towards a Post-Capitalist Theory of Value. *Capital & Class*, 33(1), 13–29.

Arvidsson, Adam. 2013. The Potential of Consumer Publics. *Ephemera*, 13(2), 367–391.

Arvidsson, Adam, Bauwens, Michel, and Peitersen, Nicolai. 2008. The Crisis of Value and the Ethical Economy. *Journal of Future Studies*, 12(4), 9–20.

Arvidsson, Adam, and Peitersen, Nicolai. 2013. *The Ethical Economy, Rebuilding Value after the Crisis*. New York: Columbia University Press.

Badiou, Alain. 2009. *L'Hypothèse communiste*. Paris: Nouvelle Editions Lignes.

Badiou, Alain. 2010. The Idea of Communism. In Costas Douzinas and Slavoj Žižek (Eds.), *The Idea of Communism*, pp. 1–14. London: Verso.

Balibar, Etienne, and Wallerstein, Immanuel. 1991. *Race, Nation, Class*. London: Verso.

Barabási, Albert-Lázló. 2003. *Linked*. New York: Plume.

Barber, Benjamin R. 2003. *Strong Democracy*. Berkeley, CA: University of California Press.

Barbrook Richard. 2008. The High-Tech Gift Economy. *First Monday* 3(12) Special Issue #3: Internet banking, e-money, and Internet gift economies. Last accessed 20 March 2020. https://journals.uic.edu/ojs /index.php/fm/article/view/631/552.

Bardhi, Fleura, and Eckhardt, Gianna M. 2012. Access-based Consumption: The Case of Car Sharing. *Journal of Consumer Research*, 39(4), 881–898.

Bauwens, Michel. 2005. The Political Economy of Peer Production. *C-Theory*. Last accessed 16 May 2016. http://www.ctheory.net/articles.aspx?id=499.

Bauwens, Michel. 2012. Blueprint for P2P Society: The Partner State & Ethical Economy. *Shareable*. Last accessed 22 July 2019. https://www.shareable.net /blueprint-for-p2p-society-the-partner-state-ethical-economy

Bauwens, Michel. 2014. Towards the Democratization of the Means of Monetization: The Three Competing Value Models Present Within Cognitive Capitalism. *The Journal of Peer Production*, 4: *Value and Currency*. Last accessed 24 June 2020. http://peerproduction.net/issues/issue-4-value-and -currency/invited-comments/towards-the-democratization-of-the-means -of-monetization/.

Bauwens, Michel, and Kostakis, Vasilis. 2014. From the Communism of Capital to Capital for the Commons: Towards an Open Co-operativism. *tripleC: Communication Capitalism & Critique*, 12(1), 356–361.

Bauwens, Michel, and Kostakis, Vasilis. 2017a. Cooperativism in the Digital Era, or How to Form a Global Counter-Economy. *Open Democracy*. Last accessed 2 May 2017. https://www.opendemocracy.net/digitaliberties /michel-bauwens-vasiliskostakis/cooperativism-in-digital-era-or-how-to -form-global-counter-economy.

Bauwens, Michel, and Kostakis, Vasilis. 2017b. Peer to Peer Production and the Partner State. *Red Pepper*. Last accessed 12 June 2019. http://www.red pepper.org.uk/peer-to-peer-production-and-the-partner-state.

Bauwens, Michel, Kostakis, Vasilis, and Pazaitis, Alex. 2016. Towards a Society of the Commons. In Walter Baier, Eric Canepa and Eva Himmelstoss (Eds.), *The Enigma of Europe: Transform! Yearbook 2016*, pp. 137–146. London: Merlin Press.

Bauwens, Michel, Kostakis, Vasilis, and Pazaitis, Alex. 2019. *Peer to Peer: The Commons Manifesto*. London: University of Westminster Press.

Bauwens, Michel, Kostakis, Vasilis, Troncoso, Stacco, and Utratel, Anna Marie. 2017. *Commons Transition and P2P: A Primer*. Amsterdam: Transnational Institute.

Bauwens, Michel, and Niaros, Vasilis. 2017. *Changing Societies Through Urban Commons Transitions*. Berlin: Heinrich Böll Stiftung.

Bauwens, Michel, and Pantazis, Alekos. 2018. The Ecosystem of Commons -based Peer Production and its Transformative Dynamics.*The Sociological Review* 66(2), 302–319.

Belk, Russell. 2014. You Are What You Can Access: Sharing and Collaborative Consumption Online. *Journal of Business Research*, 67, 1595–1600.

Bell, Daniel. 1973. *The Coming of Postindustrial Society*. New York: Basic Books.

Benkler, Yochai. 2000. From Consumers to Users: Shifting the Deeper Structures of Regulation Toward Sustainable Commons and User Access. *Federal Communication Law Journal*, 52(3), 561–579.

Benkler, Yochai. 2002a. Intellectual Property and the Organisation of Information Production. *International Review of Law and Economics*, 22, 81–107.

Benkler, Yochai. 2002b. Coase's Penguin, or, Linux and the Nature of the Firm. *The Yale Law Journal*, 112, 349–466.

Benkler, Yochai. 2006. *The Wealth of Networks: How Social Production Transforms Markets and Freedom*. New Haven, CT: Yale University Press.

Benkler, Yochai. 2011. *The Penguin and the Leviathan: The Triumph of Cooperation Over Self-Interest*. New York: Crown Business.

Benkler, Yochai. 2013a. Commons and Growth: The Essential Role of Open Commons in Market Economies. *The University of Chicago Law Review*, 80(3), 1499–1555.

Benkler, Yochai. 2013b. Practical Anarchism: Peer Mutualism, Market Power, and the Fallible State. *Politics & Society*, 41(2), 213–251.

Benkler, Yochai. 2016a. Peer Production, the Commons, and the Future of the Firm. *Strategic Organisation*, 264, 1–11.

Benkler Yochai. 2016b. Peer Production and Cooperation. In Johannes Bauer and Michael Latzer (Eds.), *Handbook on the Economics of the Internet*, pp. 91–99. Cheltenham: Edward Elgar.

Benkler, Yochai, Shaw, Aaron, and Hill, Benjamin Mako. 2015. Peer Production: A Form of Collective Intelligence. In Thomas Malone and Michel Berstein (Eds.), *Handbook of Collective Intelligence*, pp. 1–28. Cambridge, MA: MIT Press.

Bentham, Jeremy. 1907/1789. *An Introduction to the Principles of Morals and Legislation*. Oxford: Clarendon Press.

Benyayer, Louis-David. 2016. *Open Models: Business Models of the Open Economy*. Cachan: Without Model.

Birkinbine, Ben. 2018. Commons Praxis: Towards a Critical Political Economy of the Digital Commons. *tripleC: Communication Capitalism & Critique*, 16(1), 290–305.

Blanchard, Olivier, and Summers, Lawrence H. 2017. Rethinking Stabilisation Policy: Evolution or Revolution? Working Paper. Cambridge: National Bureau of Economic Research. Last accessed 20 March 2020. https://www.nber.org/papers/w24179.pdf.

Block, Fred. 2019. Financial Democratization and the Transition to Socialism. *Politics & Society*, 47(4), 529–556.

Bock, Anne-Katrin, Bontoux, Laurent, Figueiredo do Nascimento, Susana, and Szczepanikova, Alice. 2016. The Future of the EU Collaborative Economy – Using Scenarios to Explore Future Implications for Employment. EUR 28051 EN; DOI: https://doi.org/10.2760/354417.

Bohman, James. 1996. *Public Deliberation: Pluralism, Complexity and Democracy*. Cambridge, MA: MIT Press.

Bollier, David. 2001. *Public Assets, Private Profits: Reclaiming the American Commons in an Age of Market Enclosure*. Washington DC: New American Foundation.

Bollier, David. 2003. *Silent Theft: The Private Plunder of Our Common Wealth*. New York: Taylor & Francis.

Bollier, David. 2008. *Viral Spiral: How the Commoners Built a Digital Republic of their Own*. New York: New Press.

Bollier, David, and Helfrich, Silke. 2012. *The Wealth of the Commons: A World Beyond Market & State*. Amherst, MA: Levellers Press.

Bollier, David, and Helfrich, Silke. 2015. *Patterns of Commoning*. Amherst, MA: Levellers Press.

Bollier, David, and Helfrich, Silke. 2019. *Free, Fair and Alive. The Insurgent Power of the Commons*. Gabriola Island: New Society Publishers.

Bollier, David, and Weston, Burns H. 2012. Green Governance: Ecological Survival, Human Rights and the Law of the Commons. In David Bollier and Silke Helfrich (Eds.), *The Wealth of the Commons: A World Beyond Market & State*, pp. 343–352. Amherst, MA: Levellers Press.

Botsman, Ratsel, and Rogers, Roo. 2010. *What's Mine is Yours: How Collaborative Consumption is Changing the Way We Live*. New York: Harper Business.

Boutang, Yann Moulier. 2012. *Cognitive Capitalism*. Cambridge: Polity.

Bowles, Samuel, and Gintis, Herbert. 1980. Structure and Practice in the Labour Theory of Value. *Review of Political Economics*, 12(4), 1–26.

Bowles, Samuel, and Gintis, Herbert. 2011. *A Cooperative Species: Human Reciprocity and its Evolution*. Princeton, NJ: Princeton University Press.

Bowles, Samuel, and Hwang Sung-Ha. 2008. Social Preferences and Public Economics: Mechanism Design when Social Preferences Depend on Incentives. *Journal of Public Economics*, 92, 1811–1820.

Bowles, Samuel, and Polanía-Reyes, Sandra. 2012. Economic Incentives and Social Preferences: Substitutes or Complements? *Journal of Economic Literature*, 50, 368–425.

Boyle, James. 1996. *Shamans, Software & Spleens*, Cambridge, MA: Harvard University Press.

Broumas, Antonios. 2017. Social Democratic and Critical Theories of the Intellectual Commons: A Critical Analysis. *tripleC: Communication Capitalism & Critique*, 15(1), 100–126.

Broumas, Antonios. 2018. Rational Choice and Neoliberal Theories of the Intellectual Commons: A Critical Analysis. *Ephemera*, 18(3), 605–630.

Broumas, Antonios. 2020. *Intellectual Commons and the Law, A Normative Theory for Commons-Based Peer Production*. London: University of Westminster Press (forthcoming).

Brousseau, Eric, and Curien, Nicolas (Eds.) 2007. *Internet and Digital Economics: Principles, Methods and Applications*. Cambridge: Cambridge University Press.

Brown, Wendy. 2015. *Undoing the Demos: Neoliberalism's Stealth Revolution*. New York: Zone Books.

Bruns, Axel. 2008. *Blogs, Wikipedia, Second Life, and Beyond: From Production to Produsage*. New York: Peter Lang.

Brynjolfsson, Eric, and McAfee, Andrew. 2014. *The Second Machine Age. Work, Progress and Prosperity in a Time of Brilliant Technologies*. New York: W.W. Norton.

Bulajewski, Mike. 2012. An Ambitious Plan for Putting Kickstarter Out of Business. *A Blog of Philosophical Reflections & Speculations*. Last accessed 11 April 2014. www.mrteacup.org/post/an-ambitious-plan-for-putting-kickstarterout-of-business.html.

Caffentzis, George. 2013. *In Letters of Blood and Fire: Work, Machines and the Crisis of Capitalism*. Oakland, CA: PM Press.

Caffentzis, George, and Federici, Silvia. 2014. Commons Against and Beyond Capitalism. *Community Development Journal*, 49, 92–105.

Card, Claudia (Ed.). 2003. *The Cambridge Companion to Simone de Beauvoir*. Cambridge: Cambridge University Press.

Carlsson, Lars, and Sandström, Annica. 2008. Network Governance of the Commons. *International Journal of the Commons*, 2(1), 33–54.

Carter, Ian, Kramer, Matthew, and Steiner, Hillel (Eds.). 2007. *Freedom, a Philosophical Anthology*. Malden, MA: Blackwell.

Casarino, Cesare, and Negri, Antonio. 2008. *In Praise of the Common: A Conversation of Philosophy and Politics*. Minneapolis, MN: University of Minnesota Press.

Castells, Manuel. 2000. *End of Millennium. Volume 3 of the Information Age: Economy, Society and Culture* (2nd ed.). Malden, MA: Blackwell.

Castells, Manuel. 2007. Communication, Power and Counter-Power in the Network Society. *International Journal of Communication*, 1, 238–266.

Castells, Manuel. 2009. *Communication Power*. Oxford: Oxford University Press.

Castells, Manuel. 2010. *The Rise of the Network Society*. Oxford: Blackwell.

Castoriadis, Cornelius. 1987. *The Imaginary Institution of Society*. Cambridge: Polity Press.

Castoriadis, Cornelius. 1988. *Political and Social Writings Vol. 2*. Trans. and ed. D.A. Curtis. Minneapolis, MN: University of Minnesota Press.

Castoriadis, Cornelius. 1991a. Reflections on 'Rationality' and 'Development'. In David Ames Curtis (Ed.), *Philosophy, Politics, Autonomy*, pp. 175–218. Oxford: Oxford University Press.

Castoriadis, Cornelius. 1991b. Power, Politics, Autonomy. In David Ames Curtis (Ed.), *Philosophy, Politics, Autonomy*, pp. 143–174. Oxford: Oxford University Press.

Castoriadis, Cornelius. 1993. *Political and Social Writings Vol. 3*. Trans. and ed. D.A. Curtis. Minneapolis, MN: University of Minnesota Press.

Castree, Noel. 2010. Neoliberalism and the Biophysical Environment. *Environment and Society: Advances in Research*, 1, 5–45.

Clastres, Pierre. 1989. *Society Against the State*. New York: Zone Books.

Cleaver, Harry. 1979. *Reading Capital Politically*. Brighton: Harvester.

Codagnone, Christiano, Biagi, Federico, and Abadie, Fabienne. 2016a. The Future of Work in the 'Sharing Economy'. Market Efficiencies and Equitable Opportunities or Unfair Precarisation? JRC Science for Policy Report. EUR 27913 EN. DOI: https://doi.org/10.2791/431485.

Codagnone, Christiano, Biagi, Federico, and Abadie, Fabienne. 2016b. The Passions and the Interests: Unpacking the 'Sharing Economy'. JRC Science for Policy Report. EUR 27914 EN. DOI: https://doi.org/10.2791/474555.

Coleman, Gabriella. 2004. The Political Agnosticism of Free and Open Source Software and the Inadvertent Politics of Contrast. *Anthropological Quarterly*, 77(3), 507–519.

Coleman, Stephen, and Gotze, John. 2001. Bowling Together: Online Public Engagement in Policy Deliberation. *Information Polity*, 7: 247–252. http://bowlingtogether.net/bowlingtogether.pdf.

Conaty, Pat, and Bollier, David. 2015. *Democratic Money and Capital for the Commons. A Report on a Commons Strategies Group Workshop in Cooperation with the Heinrich Böll Foundation, Berlin, Germany*. Last accessed 24 June 2020. https://www.boell.de/sites/default/files/democratic_money_capital_for_the_commons_report_january2016.pdf.

Cortese, Amy. 2016. A New Wrinkle in the Gig Economy: Workers Get Most of the Money. *New York Times*. Last accessed 20 January 2019. https://www.nytimes.com/2016/07/21/business/smallbusiness/a-new-wrinkle-in-the-gig-economy-workers-get-most-of-the-money.html.

Crouch, Colin. 2004. *Post-Democracy*. Cambridge: Polity.

Crowston, Kevin, and Howison, James. 2006. Hierarchy and Centralisation in Free and Open Source Software Team Communications. *Knowledge, Technology and Policy*, 18, 65–85.

Dardot, Pierre, and Laval, Christian. 2014. *Commun: Essais sur la révolution au XXIe siècle*. Paris: La Découverte.

Davies, William. 2017. *The Limits of Neoliberalism. Authority, Sovereignty and the Logic of Competition*. London: Sage.

De Alessi, Michael. 1998. *Fishing for Solutions*. London: Institute of Economic Affairs.

De Angelis, Massimo. 2017. *Omnia Sunt Communia. On the Commons and the Transformation to Postcapitalism*. London: Zed Books.

De Filippi, Primavera. 2015a. Community Mesh Networks: Citizens Participation in the Deployment of Smart Cities. In Andrea Vesco and Francesco Ferrero (Eds.), *Handbook of Research on Social, Economic, and Environmental Sustainability in the Development of Smart Cities*, pp. 298–314. Hershey, PA: IGI Global.

De Filippi, Primavera. 2015b. Translating Commons-based Peer Production Values into Metrics: Towards Commons-based Cryptocurrencies. In David Lee Kuo Chuen (Ed.), *Handbook of Digital Currency*, pp. 463–483. London: Elsevier.

De Filippi, Primavera, and Hassan, Samer. 2016. Blockchain Technology as a Regulatory Technology: From Code is Law to Law is Code. *First Monday*, 21(12). https://doi.org/10.5210/fm.v21i12.7113.

De Filippi, Primavera, and Tréguer, Félix. 2015a. Expanding the Internet Commons: The Subversive Potential of Wireless Community Networks. *Journal of Peer Production*, 6: *Disruption and the Law*. Last accessed 24 June 2020. http://peerproduction.net/issues/issue-6-disruption-and-the-law/peer-reviewed-articles/#3554.

De Filippi, Primavera, and Tréguer, Félix. 2015b. Wireless Community Networks: Towards a Public Policy for the Network Commons. In Luca Belli and Primavera De Filippi (Eds.), *Net Neutrality Compendium: Human Rights, Free Competition and the Future of the Internet*, pp. 261–270. Basel: Springer.

De Filippi, Primavera, and Troxler, Peter. 2016. From Material Scarcity to Artificial Abundance – The Case of FabLabs and 3D Printing Technologies. In Bibi van den Berg, Simone van der Hof and Eleni Kosta (Eds.), *3D Printing: Legal, Philosophical and Economic Dimensions*, pp. 65–83. The Hague: T.M.C. Asser Instituut.

Dean, Jodi. 2009. *Democracy and Other Neoliberal Fantasies. Communicative Capitalism and Left Politics*. Durham, NC: Duke University Press.

Dean, Jodi. 2012. *The Communist Horizon*. London: Verso.

Dean, Jodi. 2016. *Crowds and Party*. London: Verso.

Dedeurwaerdere, Tom. 2013. *Sustainability Science for Strong Sustainability*. Report prepared in the context of the public tender on a Scientific Report on the Organisation of Scientific Research, with the support of the Minister for Sustainable Development and Public Administration of the Walloon Government of Belgium. Last accessed 24 June 2020. http://biogov.uclouvain.be/staff/dedeurwaerdere/2013%2001%2011_sustainability%20science-EN.pdf.

DIEM25. 2019. *Technological Sovereignty: Democratising Technology and Innovation*. Green Paper No. 3. Last accessed 9 February 2020. https://diem25.org/wp-content/uploads/2019/03/Technological-Sovereignty-Green-Paper-No-3.pdf.

Downs, Anthony. 1957. *An Economic Theory of Democracy*. New York: Harper and Row.

Dowsley, Martha. 2008. Developing Multi-Level Institutions from Top-Down Ancestors. *International Journal of the Commons*, 2(1), 55–74.

Drucker, Peter. 1968. *The Age of Discontinuity*. New York: Harper and Row.

Dryzek, John S. 2000. *Deliberative Democracy and Beyond*. New York: Oxford University Press.

Dyer-Witheford, Nick. 1999. *Cyber-Marx: Cycles and Circuits of Struggle in High-Technology Capitalism*. Urbana, IL: University of Illinois Press.

Dyer-Witheford, Nick. 2006. The Circulation of the Common [online]. Paper presented at 'Immaterial Labour, Multitudes and New Social Subjects: Class Composition in Cognitive Capitalism' conference, University of Cambridge. Last accessed 20 March 2020. https://pdfs.semanticscholar.org /5984/6c1e6e118c6762024d345795381a52259540.pdf.

Dyer-Witheford, Nick. 2015. *Cyber-Proletariat: Global Labour in the Digital Vortex*. London: Pluto Press.

Dyer-Witheford, Nick, and de Peuter, Greig. 2010. Commons and Cooperatives. *Affinities: A Journal of Radical Theory, Culture, and Action*, 4(1), 30–56.

Elliot, Brian. 2011. Community and Resistance in Heidegger, Nancy and Agamben. *Philosophy and Social Criticism*, 37(3), 259–271.

Ellul, Jacques. 1967. *The Technological Society*. New York: Alfred A. Knopf.

Esposito, Roberto. 2010. *Community. The Origin and Destiny of Community*. Stanford, CA: Stanford University Press.

Esposito, Roberto. 2011. *Immunitas. The Protection and Negation of Life*. Cambridge: Polity.

Esposito, Roberto. 2012. *Third Person. Politics of Life and Philosophy of the Impersonal*. Cambridge: Polity.

Esposito, Roberto. 2013. *Terms of the Political. Community, Immunity, Biopolitics*. New York: Fordham University Press.

Federici, Silvia. 2004. *Caliban and the Witch: Women, the Body and Primitive Accumulation*. New York: Autonomedia.

Federici, Silvia. 2012. *Revolution at Point Zero: Housework, Reproduction, and Feminist Struggle*. Oakland, CA: PM Press.

Feenberg, Andrew. 2002. *Transforming Technology: A Critical Theory Revisited*. New York: Oxford University Press.

Fishkin, James S. 1991. *Democracy and Deliberations: New Directions for Democratic Reform*. New Haven, CT: Yale University Press.

Foster, Sheila, and Iaione, Christian. 2016. The City as a Commons. *Yale Law & Policy Review*, 34(2), 282–349.

Foucault, Michel. 1969. *The Archeology of Knowledge*. London: Routledge.

Foucault, Michel. 1977. *Discipline and Punish: The Birth of the Prison*. New York: Pantheon.

Foucault, Michel. 1978. *The History of Sexuality, Vol. 1: An Introduction*. New York: Pantheon.

Foucault, Michel. 1982. The Subject and Power. *Critical Inquiry*, 8(4), 777–795.

Foucault, Michel. 1985. *The History of Sexuality, Vol. 2: The Uses of Pleasure*. New York: Pantheon.

Foucault, Michel. 2003. *Society Must Be Defended: Lectures at the Collège de France, 1975–76*. New York: Picador.

Foucault, Michel. 2004. *The Birth of Biopolitics: Lectures at the Collège de France, 1978–1979*. New York: Picador.

Freeden, Michael. 1996. *Ideologies and Political Theory. A Conceptual Approach.* Oxford: Oxford University Press.

Frenken, Koen. 2017. Political Economies and Environmental Futures for the Sharing Economy. *Philosophical Transactions of the Royal Society A* 375: 20160367. https://doi.org/10.1098/rsta.2016.0367.

Frey, Bruno. 1997. A Constitution for Knaves Crowds Out Civic Virtues. *The Economic Journal*, 107(443), 1043–1053.

Frey, Bruno, and Jegen, Reto. 2001. Motivation Crowding Theory. *Journal of Economic Surveys*, 15(5), 589–611.

Friend, Tad. 2015. Tomorrow's Advance Man. *New Yorker*. Last accessed 17 May 2017. http://www.newyorker.com/magazine/2015/05/18/tomorrows-advance-man.

Frischmann, Brett M. 2012. *Infrastructure: The Social Value of Shared Resources.* Oxford: Oxford University Press.

Fuchs, Christian. 2008. *Internet and Society: Social Theory in the Information Age*. Abingdon: Routledge.

Fuchs, Christian. 2011. *Foundations of Critical Media and Information Studies.* Abingdon: Routledge.

Fuchs, Christian. 2014. *Digital Labour and Marx*. Abingdon: Routledge.

Fuchs, Christian. 2016. Henryk Grossman 2.0: A Critique of Paul Mason's Book *Postcapitalism: A Guide to Our Future. tripleC: Communication Capitalism & Critique*, 14(1), 232–243.

Garnham, Nicholas. 2000. *Emancipation, the Media and Modernity*. Oxford: Oxford University Press.

Garnham, Nicholas. 2004/1998. Information Society Theory as Ideology. In Frank Webster (Ed.), *The Information Society Reader*, pp. 165–183. Abingdon: Routledge.

Gibson-Graham, J.K. [Katharine Gibson and Julie Graham]. 1996. *The End of Capitalism (As We Knew It): A Feminist Critique of Political Economy.* Minneapolis, MN: University of Minnesota Press.

Gibson-Graham, J.K. [Katharine Gibson and Julie Graham]. 2006. *A Postcapitalist Politics*. Minneapolis, MN: University of Minnesota Press.

Giddens, Anthony. 1994. *Beyond Left and Right: The Future of Radical Politics.* Cambridge: Polity.

Giddens, Anthony. 1998. *The Third Way: The Renewal of Social Democracy*. Cambridge: Polity.

Gillmor, Dan. 2004. *We the Media: Grassroots Journalism, By the People, For the People*. Last accessed 22 December 2019. http://www.authorama.com/book/we-the-media.html.

Gindin, Sam. 2016. Chasing Utopia. *Jacobin*. Last accessed 16 May 2016. https://jacobinmag.com/2016/03/workers-control-coops-wright-wolff-alperovitz.

Giotitsas, Chris, and Ramos, Jose. 2017. *A New Model of Production for a New Economy, Two Cases of Agricultural Communities*. London: New Economics Foundation. Last accessed 20 March 2020. https://cosmolocalization.files
.wordpress.com/2019/07/a-new-model-of-production-for-a-new
-economy-final.pdf

Godelier, Maurice. 1999. *The Enigma of the Gift*. Chicago, IL: University of Chicago Press.

Golding, Peter. 2000. Forthcoming Features: Information and Communication Technologies and the Sociology of the Future. *Sociology*, 34(1), 165–184.

Gordon-Farleigh, Jonny. 2017. Stocksy United: Brianna Wettlaufer & Nuno Silva. *Stir Magazine*. Last accessed 20 January 2019. https://www.stirtoaction
.com/interviews/stocksy-united-brianna-wettlaufer-nuno-silva.

Gorz, André. 1980. *Farewell to the Working Class*. London: Pluto Press.

Griffiths, Thomas. 2008. *Techniques of Governance in Commons Based Peer Production*. University of Melbourne: School of Culture and Communication.

Grimmelmann, James. 2010. The Internet is a Semicommons. *Fordham Law Review*, 78(6), 2799–2842.

Grossman, J. Sanford, and Stiglitz, Joseph E. 1980. On the Impossibility of Informationally Efficient Markets. *The American Economic Review*, 70(3), 393–408.

Grossman, Lawrence K. 1995. *The Electronic Republic: Reshaping Democracy in the Information Age*. New York: Viking.

Habermas, Jürgen. 1988. *Legitimation Crisis*. Cambridge: Polity.

Habermas, Jürgen. 1996. *Between Facts and Norms. Contributions to a Discourse Theory of Law and Democracy*. Cambridge, MA: MIT Press.

Hague, Barry N., and Loader, Brian D. 1999. *Digital Democracy, Discourse and Decision Making in the Information Age*. London: Routledge.

Hammerstein, David. 2019. Commons-Based Renewable Energy in the Age of Climate Change. In Sophie Bloemen and Thomas de Groot (Eds.), *Our Commons: Political Ideas for a New Europe*, pp. 25–32. Amsterdam: Institute of Network Cultures.

Hardin, Garrett. 1968. The Tragedy of the Commons. *Science*, 162, 1243–1248.

Hardt, Michael, and Negri, Antonio. 2000. *Empire*. Cambridge, MA: Harvard University Press.

Hardt, Michael, and Negri, Antonio. 2004. *Multitude: War and Democracy in the Age of Empire*. London: Penguin.

Hardt, Michael, and Negri, Antonio. 2009. *Commonwealth*. Cambridge, MA: Belknap Press.

Hardt, Michael, and Negri, Antonio. 2012. *Declaration*. New York: Argos.

Harracá, Martin. 2017. *Business Models and Organisational Forms: Searching the Edge of Innovation in Google and Amazon*. Master's thesis. Last accessed 1 March 2020. https://www.academia.edu/37170242/Business_models_and
_organizational_forms_searching_the_edge_of_innovation_in_Google
_and_Amazon.

Harvey, David. 2003. *The New Imperialism*. Oxford: Oxford University Press.

Harvey, David. 2005. *A Brief History of Neoliberalism*. Oxford: Oxford University Press.

Harvey, David. 2010. *The Enigma of Capital and the Crises of Capitalism*. Oxford: Oxford University Press.

Harvey, David. 2011. The Future of the Commons. *Radical History Review*, 109, 101–107.

Harvey, David. 2012. *Rebel Cities: From the Right to the City to the Urban Revolutions*. London: Verso.

Harvey, David. 2019. The Neoliberal Project is Alive But Has Lost Its Legitimacy. *The Wire*. Last accessed 25 March 2019. https://thewire.in/economy /david-harvey-Marxist-scholar-neo-liberalism.

Hayek, Friedrich. 1944. *The Road to Serfdom*. London: Routledge.

Held, David. 1987. *Models of Democracy*. Cambridge: Polity.

Heller, Michael A. 1998. The Tragedy of the Anticommons: Property in the Transition from Marx to Markets. *Harvard Law Review*, 111(3), 622–687.

Herman, S. Edward, and Chomsky, Noam. 1988. *Manufacturing Consent: The Political Economy of Mass Media*. New York: Pantheon.

Hess, Charlotte, and Ostrom, Elinor. 2007. *Understanding Knowledge as a Commons: From Theory to Practice*. Cambridge, MA: MIT Press.

Heverly, Robert A. 2003. The Information Semicommons. *Berkeley Technology Law Journal*, (18)4: 1128–1188.

Hill, Kevin, and Hughes, John. 1998. *Cyberpolitics: Citizen Activism in the Age of the Internet*. Oxford: Rowman and Littlefield.

Hobbes, Thomas. 2011/1660. *Leviathan*. Seattle, WA: Pacific Publishing Studio.

Hockett, Robert. 2019. Finance Without Financiers. *Politics & Society*, 47(4), 491–527.

Horkheimer, Max. 1974/1947. *Eclipse of Reason*. New York: Continuum.

Howe, Jeff. 2006. The Rise of Crowdsourcing. *Wired*. Last accessed 2 January 2017. https://www.wired.com/2006/06/crowds/.

Howe, Jeff. 2008. *Crowdsourcing: Why the Power of the Crowd is Driving the Future of Business*. New York: Crown Business.

Hume, David. 1978/1739. *A Treatise of Human Nature*. Oxford: Oxford University Press.

Hurst, Samantha. 2018. Reflective Venture Partners Announces $6.5 Million Investment in Four Blockchain Technology Startups. *Crowdfund Insider*. Last accessed 21 January 2019. https://www.crowdfundinsider.com/2018 /04/132549-reflective-venture-partners-announces-6-5-million-investment -in-four-Blockchain-technology-startups/.

Huws, Ursula. 2003. *The Making of a Cybertariat*. New York: Monthly Review Press.

Huws, Ursula. 2014. *Labor in the Global Digital Economy: The Cybertariat Comes of Age*. New York: Monthly Review Press.

Jacobs, Michael, and Mazzucato, Mariana (Eds.). 2016. *Rethinking Capitalism: Economics and Policy for Sustainable and Inclusive Growth*. Chichester: Wiley-Blackwell.

Jenkins, Henry. 2006. *Convergence Culture*. New York: New York University Press.

John, Nicholas. 2012. Sharing and Web2.0: The Emergence of a Keyword. *New Media & Society*, 15(2), 167–182.

Juris, Jeffrey S., and Khasnabish, Alexander. 2013. Conclusion. In Jeffrey S. Juris and Alexander Khasnabish (Eds.), *Insurgent Encounters: Transnational Activism, Ethnography, and the Political*, pp. 367–388. Durham, NC: Duke University Press.

Kallis, Giorgos, Kostakis, Vasilis, Lange, Steffen, Muraca, Barbara, Paulson, Susan, and Schmelzer, Matthias. 2018. Research on Degrowth. *Annual Review of Environment and Resources*, 43(1). DOI: https://doi.org/10.1146/annurev-environ-102017-025941.

Karatani, Kojin. 2014. *The Structure of World History, From Modes of Production to Modes of Exchange*. Durham, NC: Duke University Press.

Keen, Steve. 2001. *Debunking Economics: The Naked Emperor of the Social Sciences*. London: Pluto Press.

Kenney, Martin. 2014. Rethinking Labor (and Capital) in the Era of the Cloud. Paper given at the Vortrag auf dem BRIE-ETLA Annual Meeting, Helsinki, 29 August 2014.

Keynes, John Maynard. 2013/1936. *The General Theory of Employment, Interest and Money*. Cambridge: Cambridge University Press.

Kioupkiolis, Alexandros. 2010. Radicalising Democracy. *Constellations*, 17(1), 137–154.

Kioupkiolis, Alexandros. 2017. Commoning the Political, Politicising the Common: Community and the Political in Jean-Luc Nancy, Roberto Esposito and Giorgio Agamben. *Contemporary Political Philosophy*, 17(3), 283–305.

Kioupkiolis, Alexandros. 2019. *The Common and Counter-Hegemonic Policies*. Edinburgh: Edinburgh University Press.

Kleiner, Dimitry. 2010. *The Telecommunist Manifesto*. Amsterdam: Institute of Network Cultures.

Kostakis, Vasilis. 2018. In Defense of Commoning. *Organization*, 25(6), 812–818.

Kostakis, Vasilis, and Bauwens, Michel. 2014. *Network Society and Future Scenarios for a Collaborative Economy*. Basingstoke: Palgrave Macmillan.

Kostakis, Vasilis, Latoufis, Kostas, Liarokapis, Minas, and Bauwens, Michel. 2016. The Convergence of Digital Commons with Local Manufacturing from a Degrowth Perspective: Two Illustrative Cases. *Journal of Cleaner Production*, 30, 1–10.

Kostakis, Vasilis, Niaros, Vasilis, Dafermos, George, and Bauwens, Michel. 2015. Design Global Manufacture Local: Exploring the Contours of an Emerging Productive Model. *Futures*, 73, 126–135.

Krazit, Tom. 2018. How the Rise of the Internet of Things Prompted a New Feature for Microsoft's Cloud Database. *Geek Wire*. Last accessed 19 May 2018. https://www.geekwire.com/2018/rise-internet-things-prompted-new -feature-microsofts-cloud database/.

Kreiss, Daniel, Finn, Megan, and Turner, Fred. 2011. The Limits of Peer Production: Some Reminders from Max Weber for the Network Society. *New Media & Society*, 13(2), 243–259.

Laclau, Ernesto. 1988. Metaphor and Social Antagonisms. In Cary Nelson and Lawrence Grossberg (Eds.), *Marxism and the Interpretation of Culture*, pp. 249–257. Basingstoke: Macmillan Education.

Laclau, Ernesto. 1999. Hegemony and the Future of Democracy: Ernesto Laclau's Political Philosophy. In Lynn Woshma and Gary S. Olson (Eds.), *Race, Rhetoric and the Postcolonial*, pp. 129–164. Albany, NY: SUNY Press.

Laclau, Ernesto. 2001. Can Immanence Explain Social Struggles? *Diacritics*, 31(4), 3–10.

Laclau, Ernesto, and Mouffe, Chantal. 1985. *Hegemony and Socialist Strategy. Towards a Radical Democratic Politics*. London: Verso.

Leadbeater, Charles. 2010. *Cloud Culture. The Future of Global Cultural Relations*. London: British Council.

Lee, Caroline. 2015. The Sharer's Gently-Used Clothes. *Contexts*, 14(1), 17–18.

Lefort, Claude. 2000. *Writing, The Political Test*. Durham, NC: Duke University Press.

Lemann, Nicholas. 2015. The Network Man. *New Yorker*. Last accessed 13 May 2015. http://www.newyorker.com/magazine/2015/10/12/thenetwork-man

Lerner, Josh, and Tirole, Jean. 2002. Some Simple Economics of Open Source. *Journal of Industrial Economics*, 50(2), 197–234.

Lessig, Lawrence. 2001. *The Future of Ideas: The Fate of the Commons in a Connected World*. New York: Random House.

Lessig, Lawrence. 2004. *Free Culture*. New York: Penguin.

Lévi-Strauss, Claude. 1969. *The Elementary Structures of Kinship*. Boston: Beacon Press.

Linebaugh, Peter. 2008. *The Magna Carta Manifesto: Liberties and Commons for All*. Berkeley, CA: University of California Press.

Lobo, Sascha. 2014. Auf dem Weg in die Dumpinghölle: Sharing Economy wie bei Uber ist Plattform-Kapitalismus. *Spiegel Online*. Last accessed 19 July 2019. https://www.spiegel.de/netzwelt/netzpolitik/sascha-lobo-sharing-economy -wie-bei-uber-ist-plattform-kapitalismus-a-989584.html.

Locke, John. 1975/1690. *An Essay Concerning Human Understanding*. Oxford: Oxford University Press.

Lowenberg, Anton D. 1990. Neoclassical Economics as a Theory of Politics and Institutions. *Cato Journal*, 9(3), 619–639.

Lukács, George. 1972/1923. *History and Class Consciousness*. Cambridge, MA: MIT Press.

Luxemburg, Rosa. 2003/1913. *The Accumulation of Capital*. London: Routledge.

Marchart, Oliver. 2007. *Post-foundational Political Thought: Political Difference in Nancy, Lefort, Badiou and Laclau*. Edinburgh: Edinburgh University Press.

Marchart, Olivier. 2012. Being With Against: Jean-Luc Nancy on Justice, Politics and the Democratic Horizon. In Benjamin C. Hutchens (Ed.), *Jean-Luc Nancy, Justice, Legality and World*, pp. 172–184. London: Continuum.

Marcuse, Herbert. 1964. *One-Dimensional Man*. New York: Routledge.

Marsh, Leslie, and Onof, Christian. 2007. Stigmergic Epistemology, Stigmergic Cognition. *Cognitive Systems Research*, 9(1–2), 136–149.

Marshall, Alfred. 2013/1890. *Principles of Economics*. New York: Palgrave Macmillan.

Marx, Karl. 1992 [1867]. *Capital. Volume 1*. London: Penguin.

Marx, Karl. 1993 [1858]. *Grundrisse*. London: Penguin.

Marx, Karl, and Engels, Friedrich. 1975. *Collected Works* Vol. 3. New York: International Publishers.

Marx, Karl, and Engels, Friedrich. 2008 [1848]. *The Communist Manifesto*. London: Pluto Press. Mason, Paul. 2015. *Postcapitalism: A Guide to Our Future*. London: Allen Lane.

Mauss, Marcel. 1967. *The Gift: Forms and Functions of Exchange in Archaic Societies*. New York: W.W. Norton.

Mazzucato, Mariana. 2013. *The Entrepreneurial State: Debunking Public vs Private Sector Myths*. New York: Anthem Press.

Mazzucato, Mariana. 2018. *The Value of Everything. Making and Taking in the Global Economy*. London: Penguin.

McCann, Duncan, and Yazici, Edanur. 2018. Disrupting Together: The Challenges (and Opportunities) for Platform Cooperatives. Report by New Economics Foundation. Last accessed 24 June 2020. https://neweconomics .org/2018/07/disrupting-together.

McCarthy, Michael. 2019. The Politics of Democratizing Finance: A Radical View. *Politics & Society*, 47(4), 611–633.

Mellor, Mary. 2019. Democratizing Finance or Democratizing Money. *Politics & Society*, 47(4), 635–650.

Metcalfe, Bob. 1995. Metcalfe's Law: A Network Becomes More Valuable as it Reaches More Users. *Infoworld*, 2 October.

Milanovic, Branco. 2018. Will there be Postcapitalism? Review of Paul Mason's *Postcapitalism: A Guide to our Future. Global Policy*. Last accessed 15 May 2019. https://www.globalpolicyjournal.com/blog/04/01/2018/will -there-be-postcapitalism-review-paul-mason%E2%80%99s-%E2%80 %9Cpostcapitalism-guide-our-future%E2%80%9D.

Milburn, Keir, and Russell, Bertie. 2019. Public-Common Partnerships: Building New Circuits of Collective Ownership. *Common Wealth*. Last accessed 22 July 2019. https://common-wealth.co.uk/Public-common-partnerships.html.

Mill, John Stuart. 2002/1859. *On Liberty*. London: Dover Publications.

Morell, Fuster Mayo. 2010. Governance of Online Creation Communities: Provision of Infrastructure for the Building of Digital Commons. PhD thesis, European University Institute, Fiesole.

Morell, Fuster Mayo, Carballa Smichowski, Bruno, Smorto, Guido, Espelt, Ricard, Imperatore, Paola, Rebordosa, Manel, Rocas, Marc, Rodriguez, Natalia, Senabre, Enric, and Ciurcina, Marco. 2017. *Multidisciplinary Framework on Commons Collaborative Economy*. DECODE. Last accessed 22 February 2020. https://decodeproject.eu/publications/multidisciplinary-framework-commons-collaborative-economy.

Morozov, Evgeny. 2014. Don't Believe the Hype, the 'Sharing Economy' Masks a Failing Economy. *The Guardian*. Last accessed 1 February 2015. https://www.theguardian.com/commentisfree/2014/sep/28/sharing-economy-internet-hype-benefits-overstated-evgeny-morozov.

Morozov, Evgeny. 2015. Silicon Valley Likes to Promise 'Digital Socialism' – But It Is Selling a Fairytale. *The Guardian*. Last accessed 1 August 2015. https://www.theguardian.com/commentisfree/2015/mar/01/silicon-valley-promises-digital-socialism-but-is-selling-a-fairy-tale.

Morozov, Evgeny. 2018. From Airbnb to City Bikes, the 'Sharing Economy' Has Been Seized by Big Money. *The Guardian*. Last accessed 29 November 2018. https://www.theguardian.com/commentisfree/2018/nov/27/airbnb-city-bikes-sharing-economy-big-money.

Mouffe, Chantal. 2005. *On the Political*. London: Verso.

Mouffe, Chantal. 2008. Critique as Counter-Hegemonic Intervention. EIPCP. Last accessed 24 June 2020. http://eipcp.net/transversal/0808/mouffe/en.

Mullin, Chris. 2015. Review: *Postcapitalism: A Guide to Our Future* by Paul Mason. *The Guardian*. Last accessed 15 May 2019. https://www.theguardian.com/books/2015/aug/03/postcapitalism-guide-to-future-paul-mason-review-engagingly-written-confused.

Nancy, Jean-Luc. 1991. *The Inoperative Community*. Minneapolis, MN: University of Minnesota Press.

Nancy, Jean-Luc. 1993. *The Experience of Freedom*. Stanford, CA: Stanford University Press.

Nancy, Jean-Luc. 1997. *The Sense of the World*. Minneapolis, MN: University of Minnesota Press.

Nancy, Jean-Luc. 2000. *Being Singular Plural*. Stanford, CA: Stanford University Press.

Negri, Antonio. 1988. *Revolution Retrieved: Selected Writings on Marx, Keynes, Capitalist Crisis and New Social Subjects*. London: Red Notes.

Negri, Antonio. 1989. *The Politics of Subversion: A Manifesto for the 21st Century*. Cambridge: Polity.

Negri, Antonio. 1999. Value and Affect. Trans. Michael Hardt. *boundary*, 26(2), 77–88.

Newlands, Gemma, Lutz, Christophe, and Fieseler, Christian. 2016. *Power in the Sharing Economy*. Report from the EU H2020 Research Project Ps2Share: Participation, Privacy, and Power in the Sharing Economy. Last accessed 24 June 2020. https://www.bi.edu/globalassets/forskning/h2020/power-working-paper-final-version-for-web.pdf.

Norton, Jesse. 2018. How Digital Platforms Rethink their Business Models. *Kyocera*. Last accessed 8 September 2019. https://www.kyoceradocumentsolutions.eu/en/smarter-workspaces/business-challenges/innovation/how-digital-platforms-are-rethinking-their-business-models.html.

Nozick, Robert. 1974. *Anarchy, State, and Utopia*. New York: Basic Books.

Nunes, Rodrigo. 2014. *Organisation of the Organisationless: Collective Action after Networks*. Leuphana: Mute/Post-Media Lab.

Olma, Sebastian. 2015. Never Mind the Sharing Economy: Here's Platform Capitalism. *Institute of Network Cultures*. Last accessed 15 October 2015. http://networkcultures.org/mycreativity/2014/10/16/never-mind-the-sharing-economy-heres-platform-capitalism/.

Olson, Marcun. 1965. *The Logic of Collective Action. Public Goods and the Theory of Groups*. Cambridge, MA: Harvard University Press.

O'Neil, Cathy. 2016. *Weapons of Math Destruction*. New York: Crown.

Ossewaarde, Marinus, and Reijers, Wessel. 2017. The Illusion of the Digital Commons: 'False Consciousness' in Online Alternative Economies. *Organization*, 24(5), 609–628.

Ostrom, Elinor. 1990. *Governing the Commons: The Evolution of Institutions for Collective Action*. New York: Cambridge University Press.

Ostrom, Elinor. 2000. Collective Action and the Evolution of Social Norms. *Journal of Economic Perspectives*, 14(3), 137–158.

Ostrom, Elinor. 2012. *The Future of the Commons: Beyond Market Failure and Government Regulation*. London: The Institute of Economic Affairs.

Owyang, Jeremiah. 2013. *The Collaborative Economy*. Report by Altimeter Group. Last accessed 30 July 2018. https://www.slideshare.net/Altimeter/the-collaborative-economy.

Oxfam Report. 2015. Richest 1% Will Own More Than All the Rest by 2016. *Oxfam International*. Last accessed 12 May 2018. https://www.oxfam.org/en/pressroom/pressreleases/2015-01-19/richest-1-will-own-more-all-rest-2016.

Palladino, Lenore. 2019. Democratizing Investment. *Politics & Society*, 47(4), 573–591.

Papadimitropoulos, Vangelis. 2016. Socialisme ou Barbarie: From Castoriadis' Project of Individual and Collective Autonomy to the Collaborative Commons. *tripleC: Communication Capitalism & Critique*, 14(1), 265–278.

Papadimitropoulos, Vangelis. 2017. From the Crisis of Democracy to the Commons. *Socialism and Democracy*, 31(3), 110–122.

Papadimitropoulos, Vangelis. 2018a. The Rational Mastery in Castoriadis. *Capitalism, Nature, Socialism*, 29(3), 51–67.

Papadimitropoulos, Vangelis. 2018b. Reflections on the Contradictions of the Commons. *Review of Radical Political Economics*, 50(2), 317–331.

Papadimitropoulos, Vangelis. 2018c. From Socialism to Open Cooperativism: Convergences and Divergences in the Work of Castoriadis, Olin Wright and Bauwens and Kostakis. *Global Journal of Human-Social Science (F)*, 18(4), 7–20.

Papadimitropoulos, Vangelis. 2018d. From Resistance to Autonomy, Power and Social Change in the Work of Castoriadis and Foucault. *International Journal of Innovative Studies in Sociology and Humanities*, 3(11), 1–13.

Papadimitropoulos, Vangelis. 2019. Politics and the Political. *Critical Horizons*, 20(1), 40–53.

Pasquale, Frank. 2017. Two Narratives of Platform Capitalism. *Yale Law & Policy Review*, 35(1), Article 11.

Pateman, Carole. 1970. *Participation and Democratic Theory*. New York: Cambridge University Press.

Pazaitis, Alex, De Filippi, Primavera, and Kostakis, Vasilis 2017a. Blockchain and Value Systems in the Sharing Economy: The Illustrative Case of Backfeed. *Technological Forecasting & Social Change* 125, 105–115.

Pazaitis, Alex, Kostakis, Vasilis, and Bauwens, Michel. 2017b. Digital Economy and the Rise of Open Cooperativism: the Case of the Enspiral Network. *Etui* 23(2), 177–192.

Perez, Carlotta. 2002. *Technological Revolutions and Financial Capital: The Dynamics of Bubbles and Golden Ages*. Cheltenham: Edward Elgar.

Piketty, Thomas. 2014. *Capital in the Twenty-First Century*. Cambridge, MA: The Belknap Press of Harvard University Press.

Pitts, Frederick H. 2015. Book Review: Paul Mason, *Postcapitalism: A Guide to Our Future*. *Marx & Philosophy: Review of Books*. Last accessed 29 June 2020. https://marxandphilosophy.org.uk/reviews/8066_postcapitalism-review -by-frederick-h-pitts/.

Platform Coops Infographic. 2017. Last accessed 24 June 2020. https://blog .p2pfoundation.net/platform-coops-connecting-cooperatives-with-the -digital-economy/2017/08/21.

Prentoulis, Marina, and Thomassen, Lasse. 2013. Political Theory in the Square: Protest, Representation and Subjectification. *Contemporary Political Theory*, 12(3), 166–184.

Priavolou, Christina. 2018. The Emergence of Open Construction Systems: A Sustainable Paradigm in the Construction Sector? *Journal of Future Studies*, 23(2), 67–84.

Quilligan, James B. 2012. Why Distinguish Common Goods from Public Goods? In David Bolier and Silke Helfrich (Eds.), *The Wealth of the Commons: A World beyond Market and State*, pp. 73–81. Amherst, MA: Levellers Press.

Rawls, John. 1971. *A Theory of Justice*. Cambridge, MA: Harvard University Press.

Raymond, Eric. 1999. *The Cathedral and the Bazaar*. Sebastopol: O'Reilly.

Reisman, David. 1990. *Theories of Collective Action, Downs, Olson and Hirsch*. New York: Palgrave Macmillan.

Resnick, Steven, and Wolff, Richard D. 1987. *Knowledge and Class: A Marxian Critique of Political Economy*. Chicago: University of Chicago Press.

Restakis, John. 2010. *Humanising the Economy: Co-operatives in the Age of Capital*. Gabriola Island, Canada: New Society Publishers.

Rheingold, Howard. 2003. *Smart Mobs: The Next Social Revolution*. Cambridge, MA: Perseus.

Rifkin, Jeremy. 2014. *The Zero Marginal Cost Society: The Internet of Things, the Collaborative Commons, and the Eclipse of Capitalism*. New York: Palgrave Macmillan.

Rigi, Jacob. 2014. The Coming Revolution of Peer Production and Revolutionary Cooperatives. A Response to Michel Bauwens, Vasilis Kostakis and Stefan Meretz. *tripleC: Communication Capitalism & Critique*, 12(1), 390–404.

Rigi, Jacob, and Prey, Robert. 2015. Value, Rent and the Political Economy of Social Media. *The Information Society*, 31, 392–406.

Riker, William. 1982. *Liberalism against Populism*. San Francisco: W.H. Freeman.

Rose, Carol. 1986. The Comedy of the Commons: Commerce, Custom and Inherently Public Property. *University of Chicago Law Review*, 53(3), 711–781.

Roth, Karl Heinz. 2010. Global Crisis-Global Proletarianisation-Counter perspectives. In Andrea Fumagalli (Ed.), *Crisis in the Global Economy: Financial Markets, Social Struggles, and New Political Scenarios*, pp. 197–237. Los Angeles: Semiotext(e).

Rousseau, Jean-Jacques. 2002/1762. *The Social Contract: and the First and Second Discourses*. New Haven, CT: Yale University Press.

Rozas, David, Tenorio-Fornés, Antonio, Díaz-Molina, Silvia, and Hassan, Samer. 2018. When Ostrom Meets Blockchain: Exploring the Potentials of Blockchain for Commons Governance. SSRN. http://dx.doi.org/10.2139/ssrn.3272329.

Rushkoff, Douglas. 2016. *Throwing Rocks at the Google Bus: How Growth Became the Enemy of Prosperity*. New York: Portfolio/Penguin.

Samuelson, Pamela. 1990. Digital Media and the Changing Face of Intellectual Property. *Rutgers Computer & Technology Law Journal*, 16, 323–340.

Sassen, Saskia. 1996. *Losing Control?* New York: Harper Perennial.

Schmitt, Carl. 1996/1932. *The Concept of the Political*. Chicago, IL: University of Chicago Press.

Scholz, Trebor. 2012. *Digital Labor: The Internet as Playground and Factory*. New York: Routledge.

Scholz, Trebor. 2016a. *Platform Cooperativism. Challenging the Corporate Sharing Economy*. New York: Rosa Luxemburg Stiftung.

Scholz, Trebor. 2016b. *Ours to Hack and to Own, the Rise of Platform Cooperativism, a New Vision for the Future of Work and a Fairer Internet*. New York: Or Books.

Schor, Juliet B. 2015. Getting Sharing Right. *Contexts*, 14(1), 14–15.

Schulak, E. Maria, and Unterköfler, Herbert. 2010. *The Austrian School of Economics. A History of its Ideas, Ambassadors, and Institutions.* Auburn, AL: Ludwig von Mises Institute.

Schumpeter, Joseph A. 1994/1942. *Capitalism, Socialism and Democracy.* London: Routledge.

Shirky, Clay. 2008. *Here Comes Everybody*. New York: Penguin.

Siefkes, Christian. 2010. Self-organised Plenty: The Emergence of Physical Peer Production. FSConference 2010. Accessed 11 July 2020. https://keimform .de/2010/self-organized-plenty.

Simon, H. William. 2019. Economic Democracy and Enterprise Form in Finance. *Politics & Society*, 47(4), 557–571.

Slee, Tom. 2015. *What's Yours is Mine, Against the Sharing Economy.* New York: Or Books.

Smith, Adam. 1977/1776. *The Wealth of Nations*. Chicago: University of Chicago Press.

Smith, Henry E. 2000. Semicommon Property Rights and Scattering in the Open Fields. *The Journal of Legal Studies*, 29(1), 131–169.

Smith, Henry E. 2005. Governing the Tele-Semicommons. *Yale Journal on Regulation*, 22, 289–314.

Smorto, Guido. 2017. The Rules of the Game of Platform Capitalism. *CccbLab*. Last accessed 12 May 2017. http://lab.cccb.org/en/rules-game-platform -cooperativism/.

Söderberg, Johan. 2008. *Hacking Capitalism. The Free and Open Source Software Movement.* New York: Routledge.

Springer, Simon. 2012. Neoliberalism as a Discourse: Between Foucaultian Political Economy and Marxian Poststructuralism. *Critical Discourse Studies*, 9(2), 133–147.

Srnicek, Nick. 2017. *Platform Capitalism*. Cambridge: Polity.

Stalder, Felix. 2005. *Open Cultures and the Nature of Networks*. Novi Sad: New Media Center_kuda.org.

Stalder, Felix. 2010. Digital Commons. In Keith Hart, Jean-Louis Laville and Antonio David Cattani (Eds.), *The Human Economy: A World Citizen's Guide*, pp. 313–324. Cambridge: Polity.

Stallman, Richard. 2002. *Free Software, Free Society*. Boston, MA: GNU Press.

Standing, Guy. 2011. *Precariat: The New Dangerous Class*. London: Bloomsbury.

Stehr, Nico. 1994. *Knowledge Societies*. London: Sage.

Stiglitz, Joseph E. 2013. *The Price of Inequality*. London: Penguin.

Stiglitz, Joseph E. 2016. *Rewriting the Rules of the American Economy*. New York: W.W. Norton.

Sundararajan, Arun. 2016. *The Sharing Economy. The End of Employment and the Rise of Crowd-based Capitalism.* Cambridge, MA: MIT Press.

Surowiecki, James. 2004. *The Wisdom of Crowds*. New York: Little, Brown.

Swift, Adam. 2019. *Political Philosophy. A Beginners' Guide for Students and Politicians*. Cambridge: Polity.

Tapscott, Don, and Williams, Anthony. 2006. *Wikinomics: How Mass Collaboration Changes Everything*. New York: Penguin.

Tebbens, Wouten. 2017. *Legal Practices of DIDIY Hardware Technologies*. Deliverable D6.3 of the project Digital Do It Yourself. Last accessed 1 March 2020. http://www.didiy.eu/public/deliverables/didiy-d6.3.pdf.

Tepper, Jonathan, and Hearn, Denise. 2019. *The Myth of Capitalism. Monopolies and the Death of Competition*. Hoboken, NJ: Wiley.

Terranova, Tiziana. 2004. *Network Culture. Politics for the Information Age*. London: Pluto Press.

Thierer, Adam. 2009. Cyber-Libertarianism: The Case for Real Internet Freedom. *The Technology Liberation Front*. Last accessed 18 May 2019. https://techliberation.com/2009/08/12/cyber-libertarianism-the-case-for-real-internet-freedom/?fbclid=IwAR1wPcQusw7dI9VlrHwEXxgd80rLuBckfatzpbbSBAJuRm75t60OYWbPcfU.

Toffler, Alvin. 1980. *The Third Wave*. New York: Bantam Books.

Torregrosa, Marco. 2018. Platform Economy: The 4 Key Business Models. *Medium*. Last accessed 8 September 2019. https://medium.com/euro-freelancers/platform-economy-the-4-key-business-models-1fc0eda7241e.

Troxler, Peter, and Wolf, Patricia. 2016. Community-Based Business Models. Insights from an Emerging Maker Economy. *Interaction Design and Architecture(s) Journal – IxD&A*, N.30, 75–94.

Tully, James. 2008. *Public Philosophy in a New Key: Democracy and Civic Freedom, vol. 1*. Cambridge: Cambridge University Press.

Van Alstyne, Marshall W., Parker, Geoffrey G., and Choudary, Sangeet Paul. 2016. Pipelines, Platforms, and the New Rules of Strategy. Last accessed 3 April 2017. https://hbr.org/2016/04/pipelines-platforms-and-the-new-rules-of-strategy.

Van de Walle, Nicolas. 2001. *African Economies and the Politics of Permanent Crisis*. Cambridge: Cambridge University Press.

van Dijk, Jan. 2006. *The Network Society. Social Aspects of New Media*. London: Sage.

Van Doorn, Niels. 2017. Platform Cooperativism and the Problem of the Outside. *Culture Digitally*. Last accessed 30 July 2019. http://culturedigitally.org/2017/02/platform-cooperativism-and-the-problem-of-the-outside/.

Varoufakis, Yanis. 1998. *Foundations of Economics*. London: Routledge.

Varoufakis, Yanis. 2011. *Europe After the Minotaur. Greece and the Future of the Global Economy*. London: Zed Books.

Vatn, Arild. 2005. *Institutions and the Environment*. Cheltenham: Edward Elgar.

Vercellone, Carlo, Brancaccio, Francesco, Giuliani, Alfonso, Puletti, Federico, Rocchi, Giulia, and Vattimo, Pierluigi. 2019. *Data-driven Disruptive Commons-based Models*. DECODE. Last accessed 4 March 2020. https://

decodeproject.eu/publications/data-driven-disruptive-commons-based -models-0.

Vesnic-Alujevic, Lucia, Stoermer, Eckard, Rudkin, Jennifer Ellen, Scapolo, Fabiana, and Kimbell, Lucy. 2019. *The Future of Government 2030+: A Citizen-Centric Perspective on New Government Models.* EUR 29664 EN. Publications Office of the European Union, Luxembourg.

Virtanen, Marianna, Kivimäki, Mika, Joensuu, Matti, Virtanen, Pekka, Elovainio, Marko, and Vahtera, Jussi. 2005. Temporary Employment and Health: A Review. *International Journal of Epidemiology*, 34(3), 610–622.

Von Hippel, Eric. 1988. *The Sources of Innovation.* New York: Oxford University Press.

Von Hippel, Eric. 2005. *Democratizing Innovation.* Cambridge, MA: MIT Press.

Wagner, Andreas. 2006. Jean-Luc Nancy: A Negative Politics? *Philosophy and Social Criticism*, 32(1), 89–109.

Walker, Edward. 2015. Beyond the Rhetoric of the Sharing Economy. *Contexts*, 14(1), 15–17.

Ward, Michael. 1996. The Effect of the Internet on Political Institutions. *Industrial and Corporate Change*, 5(4), 1127–1142.

Wark, McKenzie. 2004. *A Hacker Manifesto.* Cambridge, MA: Harvard University Press.

Weber, Max. 1978/1922. *Economy and Society.* Berkeley, CA: University of California Press.

Weber, Steven. 2004. *The Success of Open Source.* Cambridge, MA: Harvard University Press.

Webster, Frank. 2002. The Information Society Revisited. In Sonia Livingstone and Leah Lievrouw (Eds.), *Handbook of New Media*, pp. 22–33. London: Sage.

Webster, Frank. 2006. *Theories of the Information Society.* New York: Routledge;

Wright, Erik Olin. 1985. *Classes.* London: Verso.

Wright, Erik Olin. 2005. *Approaches to Class Analysis.* Cambridge: Cambridge University Press.

Wright, Erik Olin. 2009. *Envisioning Real Utopias.* London: Verso.

Yankelovich, Daniel. 1991. *Coming To Public Judgment: Making Democracy Work in a Complex World.* Syracuse, NY: Syracuse University Press.

Žižek, Slavoj. 2008. *In Defense of Lost Causes.* London: Verso.

Žižek, Slavoj. 2010. How to Begin from the Beginning. In Costas Douzinas and Slavoj Žižek (Eds.), *The Idea of Communism*, pp. 209–226. London: Verso.

Žižek, Slavoj. 2013. Answers Without Questions. In Slavoj Žižek (Ed.), *The Idea of Communism 2, The New York Conference*, pp. 177–205. London: Verso.

Zuboff, Shoshana. 2019. *The Age of Surveillance Capitalism.* New York: Hachette.

Notes

1 For more, see https://ioo.coop/directory/, accessed 25 May 2019.
2 https://en.wikipedia.org/wiki/Stocksy_United, accessed 25 May 2019.
3 https://primer.commonstransition.org/4-more/5-elements/case-studies/case-study-fairmondo, accessed 25 May 2019.
4 https://platform.coop/about/consortium, accessed 10 April 2019.
5 https://ww2.newschool.edu/pressroom/pressreleases/2018/treborscholz.htm, accessed 10 April 2019.
6 https://platform.coop/stories/policy-recommendations-for-united-states, accessed 10 April 2019.
7 https://d3n8a8pro7vhmx.cloudfront.net/corbynstays/pages/329/attachments/original/1472552058/Digital_Democracy.pdf, accessed 10 April 2019.
8 Some prominent examples of global (digital) commons are Wikipedia, Wikispeed, Open Source Ecology, LibreOffice, Linux, Goteo, Arduino, Espiral, Loomio and Sensorica (Bollier and Helfrich, 2015).
9 https://wikihouse.cc/about, accessed 10 June 2019.
10 https://decodeproject.eu/, accessed 1 March 2020.
11 For a detailed and comprehensive analysis of the circuit of capital accumulation in Marx, see Fuchs (2011, 137–142).
12 https://stats.oecd.org/Index.aspx?DataSetCode=AV_AN_WAGE, accessed 22 September 2019.
13 https://en.wikipedia.org/wiki/Information_asymmetry, accessed 10 June 2019.

Index

B

C

Printed and bound by CPI Group (UK) Ltd, Croydon, CR0 4YY

07/07/2026

14916229-0003